I0138426

WPB

"We are not humans having spiritual experiences.

We are spirits having human experiences."

- Unknown

===

MYSTIC:

1.) One who, through contemplation, meditation, self-surrender, and prayer, seeks to attain union with the Divine Spirit of God.

2.) One who directly experiences the dimensions of cosmic consciousness, universal wisdom, and spiritual transcendence.

MYSTICISM:

The act of seeking union with God.

Mysticism was defined by Thomas Aquinas as "the knowledge of God through experience. "

MODERN DAY MYSTIC

A Psychic & Spiritual Journey Through A <u>Not</u> <u>Quite</u> Ordinary Life

MODERN DAY MYSTIC

A Psychic & Spiritual Journey
Through A <u>Not</u> <u>Quite</u> Ordinary Life

A Frank & Illuminating Memoir

By Thomas Lyons

WE PUBLISH BOOKS

UNITED STATES OF AMERICA

We Publish Books
P.O. Box 1814
Rancho Mirage, CA 92270

www.WePublishBooks.com
E-mail: WePublishBooks@gmail.com

Library of Congress Control Number: 2005925158

Lyons, Thomas
Modern Day Mystic: A Psychic & Spiritual Journal Through A Not Quite Ordinary Life

Printed in the United States

Cover design by Rhonda Clifton Lyons

Modern Day Mystic: A Psychic & Spiritual Journey Through A Not Quite Ordinary Life/ by Thomas Lyons

1.Biography & Autobiography/New Age BIO502000
2.Body, Mind & Spirit/Spirituality/General OCC036000
3.Body, Mind & Spirit/Metaphysical Phenomena/General OCC501000

ISBN-10: 1-929841-14-0   Paperback
ISBN-13: 978-1-929841-14-1 Paperback
ISBN-10: 1-929841-22-1   Hard Cover
ISBN-13: 978-1-929841-22-6 Hard Cover

First Printing, 2005
Second Printing, 2006

We Publish Books

~ DEDICATION ~

For My Kind And Loving Wife

Rhonda

My Partner And My Friend.
A Rare, Brilliant, And Beautiful Soul
In This Or Any Universe.

~

WITH SPECIAL THANKS TO THOSE WHO HELPED
ME GET THIS BOOK JUST RIGHT:

Mary Carol Winkler
Gert Basson
Rosanne Amato
Julie Gillentine
Rhonda Clifton Lyons
Gertrude Virginia Hogan Lyons
Richard Meyers

TABLE OF CONTENTS

Dedication – For Rhonda / Preface – An Interesting Life
Foreword – By Julie Gillentine / Introduction – Modern Day Mystics

CHAPTERS

An Interesting Life

A *Mystic* is someone whose very existence is an immersion in the Divine Mysteries of Life. Every major religion has its mystics scattered amongst the general population of believers and adherents. Hinduism has its yogis and seers. Christianity has its Gnostics, its "know-ers." Jews have the study of Kabbalah. Islam has Sufism. The other world religions also have their equivalents. And then, from these modern times all the way back to the most ancient of days, many true mystics have been what might best be described as freelancers.

"What is God?" "Why are we here?" and "What is the meaning and purpose of existence?" If these are the questions that daily fill your heart and mind you may be a spiritual seeker. If, however, you feel that the Divine Presence gives you regular glimpses behind the veil of life's illusions you may, in fact, be a mystic.

As best I can tell, I've been a mystic from the moment I was born. I can't remember a time when I didn't look deeply into the nature of the world around me and often see things, things that others didn't see, and know things that most others apparently didn't seem to know.

As a kid, I learned very early not to share what I saw and heard with others. When I tried to most people (family, friends, neighbors, schoolmates) responded with confused looks, blank stares, or whispers that, "Tommy's acting really strange." I was definitely a rather intense and introverted child, although I've learned to lighten up quite a bit.

Modern Day Mystic is a chronicle of a life filled with visions, out-of-body experiences, apparent visitations by ghosts and spirits, psychic experiments, and prophetic dreams that come true. But the book is also a record of my questioning exactly what all these experiences are supposed to mean and why they keep happening to *me*.

It's said, perhaps in jest, that there's an "ancient Chinese curse" whose damning words simply state: "May you have an *interesting* life."

Well, mine's been very interesting…

By Julie Gillentine

In the last fifty years leading-edge physics, or Quantum Theory, has revolutionized the way we see reality. In 1927 the great physicist Niels Bohr commented, "Anyone who is not shocked by Quantum Theory does not understand it." Forty years later, Richard Feynman, another pioneering scientist remarked, "No one understands quantum theory." Entering this domain shatters our paradigm of a solid and predictable reality. In the quantum world everything is alive with relativity and responsiveness.

The end of the twentieth century has witnessed a stunning renaissance of the metaphysical, but most people still live ordinary lives which are grounded in a firm sense of third-dimensional reality. Buildings are solid, dead people stay in their graves, UFOs don't land in driveways, and people don't travel through time.

But we hear stories, and the sense that things are not what they seem trickles into our awareness. Here and there intrepid souls are coming out of the metaphysical closet, sharing their divergent experiences from the frontiers of consciousness.

It is my sense that the borderland of the surreal somehow involves stepping out of time and space as we've come to perceive it. The rational mind alone cannot make the journey into the mystical realm. The limits of an either-or, black-white orientation cannot perceive the subtle and myriad manifestations of reality which exist outside our conventional, temporal frame of reference.

Thomas Lyons is one of these pioneers. He is a seasoned explorer on the frontiers of consciousness, and his chronicles of the mysterious and mystical in this book come from the experiences of his own life. Thomas has lived on the edge of multiple realities, straddling a nether word between dimensions and has chosen to share the diverse and sometimes startling experiences from his "not-so-ordinary life." His life has been peopled by angels, aliens, ghosts and spiritual masters and characterized by encounters that might send others screaming.

In the "not-quite-ordinary" life of Thomas Lyons bubbles of Quantum Foam emerge with clarity and truth, expressing divergent views of reality. Thomas has shown courage and penetrating insight in navigating the largely uncharted terrain of the mystical landscape. His response to his experiences shines like an early warning beacon, summoning others to look beyond their assumptions and beneath the surface. His life of psychic and mystical experiences stretches our mental limits of what's possible for all of us. *Modern Day Mystic* is not just a riveting memoir of an unusual life but also serves as a prelude to what awaits humanity.

Many readers will sit back in their chairs and exhale a huge sigh of relief, realizing they are neither unique, weird, or alone. Others may feel a profound disquiet as the edges of their solid world begin to dissolve. For me, *Modern Day Mystic* came as a welcome confirmation of my own strange-but-true experiences that I haven't found courage to share.

The path of the mystic involves lessons of discernment, compassion and non-judgment and is a sojourn of healing and synthesis, learning to see an ultimate unity. Along the way fear, ego and moralistic judgment must be surrendered. Eventually we recognize guidance and learn to trust this inner knowing.

I believe the chronicles of Thomas Lyons, modern day mystic, echo the words of the great mystic and teacher Paramahansa Yogananda who said to his students, "I come not to entertain you with worldly festivities but to arouse your sleeping memory of immortality."

We are challenged to wake up and remember our true selves so that we may remake the world in a grand and loving design. Thank you, Thomas, for shining your visionary headlights into the future.

Julie Gillentine
Winter 2005

{Julie Gillentine is an award-winning author and astrologer. Her books: *Messengers*; *Tarot & Dream Interpretation*; and *The Hidden Power Of Everyday Things* (co-author) are available in bookstores, through online booksellers, and at: http://www.QueenOfCups.com.}

Modern Day Mystics

We live in a time of extraordinary change that is unprecedented in the known history of our world. This is very scary and threatening for some people and an exciting adventure for others. As I continue to be both an observer and a participant in this period I've determined that I have something of value to offer, my life experience as a mystic.

My experiences might be classified along with that guy who's been struck by lightning five or six times and is still alive to talk about it. A skeptic to this man's experiences might challenge him and say, "Prove that you're periodically struck by lightening! Let's see you get struck by lightening again!" Well, it generally doesn't work that way. Profound mystical experiences, like artistic inspiration or scientific revelation - events sometimes likened to being "struck by a bolt of lightning" - are not something most of us can create on demand. To those who don't normally have any sort of metaphysical awareness, mystics, people who perceive everyday life as transcendental and filled with meaning, might appear kind of strange. Those who live outside the mystical loop may even choose to view all claims of supposed metaphysical experience as fraud, self-delusion, or signs of mental illness. Others view these same mystical individuals with utter amazement, or as spiritual lights in a world lost in darkness. The thing to remember is that these mystical types are just people, like anybody else, regardless of how they experience reality.

Frankly, if the experiences detailed in this book hadn't happened to me, I probably wouldn't believe half of them. But they have happened to me and so here I go. At the end of the day, the principle difference between the likes of me and many others in our world is simply that I regularly pay very close attention to that subtle sense of knowing, those curious coincidences, and those gut feelings that inform each of us that something mystical is, in fact, occurring in our lives. Virtually all my life people have told me, "You ought to be a teacher," and it seems that is exactly what I am. However, many times during the writing of this book I've had to ask myself, "Are you really going to tell people about that?" Well, in fact I have edited myself, more than I would like to have in a perfect world, but for the most part I've let this book become what it seemed to naturally want to become.

Many spiritual books available today are mostly regurgitations of somebody else's philosophy. Others set up a particular personality, whether human or supposedly supernatural, as the All-Knowing Wise One we should all be following around like small children after their parents. However, the spiritual teaching, "We must become as little children in order to enter the Kingdom of Heaven," does not mean that we should be letting somebody else do our thinking for us, as if we had no capacity to question and learn for ourselves. The fact is most children are natural mystics. Just observe very young children, and you'll notice they are constantly exploring and seeking to learn all their environment has to offer them. These newly incarnated souls know instinctively to trust the evidence of their senses, both the normal physical senses and their extra-sensory perceptions, no matter what those senses may be telling them. It's usually only when they've gotten a bit older, and are in the process of socialization, that they finally acquiesce to somebody else's definition of reality. This, after being told repeatedly by their elders that they are "wrong," that they must "stop lying," that they're "imagining things," and that what they are seeing and experiencing is "not real."

But why, aside of this socialization process that demands a child join in the world of the majority, do most of us not normally see through the supposed *veils of illusion* into other worlds and other realities if they really do exist? Well, it seems that even though our sense of separation from the Divine may ultimately an illusion, it is also a very *purposeful* illusion. For instance, how would any of us function in this world if we kept bumping into other equally valid worlds all the time, especially when cutting-edge scientific theory now tells us that the number of other possible realities may be infinite by any human measure? And what of the unique human experiences allowed for by the sense of individuality, when we feel ourselves separate from our Divine Source. In order for us to know the wonder and joy of human love, a man for a woman, a child for its grandparents, our best friend for life, it first requires a perception of separate-ness from that other.

The reason I've written this book is that from the time I was a small child I've had encounters that have shown me greater dimensions of reality than I was otherwise taught to believe existed or could exist. In these pages I seek to share as much of the wisdom, wrought from experience, as I feel I have to offer, in the hope that it may be of value for those who are seeking to understand their own such experiences. It is my sincere belief that, by consistently paying attention to that which the Universe/God/Goddess/Great Spirit shows to each of us, in the subtle whispers and connections of everyday life, we can each gain a greater understanding of the mystical world and of the magical reality in which we are all daily immersed, whether or not we recognize it.

If you're trying, but not quite there yet, perhaps with a little effort, patience, and faith in yourself and in the Divine Spirit, you will wake up one day and recognize that too have become a Modern Day Mystic.

Thomas Francis Lyons Jr.
Winter 2005

CHAPTER ONE

The Man Who Wasn't There

I can't say when I first became aware of his presence. He was always there throughout my childhood, just out of sight. I knew he lived on the other side of the world in a place called Egypt, by the Nile River. When I thought of him I could see over the round curves of the Earth and feel his presence emanating from that corner of the globe. Yet when I really needed him he would immediately appear at my side.

He appeared in the black robes of a priest, though unlike the Roman Catholic priests of my childhood he wore a headdress and black veil that fell on either side of his face. He had a full black beard and brown to olive skin at a time when all the priests and ministers where I lived were white and clean-shaven. His eyes were so deep and penetrating that looking into them was like looking into the depths of the Universe.

I wasn't certain if he spoke English, my language. That I supposed might be one of the reasons he didn't talk with his mouth but communicated directly to my mind from his mind. I also understood that direct mind-to-mind communication was a more effective way to ensure the other person understood exactly what you were intending. This was all quite clear to me long before I entered kindergarten.

On the occasions when he would materialize before me my mind would undergo an expansion and I would once again remember that he was my teacher and I was his student. It had been so for many centuries. As a child I never had a name for him. When one's greater existence is understood to continue lifetime after lifetime, in and outside of time and space, names sometimes become unimportant. It would be more than thirty years before I learned that he had a name, a name known by millions of others around the world, and that the same mysterious spiritual Master had been appearing to others since long before I was born in a New England city hospital in 1958.

When I was very young I generally thought of him as the Man. I would look up from my normal child's perspective and suddenly find him standing before me. I would think, "Oh, the Man's here again." It was a natural thought process as I was accustomed to referring to all men I didn't know as family or neighbors in the same fashion. "Look at what the Man's doing, Mummy," I would say when referring to the actions of a garbage man, a carpenter, a mailman, a pharmacist, etc.

At the times the Man appeared I would have to stretch my normal little boy consciousness to encompass the much greater being I knew I was outside of Earth's normal time and space boundaries. We are all in fact much greater beings than we generally understand ourselves to be but it takes an expanded awareness to see it. In the end a consistently expanded awareness encompassing one's larger self and one's truer place in the dance of life is perhaps as reasonable a definition of spiritual enlightenment as any I can offer.

When the Man would visit with me I consciously knew so much more than I would normally about the true nature of life and spirit. After he departed my consciousness would slowly shrink back down to its normal little boy size. But each time the lingering memory of what had transpired when he was there with me remained. The earliest clear memory I have of him is from a near-death experience I had at the beach. A near-death experience is you're your body apparently dies and your spirit leaves but then later returns with the memory of having faced death from the other side.

~

According to my mother I was just two years old the day I drowned in the Atlantic Ocean. The place was Falmouth, Massachusetts a few miles from Martha's Vineyard. My eldest sister Kathy was in the water and my mother was changing my brother Bob's diaper when I saw a really pretty wave rushing to shore. I knew if I waited for an adult to take me I would miss out. I decided to go for it on my own.

I sprinted to the water but found it too shallow to give much of a rush. Without hesitation I ventured further into the sea. The power of the deeper water was much greater than I had expected. Then the powerful tide started pulling out, taking me along with it. Trying to resist I dug my feet in but the heavy water stole the sand right from under my feet. As it tipped me over into the rushing water I understood why everyone had warned me about not getting caught in the undertow. "This must be the undertow," I thought to myself. It made sense. The water had gone right under my toes.

As I went under I wondered why there had to be an undertow to spoil everything. It didn't seem fair. As I instinctively held my breath to keep the water from pushing into my lungs my mind questioned the entire design of this world. "If there were undertows at the beaches and cars in the street that could hurt you what other poorly thought out things might exist in this place?" I wondered. "Hadn't the Great Wise Spirit thought through the consequences of making things so dangerous and painful here? Couldn't *They* have done a better job?"

My body somehow drove itself above the surface. "That wasn't hard," I thought. "Maybe it all worked out if you just gave it a chance?" My legs searched for a place to stand but the land was now too far below me. My arms tried to help, but I went under again. Salt water poured into my nose and down my throat. Now the body's natural desire to survive forced me to pay it my full attention. Sorting out the *meaning* of it all would have to wait.

I thrashed wildly at the dense water trying to get back to the surface. I knew I had to go up to get to the air but I could no longer tell where up was. I could see where the underwater currents were flowing the strongest. The water there seemed somehow darker and thicker than the rest of the water as it moved in long strands in certain places. I surmised the sun's light must reflect differently off the varying parts of the water creating those visual effects. My mind was wandering again.

A blind urgency brought me back to the task at hand. I was suddenly afraid or more correctly my *body* was afraid and I was now strongly identifying with it. I fought the water as it filled my lungs but it wasn't long before the water won and I couldn't fight anymore.

I felt my body go limp and release me from its confines. I looked up at what I thought for a moment was the sun above the water but then I realized that it wasn't the sun. It was the light. As the light grew brighter I was filled with an overwhelming sense of joy. Effortlessly I moved towards it. I recognized it now. The light was the Source I had come from. The light was the way home. That I was going home so soon came as a surprise. I'd expected to have to stay here a lot longer. But there was the light before me and there I was beginning my return.

Suddenly the figure of a Man moved in front of me. It was my teacher. As I maneuvered around him the Master moved, blocking my path to the light once more. "Get out of my way!" I thought angrily. "You can't leave. You have to go back," were the thoughts that came from the Master's mind to mine. "But I want to go home," I thought back. "You have work to do here. That is why you came," were his mental impressions to me. "It's too soon for you to leave this place." I withdrew my objections, realizing he was right. It wasn't my time.

Then someone *physical* moved towards me, and everything went black. Then I found myself back inside my body, but it wasn't working anymore. It had drowned. I seemed to exist not quite in the physical or back in the light. Instead I was trapped somewhere in between. Going to the light would be fine. Going back to living in that body was perfectly acceptable. But staying with a body that was dead and stuck between the two worlds was not a place I wanted to remain.

I looked again for the light but couldn't find it. Then the body was alive for a moment. I felt coarse wet sand scraping against me. It hurt and I was furious at whoever was doing this to me. Then I realized someone was pulling my body out of the ocean. I blacked out again.

I awoke painfully for an instant as a woman was forcing the water out of my chest. The heavy salt water made me feel sick inside. People were talking excitedly all around me. The woman bringing my body back to life was my Aunt Shirley. As more seawater was pushed out my body lost consciousness again and I returned to the now welcome blankness, knowing that the body would be fine in a little while.

The truth was once I had completed the actual drowning part of the experience I hadn't really wanted to be rescued anyway. In retrospect I'm happy that I was. Curiously, even though my mind was not afraid of returning to the light my body was afraid of its own death. Because of that drowning experience I would be over forty years of age before I would finally brave the ocean waters again and learn how to swim.

CHAPTER TWO

My Mother, The Mystic

My mother Gertrude Virginia Hogan, Trudy to her friends, was a young bride with a baby on the way at the time of her father's death. Her father's illness from an inoperable brain tumor and his final awful death would devastate their entire family.

A year or so *after* her loving father's untimely death my mother was to have a disturbing visit from her now dead parent. The visitation happened one night, as Trudy and her husband Charles "Buddy" Andries were asleep in her mother's house. Buddy was a wonderful man loved by all but was regularly disturbed by horrible nightmares of the grisly action he'd seen as a soldier in World War II. Night after night he'd sit bolt upright in bed searching for his gun. Over and over he'd discover his friends and comrades dead on either side of him, their throats slit by enemy insurgents who had slipped into their encampments under cover of darkness and killed a few men here and there while leaving the rest to fear for their lives when they awakened.

That prophetic night, my mother awoke to find her dead father standing by the bed. "What're you doing here, Pa?" she asked him. "I've come for Buddy," her father's ghost said back. Trudy turned to look at her sleeping husband. In her vision Buddy's body appeared as if he were a corpse. She screamed and the entire house was awakened.

As people rushed in the room, they saw a fire burning in the metal wastepaper basket where my mother had seen the spirit of her father moments before. This was extraordinary because in life her father had been a daydreaming chain smoker who had actually caused a few unintentional wastepaper basket fires in his day. No one else in the household smoked.

~

A couple of months before the fateful visit by her deceased father's spirit, my mother had a shocking premonition of the tragedy that would soon befall her. She had recently given birth to her first child, my sister Kathleen. While looking over photographs at her husband Buddy's family home she found herself saying aloud, "I'll have to have copies of these pictures of Buddy made for Kathy so she'll know what her father looked like when she gets older." The shock of what those words meant went through her like a knife.

Two weeks later when she got the news that Buddy had been hit by a truck while crossing the street she knew that he would not survive his injuries. Her father's spirit had come to take Buddy to the other side, a place where he would hopefully be freed from the pain and horrors of war that had haunted him so deeply until the day of his death.

~

My mother would probably never describe herself as a mystic, but from the time she was a little girl she's had strong feelings about things that somehow turned out to be correct. As an adult she would occasionally have visions of the future that would come to pass, visitations with ghosts of people who had died, and would twice be declared dead in a hospital while experiencing what would come to be known years later as *near-death experiences*.

~

Seven years after the death of her first husband my mother was to meet and marry the man who would become my father, a brilliant, handsome, wild rogue named Thomas Francis Lyons. The son of poor Irish Immigrant parents, my Dad was a charming, domineering, controlling, and sometimes violent man, who had considered careers as both a Jesuit Priest and as a Massachusetts State Trooper. A high school dropout with a genius I.Q. my Dad was also a *closet mystic*. He had an insatiable passion for knowledge and learning in the areas of history and religion, as well as a propensity for living on the wild side and for experiencing the occasional psychic vision of his own.

These kinds of abilities often run in families, it is said.

CHAPTER THREE

A Vision In Church

In my first year of life one of my favorite things was to attend mass at Saint Williams Church in Tewksbury, Massachusetts with my family. Those were the days when our Dad used to come with us. Saint Williams was a Roman Catholic Church, although at the time I didn't know there was any other kind. The year was 1959.

I remember one particular Sunday morning when a wonderful *vision* opened up before my eyes. As I gazed rapturously at the scene before me *another mass* appeared superimposed over the regular ceremony. In it I saw many of the same people who were sitting alone had really come to be close to others who were also alone or feeling lonely.

The Priest in my vision had come down from his place at the altar and was ministering to a very elderly woman. The woman was close to death and very much afraid of dying. Above her and in the air around her I saw spirits in the form of angels. Beside her sat members of her family, people who had already passed over the bridge of death and who were waiting for her. They had all come, angels and human spirits alike, to help the old woman make her transition to the other side.

I looked around and determined I was the only one who could see the vision. I ran to my father gesturing wildly as I described the scene of my vision in great detail. I explained what everything meant and how I understood that what I had been shown was the *real mass*, the true spiritual reason we were all gathered there together.

My big burly father, looking more awkward than I ever remembered, patted me on the head uncertainly saying, "There, there Tommy. It's alright. Everything's going to be okay." I became furious at his dismissal of the important revelation I was sharing with him. I tried to communicate, "Listen to me! This is important! This is so wonderful!" I declared. But as I *thought* these words in my head I heard my one-year-old baby's mouth trying to make the correct sounds of the words. I realized all my little voice was saying was, "Blah, blah, blah, blah..." in typical baby talk. "Oh, that's right!" I thought to myself. "My mouth hasn't learned how to talk yet."

CHAPTER FOUR

A Visit From Santa Claus?

How do people tell the difference between fantasy and reality? This is an issue that comes up again and again in the world of psychic, spiritual, and mystical experience. Did you really receive a visit from your dead grandmother or was it just a dream? Did you actually know your best friend had been in an accident or was that terrible feeling you had about them in your gut just a strange, yet unrelated coincidence?

The following story would be nothing more than a simple, fanciful childhood memory if it didn't have a greater significance with respect to altered states of consciousness, dreams, and visions. Like many young children I saw things that the grownups and older kids couldn't see. I had this apparent visit from Santa Claus when I was only four years old so the fact that nobody else in my family had this experience didn't bother me. What did bother me was when I realized that logically speaking what I'd experienced could not have happened at all.

~

It was Christmas 1962. We younger kids didn't know it but our father used to play Santa Claus for some local charities. My Dad was a big burly man with a ruddy complexion, twinkling blue eyes, and a larger than life presentation so he made a very convincing Santa. One of our father's friends also made the rounds as Santa each year. That particular year they made a deal to play the role at each other's homes. I still remember Santa's appearance in our living room as one of the highlights of my early childhood. It was truly magical.

When Christmas Eve came I was still lost in the blissful trance of wonderment. "This is the chair Santa sat in," I remember thinking. "He put his feet right there on the floor." I went to bed that night certain that this would be the most magical and marvelous Christmas I had ever known. It would in a way turn out to be just that.

Late that night I awoke with a start. I was sure I had heard them, Santa's reindeer. I looked across the room to my brother. "Bobby!" I said. No response. I shook him gently. "Bobby, did you hear that?" I so much wanted to share this with him. Bobby didn't move a muscle.

Then I heard them again. *"Jing, jing, jing, jing."* Those were sleigh bells! They had to be! I turned to the window to scan the sky for Santa's sleigh. Across the street I saw a giant full moon shining over the dozens of snow-covered houses in what appeared to be a cozy little village. All the chimneys were billowing out a friendly smoke. Somewhere in the back of my mind it occurred to me that there was only one house across the street from us. But the sleigh bells jingled again and suddenly it didn't matter what might be true in the daytime. This was happening now! This was what was real!

I rushed to the window as the silhouette of Santa's sleigh and his magic reindeer made its way across the giant full moon. Then there was a heavy "thump" on the roof. I knew the sleigh had landed and that Santa was about to come down our chimney! I sneaked down the staircase, just far enough to peer through the banister into the living room below. There was Santa Claus. My head felt dizzy. My heart raced. It was beyond belief to catch him on his yearly rounds. But inside I knew something was wrong. Something wasn't right about all this. I wasn't supposed to be witnessing this.

Then our eyes met, Santa's and mine. Now I'd done it. All the adults had told us we weren't allowed out of bed on Christmas Eve. Horrified by what I'd done I bolted up the stairs and dove under the covers of my bed. "If Santa catches you out of bed he'll take all your presents away and leave you nothing but a lump of coal in your stocking." Those familiar words of warning stung in my ears.

When morning came I was too afraid to get out of bed. Whenever one of my brothers or sisters came to my room to wake me I pretended to be asleep. They tried and tried but I wouldn't budge. Finally my father's voice reached out to me from the living room below. "Tommy," he said kindly but very firmly, "Come down stairs and join the rest of the family. Now."

My sister Kathy began to read the names off the tags and hand out gifts. I dreaded what was to come. After six or seven names my name was called. "How could this be?" I wondered. "For Tommy from Mum and Dad," my sister said. That explained it. I stared at the oversized stockings hanging from the fireplace mantel. "Was mine filled with coal this year?" I wondered. I couldn't tell from where I was. Actually a part of me thought it might be interesting to get a few lumps of coal. I had never seen coal except in storybooks. It might be neat to have some. And then it happened. "A present for Tommy, from Santa," Kathy announced. I could hardly believe it. Had Santa left me just one present out of compassion?

With a new confidence I made my way over to my stocking. Inside I found various tiny gifts, but no coal. My heart leapt with joy. But still I was left to wonder, "Why hadn't my gifts been taken away? Was it possible the stories the adults told us weren't true? Could they have been lying to us for some reason?" I considered the possibilities. "And why did an entire village of houses appear across the street last night, houses that I know aren't there in the daytime?" I went upstairs and double-checked from our bedroom. The village I'd seen across the street hours earlier definitely wasn't there. "What had happened to it?" I wondered. "Perhaps the village is only there at night?"

I was only four years old that Christmas day and up until that time I hadn't had any good reason to question the apparent evidence of my senses. Sure I'd had my visions but they had always made sense in the end. They'd shown me truths about life and taught me things that I needed to know to live in this world. This supposed nighttime visit from Santa and his reindeer however didn't make sense at all and that uneasy reality stuck with me throughout the rest of my childhood years. I had learned an important lesson, that it was possible to be fooled by one's own senses.

When I got a little older I would come to understand the difference between a very vivid dream and an actual vision. I would come to understand that some dreams were filled with meaningful content and that others might be simply pure fantasy. Further I came to know that dreams can also be symbolic in nature or that they may even represent contact with other beings in other realities. The trouble comes about when children grow up to be adults and they still don't know how to tell the difference between a true mystical or spiritual experience, a merely symbolic image sent from the subconscious mind, and a purely wonderful and silly dream that holds no real value other than the delightful experience of the dream itself.

CHAPTER FIVE

JFK & The Color TV

It was early afternoon on November 22, 1963. Although I was enrolled in kindergarten I was at home with my mother that day. As I watched my mother making cookies the announcement came over the radio: President John Fitzgerald Kennedy had been shot. My mother froze in horrified disbelief. Then she began to cry. As she staggered across the room a vision of the assassination began playing in front of my eyes in vivid color and full detail. I watched the entire sequence of events in Dallas as if they were images captured from a far away television camera. I knew I was seeing the attack just as it had happened.

Later that afternoon as the television played the news footage of the assassination of our beloved President I saw the images on the TV just as they had appeared to me at the moment of the radio announcement. They were the same images in the same sequence from the same perspectives and in the same vivid colors as I had witnessed hours earlier in my vision. I concluded that I had picked up the invisible television signals that I knew flew through the air everyday. As I watched the news with my family, however, I noted no other images were shown in color. Everything else on the TV was in black and white. As the days, weeks, and finally months passed I kept a lookout for other programs, commercials, or special bulletins broadcast in color. There never were any.

Five years later in 1968 our neighbors got their first color TV. I stood in awe of the brightly colored images, finding it difficult to handle the sensory overload of the added color to the shows and commercials I knew so well. Less than a week later my Dad responded by bringing home our very first color TV. As I watched the new color images with my family I remembered having seen the news footage of Kennedy's assassination in full color on the TV back in 1963 and then searching the set for color images other than that of President Kennedy's murder. I realized that we probably hadn't had a color TV at that time. I checked with my parents. They assured me we had never had a television that could show color images until today. Even though color TV receivers had been available to Americans since about 1954 very few American homes had color TVs until the late 1960s.

CHAPTER SIX

My Mother Crosses Over & Then Crosses Back

My mother was almost forty-one when she gave birth to her seventh and final child. It was a stressful pregnancy and my mother was dangerously weak towards the end. Poor little Larry was born with substantial birth defects, a clef pallet, and a heart that had developed outside of his body. These sorts of problems were not the kind the medical profession was as yet equipped to handle back in 1965.

My mother had bled profusely during the delivery. Afterwards the bleeding wouldn't stop. The doctors gave her one blood transfusion after another but the blood just went in one part of her body and poured out another. Somewhere in the midst of it all she found herself floating high above her body. For quite some time she watched from above as the doctors and nurses down below worked frantically to save her dying human shell. Finally a Catholic Priest was brought in and she was given the last rites of the Church. Trudy Lyons would not survive the day.

When her body finally stopped fighting it came as a relief. She found herself moving rapidly through a tunnel with a beautiful light shining at the other end. As she approached the light a profound and joyous peace enveloped her. It was over. But in her heart she was troubled that she was leaving. "How can I do this to Tom?" she asked herself. "How can I leave my husband all alone with seven children?"

She knew my father's own mother had died in childbirth and left my paternal grandfather with six boys to raise on his own. She knew how much emotional damage the loss had done to his family, how the boys had grown up hard and wild without a gentle female example around to teach them balance and how their father had turned to ruling his house with an iron fist. She also knew how my father's father had never forgiven his wife for dying on him and leaving him all alone.

As she struggled with her dilemma a Figure reached out to my mother from the light, its spiritual hands touching her shoulders though she could not see its face. The Presence was kind and comforting. My mother didn't want to go back to the world. She wanted to go into the light. But she also wanted to do the right thing. Finally a voice spoke from the light, not in words but directly to her mind. "It's not your time," it said. "You're going back." When my mother's spirit returned to her body it started breathing again and her heart began to beat. During her spirit's absence her body had been declared dead, left for a couple of hours, and was finally being wheeled down the hallway to the morgue when my mother returned to it. The event is recorded in medical history.

My father was very different for a few months after my mother's brush with death. He became kinder, gentler, and more understanding. But ultimately the gentleness didn't take. My father would eventually mellow in the final years before his death but that was still decades ahead in the future. My brother Larry's tiny incomplete body managed to survive for two months before he finally went back into the light to which we all must return.

It would be seven years before my mother would share this event with me and only then on the day that she had seen the ghost of the old woman walking through the house and saw me stop to let the elderly ghost pass by. Once my mother and I began sharing stories of our otherworldly encounters with each other our lives became a little richer and our bond a little closer. These were, after all, not the kind of things you normally talked about in those days.

Later in 1975 my sister Mary Alice would give our mother a copy of a new book called Life After Life by Raymond A. Moody Jr., M.D. The book was filled with descriptions of people who'd had experiences just as my mother and I had of a brush with death, followed by seeing a light, and of a presence sending them back to the world of the living. Such encounters were to become know as Near-Death Experiences.

13

CHAPTER SEVEN

Our Family Pet Meets His Maker

Another strong memory I still retain of the spiritual Master that visited me throughout my childhood was from the day our dog Pepper died.

Pepper would be one of several dogs that would die in the role as our family pet. This was because our father had this penchant for finding cats and dogs that had been terribly abused by their former owners and then bringing them home for us to love and care for. These psychologically damaged little beings would manage live with us in their pain and confusion until the day they would finally do something too crazy, too dumb, or too violent and succeed in getting killed. As you might imagine this put my siblings and I off from becoming pet owners for many years. Our mother has never gotten another pet.

Pretty much since the day our Dad brought us Pepper, a tall lanky dog with constant nervous energy, we all agreed the dog was nuts. He would be silly and playful one minute and then turn strange, scary, and threatening the next. We never knew if we were going to get the happy puppy version of Pepper or the psycho crazy version. We learned quickly to steer clear of him for our own safety. Our mother of course was stuck with caring for him as best she could.

Pepper finally met his end one day while harassing and threatening the men in a massive city garbage truck. As the men drove away Pepper made the fatal decision to attack the ten-ton truck with his teeth. I was just a few yards away when Pepper's body rolled under the giant right front tire and then under both sets of double tires at the rear. As the other kids and the garbage men gathered around the crushed body of our now former pet I ran back to our house on Helvetia Street and plopped down on our living room couch. Finally I started to cry.

As the tears poured down my face I felt a firm male hand on my left shoulder. I looked up to see the Master of my visions, my teacher, standing beside me once again. The Master appeared as he always did in the black robes of a priest with a black headdress and side veils. He always looked the same to me, an intense, highly intelligent, bearded man in his mid-thirties. Year after year he never seemed to age. It would be some twenty years in the future before I would see a picture of another man in exactly the same kind of priestly garments. They would turn out to be those of a Coptic Priest, the Coptic Church being the ancient Christian Church of Egypt. Egypt, you might remember, is the place I saw the Master living in my visions.

His lips never moving the Master impressed his question on my mind, "Why are you crying?" The connection from his mind seemed to cause an expansion inside my own. "I'm crying because a little boy is supposed to cry when his dog dies," I responded. With this admission a flood of understanding came over me. I knew that Pepper had been a tortured animal. His mind had been filled with fear and confusion with the phantoms of past abuses attacking and hurting him over and over again. With his death Pepper had been released from the pain of his damaged nervous system and twisted mind. Freed from his temporary physical form his spirit could now return to the great mystery where it could finally heal and prepare for the next stop on its soul's journey.

I looked into the eyes of my teacher and thanked him for this gift of understanding. He impressed on me that I could have figured this out for myself if I had just looked deeper into the truth rather than reacting, as convention and fear would have me do. I felt a bit embarrassed at this communication, as I knew he was right. I had after all been coming to this world time and time again for many thousands of years. This was a very simple level of understanding about the nature of life and death that I shouldn't have to be tutored on any more.

"Next time, call me about something important," was the final message from his mind to mine. And then he was gone. The next time it would be important. It would be a matter of life and death. Mine.

CHAPTER EIGHT

A Broken Jaw & Thinking I'm Dead

My sister Mary Alice is a year older than me. When we were very little we were practically inseparable. But by the time I reached the third grade and she'd reached the fourth she had her life and I had mine. The tensions that often develop between siblings reached a peak one day as we were heading home from Saint Williams Elementary School. I caught up to her and her friends on the two-mile walk home and things got ugly.

The tensions between us quickly escalated and at a certain point she swung her canvas book bag filled with hardcover schoolbooks and landed a solid strike on my jaw, hitting me so hard she almost knocked me off my feet. I was dazed for a moment, then looked down and saw blood pouring out of my mouth down my clothes and pooling below me on the street at my feet. At the sight of my blood my nine-year-old sister and her friends screamed with fright and ran away, leaving eight-year-old me to make the remaining mile and a half trip home alone with blood coming out of my mouth the entire way. By the time I got home I was in shock due to the amount of blood loss. I was also a little scared because the bleeding hadn't stopped.

My mother took one look and me and called my father at his work. When my dad got home he was furious his day had been interrupted. I was holding an ice pack to my jaw, tears still on my face. "Stop that crying or I'll give you something to cry about!" he yelled, raising his enormous right hand to hit me across the face. My mother thrust herself between my father and me. "Tom!" she yelled at my father, "Don't you dare hit that child!"

Less than an hour later our Family Dentist informed my parents that I would have to go to the hospital for surgery. My sister's canvas bag of hard-covered schoolbooks had managed to hit me just right and had fractured my jaw. With this news my dad finally calmed down towards me. He hated it when one of his sons cried for any reason whatsoever. Even though we were just little children he saw it as a weakness, one that had to be nipped in the bud for our own good. It wasn't until many years later that I learned my iron-fisted father had once been a gentle quiet little boy who loved to read, just like me. His sweet thoughtful demeanor had made him a target for the violent Italian immigrants kids that regularly made war with the Irish immigrant kids in my dad's neighborhood. My father had learned to survive by becoming the hardest toughest kid in town.

Once I was settled into the hospital that night I began to pray, not for myself but for my sister. I was afraid my father would vent his anger on her when he got home. As it happened my prayers were answered. My dad never laid a hand on her.

The next morning a nurse wheeled me off to an operating room. Without telling me what was about to happen, a doctor put a mask attached to a hose firmly over my nose and mouth and told me to "breath normally." But I couldn't breath. There wasn't any oxygen coming from the hose. I told the doctor there was no air but he ignored me. When I tried to pull the mask from my face he clamped down harder, clearly annoyed that I was wasting his time.

I began to fight because I was getting dizzy and I was afraid I was going to suffocate. The doctor called for help. Several attendants grabbed my four limbs and my torso and held me down against the operating table. As I lost consciousness my final thoughts were, "You stupid idiots! You just suffocated an eight-year-old boy to death!" I also wondered with a kind of morbid amusement at just how they were going to explain my death to the authorities and to my parents.

~

At first everything was black. There was no sight, no sound, and no sensation of any kind. Then I found myself floating in the air above my body. The doctors below me were working on my jaw as if nothing were wrong. "How can they not notice I'm not breathing?" I wondered. "How did they get to be doctors and nurses in the first place while being so incredibly unobservant?" After a while I returned to the nothingness. I faded in and out of existence for an unknown period of time. Finally I returned to my corpse. Once back inside all was black and dead. No sight, no sound, no feeling. "Is this it?" I started to worry a little. "Could this be the end? Isn't there supposed to be a light for me to go to? Am I going to be stuck this way forever?"

It seemed like forever before a hint of sound finally came my way. It was a strange sound, garbled and distorted, but it was sound nonetheless. I hoped this wasn't a bad sign. A while later a slight shadow gave me hope that some kind of sight from beyond the grave might be possible. An eternity of nothing seemed very unappealing. I tried to move some part of my body, any part, but with no success. Then I began to sense my physical form. It felt cold and stiff. Slowly I sensed more light, more sound, and possible movement around me. I tried to talk but my mouth wouldn't open.

As the drugs wore off my normal senses slowly returned. Later when I questioned a nurse I learned that the mask over my face had been a gas mask with a special gas to knock me out, and not an oxygen mask like I'd seen on the TV doctor shows. The gas had put me to sleep and shut down my senses. My body had been strapped to a table and my mouth wired shut with metal wires so my broken jaw would heal properly. That is why I wasn't able to move or speak. I asked the nurse why no one had bothered to tell me what to expect on the operating table, as it would have spared me all that fear and confusion. "The doctors are very busy men," she explained. "They don't have time to waste with children."

Through it all I had managed to learn something quite interesting. Apparently I could leave my body without being close to death and it would still be waiting for me when I returned. All I had to do was get back inside. This new discovery would set me up for many out-of-body experiences throughout my childhood.

~

Eight weeks after my broken jaw surgery I was brought to a dental surgeon's office to have the stabilizing wires sewn throughout my jaw and gums removed. This time when I was given the gas I was ready for what was to come. This time I didn't fight or resist. Instead I focused my mind in order to remain as conscious as I could.

As the gas took effect I held my focus and my mind remained clear. I felt a strange pressure building up in my spinal column increasingly focused at the base of my neck. Just as I thought the energy in my spine couldn't be compressed any further I felt a sudden release of the pressure and heard a loud "snap" in both of my ears. An instant later my consciousness was catapulted out of my body. I felt my mind sailing at high speed through the floors of the medical office building. In less than a second I had exited through the roof and found myself soaring through the sky high above the city below me. Now this was worth a broken jaw!

It seemed that a spirit version of my body had come with me. Years later I would learn that mystics sometimes referred to this as the "astral body" an energy body-double that we take with us when we travel outside of the normal time and space restrictions. I found control of my flying spirit body was quite easy to manage. It felt completely natural as if I'd done this many times before but couldn't quite remember. I flew at will over the city, able to see other towns and cities far off as I went higher and improved my vantage point. I dive-bombed at tall buildings and swept under bridges like I was Superman. After a bit more playing, some part of me left for a while and went to another dimension of reality. I don't know how long I was gone but I managed to come back to this dimension before the anesthetic wore off.

Once back in the normal world, albeit still in my astral body, I flew around the city looking into windows and moving through walls just to see what it felt like. Finally I felt a tugging sensation on my spine. I knew it was time to go back to my physical body. The anesthetic was wearing off and my body was regaining consciousness but without my mind there to direct it my body was having trouble functioning.

I re-entered the medical office building through the roof and returned to my body via the path I'd used on the way out of it. Once I'd settled in I felt the effects of the drugs that had not yet completely worn off. My senses became dull and clouded and remained so until the drugs were gone from my system. But I didn't focus for long on the drug's effects. I focused on what I had just achieved. "If I can fly through the sky in an invisible spirit body," I wondered to myself, "what other secrets does the world just behind the veil of everyday reality hold for me to discover?"

CHAPTER NINE

Hundreds Of Visions Of The Past & The Future

Growing up can be hard on any child, but for those hypersensitive to everything around them it can be especially so. I loved my family but felt distant from them most of the time. My father called me a dreamer who'd better wake up to the real world. My siblings called me weird and wondered why I couldn't act normal like other kids.

The mystical experiences that peppered my otherwise melancholy existence ultimately made me long for a life in the worlds beyond this reality. Finally at the age of six, I decided to leave home and go in search of a better life. Early one summer morning I put fruit and crackers in a large square handkerchief and tied it on the end of a stick, just like I'd seen the hoboes do on TV. I would need these provisions for my journey. I walked until I arrived at Nehill's Drugstore. I'd never walked farther than Nehill's, not even with my mother or my sister Kathy. Everything after Nehill's was the great beyond. As I stood there I realized that I had no money, no skills, and I was only six years old. Striking out on my own would have to wait until I was older.

But my deep unhappiness only worsened with time. Three more years of loneliness and despair about the sad state of the human race found me at rock bottom as I approached my ninth birthday. One day as I watched a truck rush by on the street in front of our house I decided to end it all and forcibly return myself to the Source of All Life where I hoped to find the peace and happiness I so lacked in this physical dimension. I took my position behind a large tree by the road and prepared to die. As I waited for a truck to throw myself in front of I felt firm hands on my shoulders. I turned to see the spiritual Master teacher, the Coptic Priest from my visions, standing behind me. "You can't leave," he said to me with his mind, "you have something very important to do with your life. It's why you came."

I knew what he was talking about. I had come to teach people about the reality of God and to help them understand the greater meaning of the sacrifice and life of Christ and other great spiritual masters. I had come to help pull away the veil of illusion, to help others catch a glimpse of the Divine Mystery that lies behind all physical form. I had always known this. But it was taking so long! It seemed like I'd already been here forever and my body was still small and vulnerable. The distant future of mature adulthood and my life of service seemed too far away to bear. "But I want to leave," I said to him. "This is a terrible place! The people here are so angry and lost and empty. They'll never understand anyway!"

"You can't leave," he said again as he led me away from the road. I wondered what people would think if they saw this dark bearded Master in black robes, headdress, and flowing veil in the front yard of our four bedroom New England colonial style house. I looked around and realized that any onlookers would only see a little boy standing in a daze by himself. This was vision. It was happening at another level of reality, far beyond the ability of most people to see. This very truth I knew was part of what I was here to share.

As I made a final attempt to argue my right to leave this world my Teacher tapped me in the center of my forward and several dimensions of time and space opened up before me simultaneously. I saw lives upon lives that I had lived in the past in many different realities. I saw that he'd been my spiritual teacher for several of them and that I too was a teacher for those who were not yet at my level of understanding. Those lives were not all in this world, but existed in many other levels and dimensions of Universe. The vastness of it all was astounding and yet also quite matter-of-fact to me. I knew all this. It was just that this dense physical form made it difficult to remember the Greater Truth. I watched as visions of ancient times past flowed before my sight. The visions carried me almost to the present, but then slowed down so that I could focus on a particular place and time in the late 19th Century.

"Remember," my teacher said as the images from this other life burned into my little boy's memory. "Remember." Before my eyes I saw New York City in November of 1875. Men and women in evening dress were gathered in a wood-paneled apartment. They were assembled there for a specific purpose. It was all very familiar. My teacher directed my focus to one of the men in the crowd. The man's face became artificially large before my eyes and took the form of a pose, as if for a portrait or a photograph. It seemed that I was to remember the exact pose that he was in. He was a white man in a brown suit. He had a beard and a kind, intelligent, and thoughtful face. "Remember," my teacher impressed upon me again. My mind took a snapshot of this

21

man and the pose he was in. I would remember him.

A map of the world appeared before me. I watched as a line traced the significant travels of this man's life over various parts of the globe, like I'd seen done on maps in old movies when they wanted you to know where the characters where traveling to. The lines started in Ireland, crossed the Atlantic to America, stabilized in New York, and then moved back and forth from New York to Boston. The line also went into parts of South America and thinner lines went out like tributary branches to additional cities in the U.S. The lines returned to New York and then headed back across the Atlantic to England. From there they traced down the European coastline around the continent of Africa to a city on the west of India and then on to another place on the eastern side of the same subcontinent. I saw that he eventually returned to the United States after this final stop in India.

After all this was shown to me, my focus was pulled away and back to the original room of people in New York City in the fall of 1875. I would come to know some of the people from this group in my current lifetime as he had known them back then. We had work to do together. With a rush of happiness and understanding I realized that I was not alone in all of this. There were others. Many others. Someday I would have friends and they would understand the same things I understood. I felt foolish that I had been so lost in my own sense of responsibility and purpose that I had imaged that it was all up to me.

As I walked back to the big tree on our front lawn with my teacher beside me I was still tempted to jump at a passing car. All these visions of other lives and other worlds had only made me want to leave this unhappy one and find a better one to settle into. My teacher knew my heart and pulled me again away from the road. In his hands he manifested what looked to be an ancient scroll made of skin or parchment with wooden rollers on the ends. As he placed the scroll in my hands I saw visions of hundreds of events from my past, my present, and from my future in this current lifetime all simultaneously revealed to me in the scroll.

I saw my unhappiness was not at its end. There would be many pains and cruelties and difficult times ahead for years to come. I saw that I would finally have others I could call friends as I entered my teenage years. I wouldn't have to wait until adulthood to end this bitter loneliness. I saw that when I was grown up my life would take many different paths as I continued to study and learn the secrets of the world around me. The older I saw myself in the visions the less the specifics of my future seemed laid out for me. There were many possibilities. The visions finally led me into my early forties where I saw I would change my focus and prepare to introduce myself to the world. In some ways it seemed a terribly long time to wait to do what I'd come here to do but now I knew that there would be joys and happy times and wonderful things to learn and see along the way. It would all turn out to be worth the trouble. I decided I could do this life.

I looked into the eyes of my Teacher. He knew that I would stay. I psychologically prepared myself for all the hurts and pains that I had seen were to come and made an inner commitment to see it through. I had been through worse in other times. With the crisis resolved my teacher was gone from my presence as mysteriously as he had arrived. I sensed his focus was now more fully on his work in Egypt and that there were others like me in different times and places that he was also giving his energy, support, time, and attention to. I determined that I would not bother him again if I could help it. Although my body was that of a child, my spirit was not.

As the years passed I would remember the scroll and the promises for my future. Again and again throughout my childhood I would recognize something that was happening as another of the events shown to me in the visions of the scroll. Just another bump in the road, I would remember. This too would pass. Later in my adult life I would meet and get to know some of the souls whose lives I had seen in the visions of the past delivered to me on that lonely day on my parents' front lawn. It would be almost twenty-five years from that day before I would open a copy of a mystical book published in the 1890s and see a photograph of a bearded man in a suit (the author of the volume) and recognize him and his exact pose as the man I was asked to remember from my vision when I was a boy. He name was William Quan Judge and in November of 1875 in an apartment in New York City he was one of the founders of the Theosophical Society, an organization founded to share the spiritual truths of all the world's religions. At a time of great social division and rampant prejudice across the globe this new Theosophical Society declared the oneness of all peoples and the equality of all regardless of race, sex, religion, national origins, education, social status, or economic circumstances.

CHAPTER TEN

The Great Wall & The Silver Cord

Once I knew how to go out-of-body and fly around the neighborhood I did so quite a bit, especially in my elementary and junior high school years. The actual leaving my body part almost always happened when I was asleep. However the coming back in for a landing part was often a very awake and aware process and quite a lot of fun actually.

Most mornings before I was able to wake up and get out of bed I would first have to intentionally re-enter my body. I would typically find myself back in my bedroom hovering high over my bed with my astral face and astral body pressed against the ceiling. The recognition of my face against the ceiling was my daily signal that I had returned from whatever flying around this and other dimensions of reality I'd been doing during the night. The particulars of where I'd been and what I had been doing often faded from memory very quickly, the way most people's dreams do, as I focused on my morning ritual of reintegrating my conscious awareness and the astral version of body with the three-dimensional physical version of my self.

I would usually look down over my astral right shoulder at my sleeping body below and then gently float down to become one with it again. Often my consciousness became blurry or foggy once I was back inside. I later understood this fogginess was in large part due to my becoming increasingly hypoglycemic through childhood. That is I had a serious blood sugar imbalance that would cause my brain to start the day with too low a level of blood glucose for it to function sharply and clearly until I had something to eat.

When I was ten we moved from the increasingly urban Tewksbury, Massachusetts to the more rural Pepperell, Massachusetts. I went from attending a very rigid and academically demanding private Catholic school to attending a comparatively lax public school. It wasn't a bad public school it was just that the curriculum was literally a couple of years behind the one offered at the parochial school I'd just come from. A large part of my parents' rationale for moving us to a smaller town was that Tewksbury was becoming a dangerous place for kids. Ironically for me the little town of Pepperell, with its children of small farmers and paper mill workers, was a much more violent and cruel place than the outwardly more threatening urban town we'd left behind. And like the residents of many insular small towns or inbred city neighborhoods around the globe these folks didn't take kindly to strangers, or at least not to strange otherworldly kids like me. Being able to go to sleep and leave my physical life behind me was one of the things that kept me going during the toughest emotional times.

One night I was exploring the higher dimensions, pushing as hard as I could to see just how far I could go in expanding my consciousness, when I came upon what appeared to be a massive gray wall. This great wall I knew was the manifestation of an idea, a translation by the human mind into concepts it could grasp and approach, of a much greater meaning and deeper reality. According to many of the great mystic philosophers and a growing number of today's theoretical physicists this could also be said to be true of our own world.

After studying the wall, I tried to get around it but it appeared to go on forever. It seemed infinitely high and infinitely low, stretching beyond all visual limits on either side. No matter how fast I moved in any parallel direction the wall just continued on without end. I knew the wall had to be either an actual cosmic barrier or a psychological one that was meant to keep me and other mystic travelers from straying too far from the dimension of reality I had been regularly swimming through, presumably for the safely of our fragile human psyches.

But I still wanted to know what was on the other side. I willed myself to get beyond the barrier and instantly I passed through. Although the wall appeared to be basically the same smoky gray monolithic barrier on the opposite side as it had seemed from my earlier vantage point this other reality I had apparently entered on to the periphery of felt alarmingly foreign. Terror struck at my heart almost immediately upon my arrival. My great desire to explore this other reality quickly gave way to a fear that I didn't know where I was or how to get back to where I had come from. I searched the wall for a way back through but found none. I tried to will myself briefly to the other side to prove that I could safely go back and forth between the two dimensions at will before venturing any further into this new world. But my now shaky will yielded no change of position. I began to feel as a claustrophobic must feel when they find themselves in an enclosed space with no obvious way out. I began to panic.

With fear almost overwhelming me I felt a sudden tug at my spinal column as if my spine was part of a long cord that extended far away from my astral body. I looked behind me and saw what appeared to be a long silver cord attached to my spine. I mentally followed the cord to see where it led and to discover what I might be tethered to. My mind followed the tether and found it was attached to my physical body still asleep in my bed. As action follows thought the cord pulled taut and almost instantly I was snapped back into my body across all barriers and dimensions of time and space, like the end of a carpenter's tape measure let go of and snapped back into its metal chamber. I landed in my body with a thud and sat bolt upright in my bed, my body drenched in perspiration and me shaking like a leaf.

What I'd just experienced had scared the crap out of me. At the same time it had taught me something new: that there was a cord of energy or of consciousness that kept you connected to your body while you were away from it. That was how you could always find your way back. But deep inside I also knew that it was possible to break that connection and to lose your way back. This could result in a catatonic coma state with the body still alive but dysfunctionally separated from the mind. The inner knowledge of this possibility was part of what had terrified me in that other realm.

Years later I learned some mystics have taught that such a cord exists and that breaking the connection to the physical can result in insanity. In such a broken state the body remains alive but without the rational mind there to govern and inform it about our normal world. It is also taught by some mystical schools of thought that this connection of the astral to the physical is what is severed at the moment of death. As a young adult I would read many books on such subjects and learn that this awareness of a silver cord connected back to the physical body was a common element in many out-of-body experiences.

As my early childhood years transitioned into my teenage years I largely stopped remembering my nightly excursions. My focus was elsewhere. Instead I would intentionally experiment with the power of the mind in my daily waking life. I would also spontaneously experience numerous other interesting phenomena, many of them while fully awake and walking around.

CHAPTER ELEVEN

Giving Peace A Chance

When I was about six or seven I was given a bag of those small plastic green army men to play with. As I looked at them, I felt there was something wrong. I wondered how to fix it, and then I knew. I got a kit with many different colored hobby paints and small brushes. I then took a pair of scissors and proceeded to cut all the weapons off the army men. I removed handguns, grenades, rifles, knives, and bayonets. Then I painted different types of clothing on the little men so that they could have other careers; doctors, teachers, farmers, businessmen, etc. During my teenage years in the early 1970s I found myself questioning my place in the world, getting very interested in girls, and considering the likelihood that I would be drafted to fight in the Vietnam War. I decided I would be willing to serve as a chaplain or as a field medic helping the wounded and the dying but I knew in my heart that my place in this life was as a healer and not as a destroyer of life. Perhaps because of my early near-death experience I found I was not afraid to die. It was ironic that I who'd had so many other fears as a child found that death in war didn't count among them. In addition the visions I'd been shown in the scroll hadn't included my going to war. As it happened, America pulled out of Vietnam and the military draft was cancelled shortly before I became of legal age for military service.

My junior and senior high school years would include different types of mystical experiences. One day when I was about twelve my sister Kathy asked me what I thought of the concept of reincarnation. As she offered her own thoughts on the subject my consciousness was swept away into an elaborate vision of an apparent memory of living in another time on another place on the globe and with a very different adult body than the one I would grow up to have in this life.

At first I was confused because, except during those experiences when my everyday consciousness would expand to include a much greater understanding, I didn't actually believe in reincarnation. It wasn't even something I thought about. Nonetheless her questions had started another vision going and soon I was following a stream of memories back to a very ancient time. There I found that the "I" that I was then was a teacher in a major school of philosophy and mystical thought.

The architecture around me was more like that of ancient Greece or Rome than anything of the twentieth century, yet distinctly different and much more high tech than anything from either of those civilizations. The high tech aspect caused me to wonder if I was seeing the future rather than the past. Nothing I'd been taught in school had even remotely suggested that a time of greater antiquity could have had a more advanced technology than ones that came so far after it. It was still a few years before I would hear the stories of ancient Atlantis from the psychic readings of American mystic Edgar Cayce and the tales of a technologically advanced civilization lost ages ago.

My own apparent memories (of Atlantis?) included many scenes from this other life culminating with the destruction of our world in a war that came from the air. There was a point where I knew that I would be dead within the hour. I made the decision to spend what time I had left aiding the casualties of that terrible war rather than going inward to prepare for my own death. My last memory is of holding a dying man's head cradled in my hands, helping him in his soul's transition to the other side of consciousness.

The chronological scenes from this apparent distant past of humanity made it clear that this near total destruction of our civilization had been coming for some time. Evil people who wanted power at any cost and others who had simply bought into the "us and them" war mentality had steadily brought this death and horror on us all over the course of several years. It all could have been avoided of course, but those who wanted their way no matter what the sacrifice of human life finally pushed the envelope just a little too far and it all blew apart. As best I could tell we'd been fighting a war using a combustible gas as a major weapon of terror and destruction. These giant-sized bombs were somehow dropped from the air and ignited just above or at the surface of the Earth, destroying everything at ground level with fire and a massive explosion. In a final critical miscalculation, a number of these gas weapons were exploded too near a fissure in the ground igniting natural gas pockets just below the Earth's surface. This caused a chain reaction across large parts of our world, burning up much of what was in the lower atmosphere including a significant part of humanity.

According to my vision, a great civilization was laid to ruin in a matter of hours and those who survived were thrown back into Stone Age levels of struggle and survival. Further I saw that this same kind of near total annihilation of our world was also a possibility during my current lifetime if our desires for power, wealth, and personal selfish convenience were not reeled in. I saw visions of war reaching out to the world from the Middle East unfolding in the first ten to twenty years of the 21st Century unless we made more positive choices as a species. In the apparent futuristic part of the vision, I saw death and terror in the early 21st Century as people fought for religion, ideology, and power. Sadly this scenario seems to be exactly what's unfolding today. I very much hope that we will be able to minimize the worst of what could be. It's in our own hands, really.

Whatever weapons some ancient civilizations may have possessed that could have wiped the evidence of its very existence off the face of the Earth, I have no doubt our current stockpiles of nuclear, biological, chemical, and conventional weapons are far more destructive than anything I saw in my visions of the apparent ancient past of our world. I was particularly disturbed by a news story of the new giant combustible gas weapons introduced to the world at the beginning of the 2003 U.S. invasion of Iraq. The giant bomb is called a MOAB, for Massive Ordinance Air Burst. MOAB's nickname in the U.S. military is the Mother Of All Bombs. The MOAB is the world's largest non-nuclear weapon in existence. It weighs 21,500 pounds and is about the size of a small truck. According to newspaper accounts it's guided to the earth by a parachute. When it reaches its destination it releases a highly flammable mist, which is then ignited by a conventional explosive. The bombs are exploded just at or above the earth's surface and destroy every living and non-living thing at ground level, just like the weapons I'd seen in my vision as a child where images of the ancient past and the near future were shown to me simultaneously.

At various times over the years I've had visions of other apparent lifetimes I've lived, some of which included the life of a warrior. I've seen my greater soul living lives carrying sword and dagger, bow and arrow, manning artillery cannon, and with charts and maps in hand as a battlefield strategist. But the description of this brand new bomb is too close to the images from my childhood visions not to cause me to wonder just how close to the annihilation of humanity we may taking ourselves once more. Maybe it's time we all thought about giving peace a chance?

CHAPTER TWELVE

Uri Geller & The Broken Watch

When I was a kid I was fascinated by the magicians I'd see on TV. "How did they create those illusions?" I wondered. "What were the mechanisms behind their tricks?" I read the classic Joseph Dunninger's Complete Encyclopedia of Magic from cover to cover learning all of the foundational principles of a stage magician's illusions. I also ordered every professional magician's magazine and every catalog of magic tricks on the market and learned all the basic principles of sleight-of-hand and stage illusion. I was determined to decipher how each and every illusion was accomplished. I figured out that if you studied the photos and drawings and combined that with an analysis of the exact wording in the descriptions of each trick a clever person could figure them out. As I was a kid with no money to buy these effects so I had to count on being clever.

Around that same time two professional magicians would come to prominence on the world stage in the debate over whether or not *real magic* actually existed or whether it was all just illusions perpetrated by con artists on the gullible masses. The two magicians were James Randi and Uri Geller. Randi (born Randall James Hamilton Zwinge, according to an Internet biography) was a fierce devotee of the famous magician and escape artist Harry Houdini. The Amazing Randi as he called himself had evidently patterned his entire professional life after the magic icon from the first half of the twentieth century. In the first part of his career he performed all the same stage tricks and escape artist feats as Houdini, such as underwater and straightjacket escapes. After that Randi moved on to trying to expose all psychics, mediums, astrologers, etc. as fakes and phonies in homage to Eric Weiss' (Harry Houdini's real name) personal journey through the false mediums and con artists of his day. Houdini himself had worked as a fake spirit medium in his early years, yet tried desperately for years after his beloved mother's death to contact her deceased spirit using mediums.

Ultimately James Randi was to find much greater fame and fortune as a professional debunker of mystic phenomena than he had ever managed as a performer and so he became the Western world's foremost professional naysayer on all topics psychic and spiritual.

Interestingly of all the supposed psychics and mediums Houdini visited, one of the only ones he was unable to expose as a fraud was the American trance medium Edgar Cayce. Houdini was reportedly astounded by the mystical abilities of the "American Prophet" according to records from the time kept by Cayce's family.

On the other hand, the Israeli-born magician Uri Geller was to become the Amazing Randi's unofficial public nemesis. In the early 70s Geller came to the attention of the world as a man with apparent telekinetic abilities, one who was able to effect a change in physical matter by the force of his mind and will. Geller was the original "spoon-bender" who could twist solid metal with an unseen power that we supposedly all innately possess. One day I turned on the Merv Griffin Show, a popular TV interview and entertainment program, and discovered Uri Geller was the main guest. Geller proceeded to demonstrate his ability to alter the shape of solid objects like metal spoons for the studio and television audience. Then Mr. Geller directed viewers at home and in the studio to join him in an experiment. "During the commercial break," he said, "bring out any old broken watches or clocks you might have and hold them up. Those watching at home should hold them close to the TV." As it turned out I had just such a broken watch, one my father had given me years before.

I ran upstairs at the commercial break and took the old watch from my top dresser drawer. Although the very old watch hadn't worked since I'd gotten it I really liked it for some reason, so every few months I would take it out and fiddle with it, trying to get it to work. A couple of years of winding, rewinding, and prying it apart to see what might be wrong on the inside had yielded no success. When Geller came back on the TV I was sitting directly in front of the screen with my old watch in hand. He told the studio audience to hold up their broken watches and for us at home to do the same. As I held my hand up to the television I looked at the still motionless watch face and thought how wonderful it would be if it could actually keep time. As Geller sent out his special energy I felt it. I was certain of it. It was a low level vibration that seemed like a kind of electricity. When the experiment was done, TV audience members claimed that their watches and clocks were now working. My old watch was also running for the first time in years. Curiously, as I was editing this book, I mentioned this experience to my wife. As it turns out she too had had the same experience with Uri Geller and a broken watch.

During the days following the TV broadcast I searched out every old broken watch and clock I could from family, friends, and neighbor homes and brought them back to our living room. I wound them up, shook them, and held each of them up to the rays of the television set under the theory that perhaps the radiation from the TV may have been the real trigger. No other timepiece ever started working again, only the one Uri Geller had somehow touched across space and time.

Years later, I would ask my father why he had given me an old watch that he knew didn't work. It seemed a strange sort of gift. My Dad, who was a bit of an amateur astrology buff, said he had read that those born under the Sun Sign of Cancer were typically fascinated by history and often had a love of old things from other times. In his mind an old timepiece seemed a perfect gift for his young Cancer son, even one that didn't work. Amusingly, he was right. I did love it, and for all the reasons astrology suggested.

Not surprisingly, professional skeptic Randi called Geller a fraud and a huckster and continues to do so to this day. To be fair to the efforts of Mr. Randi and others like him there are quite a number of frauds, fakes, con artists, and self-deluded people out there all claiming to have something to offer of a spiritual or supernatural nature that they really don't possess. Some make such claims for money, some for the attention, and some of them really do have some level of psychic or mystical ability. As for the professional debunkers, I figure the simple, gullible, and vulnerable among us can use whatever protection they can get from those who would use, abuse, or take advantage of their overly trusting natures. It is my belief that not everybody needs to look behind the veils of this reality into the other worlds of possibility for their lives to be complete. It seems to me that there are plenty of wonderful things to see right before our everyday eyes. Presumably, that is why we are all *here* rather than *there* in the first place.

As for the potential dangers of evil influences creeping into one's life through the exploration of the unknown, the occult, and the mystical it is my personal experience that such dangers do indeed exist. If you don't feel safe or comfortable looking into the more mysterious corners of the human psyche, consider that just maybe you don't really need to know what's there after all.

CHAPTER THIRTEEN

Three Days Out Of Sync With Time

Between the ages of eleven and thirteen I began a more active exploration into the larger questions of the spirit. I read books on India, UFOs, astrology, the Rosicrucians, mind control, the Mormon's sacred texts, Bible prophecy, and others. One day I came across a magazine article on the power of the mind. The author described a number of mind-over-matter techniques, which culminated with his going to a dartboard and throwing three bull's eyes in a row by visualizing in his mind that he could and would do so. I was very excited at the implications for the powers of the mind and immediately ran up to the attic of our old house to try the experiment on the brand new dartboard we'd just gotten a few days before.

At that age athletic ability and physical coordination were not yet among my skills and my brief attempts at throwing the darts a few days earlier had mostly resulted in my missing the board entirely and hitting the wall. Some of my darts had even landed on the wrong wall. My brothers had decided it was safer to leave the room when it came my turn at throwing the darts.

But as the moment would have it I'd just read the magazine article on mind power and was momentarily convinced I could and would do this. I went to the attic, grabbed three darts and took a position on the other side of the attic as far away from the dartboard as I could go. I threw the first dart absolutely certain it would hit the center of the bull's eye. It sailed across the room and landed dead on the bull's eye. Without hesitation I threw the second dart. It too hit dead center on the target. As I moved to throw the third dart, a tiny bit of doubt bubbled up to the surface of my mind. "Could I really be doing this?" a part of me wondered. "Could I really do it again?" The third dart left my hand, touched by that small amount of uncertainty. That dart landed just off the center of the target. I knew that certainty had brought the first two darts home to the bull's eye and that uncertainty had created its own result. In each case the mind manifested exactly what it expected to.

As interesting and informative as my little experiments would prove to be most of my lessons would continue to come to me completely spontaneously. One such lesson started right in the middle of my ninth grade geography class. As our geography teacher lectured at the front of the classroom, I saw a completely different series of events taking place superimposed over the normal three-dimensional time-space reality the rest of the class was experiencing. As our teacher continued to speak, I saw an alternate version of him turn and begin writing on the chalkboard. As the apparent ghostly version of my teacher wrote on the board a ghost version of a math teacher showed up at the closed hallway door and looked through the door's glass window at our geography teacher. In the superimposed version of reality, our teacher went to the door and engaged the other teacher for about a minute or so. Eventually the ghostly version of the math teacher went on his way and out through a doorway connected to the next classroom.

Once this ghostly alternative sequence of events was done our teacher turned to the board and began writing and moving exactly as he had in my superimposed vision. Right on cue, the math teacher appeared at the door and the entire order of events took place in real time just as I had seen them transpire in my ghostly vision, complete with the math teacher leaving through the same side classroom door. I shook my head and wondered how I'd managed to see into the future like that, but even more I wondered how and why I'd managed to see just three to four minutes forward in time? What was the point?

About a half hour later, as I was about to chalk up this out-of-sync with time experience as just another interesting bit of psychic entertainment and a mini-lesson on the malleability of what we generally think of as solid mechanistic reality, it happened again! The next out-of-sync with time experience was no more remarkable in its content than the one in geography class with the visiting math teacher. What was remarkable was that these events continued to happen all day long and into the night, right up to the moment I went to sleep.

When I awoke the next morning my first thought was, "Was that it or will this phenomenon continue to happen to me again today?" Within a few minutes the next out-of-sync vision of the near future superimposed over regular time occurred as my brother Bob and I were getting ready for school. "Cool," I thought to myself.

The affect continued for the rest of that second day and through the following day as well. On the morning of the fourth day I waited patiently for the affect to kick in but it did not. This was fine with me. Although a fascinating lesson on the mutability and flexibility of time and space there was nothing else really going on of interest in the visions and quite frankly watching one superimposed future vision after another after another all day long was making it difficult to focus on regular reality and to get anything done, especially my school work.

What's the lesson to be learned from this particular extracurricular tutorial? It might best be encapsulated by quoting the extraordinary writer known to time as William Shakespeare – "There are more things in Heaven and Earth, Horatio, than are dreamt of in your Philosophy."

Don't take it for granted folks that all those learned people out there know all the secrets of the Universe just because they may like to think they do. And just because somebody wrote down what they believe to be true in some officially important book – whether it be a scientific book or a holy book – it still doesn't make it so if it isn't so. I remind you that such caution goes for this book as well. Trust the evidence of your own senses and you may find that you can see a whole lot farther and deeper into the worlds around you than you ever thought possible.

CHAPTER FOURTEEN

A Ghost In The Hallway

Up to age fourteen I'd pretty much kept my mystical world to myself. After all, nobody ever talked about such things in regular society and the only place you heard about them was in church or in scary stories. Then one day in our upstairs hallway I found someone who understood. My mother.

I'd been looking at something from the windows of my brothers David and Jim's bedroom at the rear of the house. As I walked out of their room I stopped suddenly in my tracks. The air in front of me seemed somehow denser as if there was someone or something in my way. I waited more than ten seconds for the space to clear before moving on. As I continued down the hall I saw my mother at the bottom of the staircase on the first floor, her eyes watching me with utter disbelief. As I busied myself in my room I could feel her wanting desperately to talk with me. Finally she made her way up the stairs and timidly approached my bedroom door. "Tommy, can I talk with you?" she asked awkwardly. "Sure, Mum." I said. And so the conversation began.

As it turned out my mother had seen the ghost of an elderly woman, one she'd seen in the house before, sitting in a non-existent chair. (Perhaps one from the past?) When the old ghost got up from her ghostly chair and started up the front staircase my mother had followed her to see where the ghost was going. When the woman got to the top of the stairs my mother saw me rush out of my brother's room and then stop dead in my tracks, apparently to allow the elderly ghost time to pass by. Once my mother shared with me that she could see ghosts from time to time and that she had other visions as well, I finally felt I had a friend. A decade later as my family was packing to move from that house my mother told me the old woman's ghost had visited her one final time to say goodbye and to wish her and her family well for the future. As my mystical encounters continued I soon had another amazing experience to talk about, one that I attempted to share with my brother Bob. Years later, Bob would admit to me that at the time he thought I'd gone completely crazy, which of course was why I didn't tell people this stuff in the first place.

CHAPTER FIFTEEN

Aliens In My Bedroom

This is the story that inspired me to write this book. Actually this book started out as a magazine article that was going to be my take on the UFO phenomenon. After my own Close Encounters in 1972, described in this chapter, I looked deeply into many similar accounts. After years of research I felt I had a valuable perspective on the truer nature of these apparently otherworldly experiences. Then the intended article quickly started becoming an entire book, and so here we are.

My first encounter occurred while I was running laps outside of our high school late in the afternoon on a spring day. Not an unusual thing for many kids, but highly unusual for non-athletic me at that age. The endorphins released in my brain gave me what I suppose qualifies as a classic runner's high. It was while enjoying that biologically induced state of bliss that I looked up and saw it. It appeared as a large, circular, shiny metallic object silently sitting dead still in the sky. I stared at it intently. The top and bottom tapered away from the wider midsection and it had what appeared to be round regularly spaced windows or portals around its midsection. Its physical appearance was very much the standard image of a flying saucer, just like the ones depicted in old movies from the 1950s. I knew the look well. I'd done a term paper on the subject when I was in the eighth grade.

I looked around and saw many people close by deeply involved in other things. There were two baseball games in progress as well as a track and field event. As best I could tell I was the only one who saw this object in the sky. This I found to be most interesting. After a couple of minutes of my watching it and it doing nothing in particular I felt a sudden rush of energy go through me. "They saw me," I thought to myself. At that the energy of the unidentified floating object shifted subtly, or so it seemed to me, and then it silently moved behind the only cloud in the otherwise clear blue sky. I waited for a few minutes to see if it would come out again, but it did not.

After the experience I wandered inside the largely abandoned halls of our high school, feeling a bit dazed and wondering why I had had this particular experience and what it might mean? In my wanderings I came upon the open classroom door of my geometry teacher, Arthur. Arthur was one of my favorite faculty members and felt more like a kindly father or older brother than a standard authority figure. Arthur immediately saw that I was troubled and offered his patient ear. Soon I was drawing a picture on his blackboard of the object I had just seen and was giving him the details of the experience. He studied the drawing for a few moments and then preceded to tell me of a UFO experience he and several of his comrades had had while they were enlisted in the United States Air Force.

I went home that day telling no one else about the experience. I was not quite sure how it fit in with my other more spiritual experiences. I had never thought to put supposed UFO encounters in the same category as seeing angels and spirits. After I finished my homework that same night I put my books away and shut off my bedside lamp. My brother Bob, sitting up on his bed a few feet away, continued with his homework. Seconds after I lay down on my pillow I felt a strong pulsing vibration coursing all through my body and heard a strange whirring sound in my ears. I looked over at Bobby but nothing unusual seemed to be happening to him. Next the front wall of our house seemed to disappear before my eyes. I could now see the trees on our front lawn and the night sky above it. I watched and listened as cars drove by our house on Main Street, their headlights illuminating the road before them.

Bob, still engrossed in his schoolbooks, adjusted his bedside lamp, turned a page, and continued reading as if nothing else was going on. "How can he not notice," I wondered, "that the front wall of our house, only inches away from the left side of his body, has ceased to exist?" I tried to call out to Bob so that he would look up and see what I was seeing but I couldn't make a sound. I tried to sit up but my body would not respond. I seemed to be paralyzed. The whirring sound grew louder in my ears as a spaceship appeared about thirty feet over our front lawn, sitting dead still in the air. The intensity of the energy increased along with the sound. "Surely," I thought, "Bobby will see the ship and the missing wall if he'll just look up from his homework?" While I thought this, I realized there were plenty of cars driving by our house and none of the drivers seemed to notice the fifty-foot UFO hovering above our front lawn.

Just then I seemed to see inside the ship. There were two of them. I understood they had come expressly for me. They linked into my mind and started probing around inside my unconscious. This intrusion into my psyche frightened me. I felt extremely violated that somebody appeared to be in control of my body and able to access my mind. Slowly I became aware of an apparent dialog going on between them and some other part of my larger self, a conversation the smaller more personal part of me couldn't listen in on. The fact that I was being shut out of this otherworldly communication finally infuriated me. I focused all my will and silently screamed inside my head for them to "GO AWAY!" At that forceful expression of will everything stopped and was immediately back to normal. The ship was gone, the front wall was back, and I was once again in control of my body. I jumped out of bed and opened the window shades to the front yard. I searched outside for signs of the ship or of some kind of impression made on the grass below it. Nothing. I asked my brother Bob what he'd seen or felt. He hadn't seen or felt anything. I told him what had just gone on. He looked at me like I was mad.

The next day, I continued to try to understand what had happened and why. The fact that Bob had been only a few feet away from me during the events and had seen and heard nothing made it clear to me that what had happened had not occurred in the normal three-dimensional physical world. This I found intriguing. Presumably the ship I'd seen in the sky in broad daylight earlier the day before had not actually been there in this dense physical universe, either. I realized that my brother's presence had been key to the lesson I was being asked to learn, for if another person had not been present in the same room with me the entire time all of the evidence of my senses would have told me that what had happened had been completely real. My brain would have had no reason to believe otherwise. The old expression "seeing is believing" was strangely applicable and yet not applicable to the situation.

Had I not already had so many other visions and had I not understood that these experiences were ultimately happening at another level of reality I would probably be insisting to this day that what occurred that night was completely real in the normal sense of that word. Perhaps I'd have become part of that subculture of alien abductees, telling my story under hypnosis and demanding the government tell us the "truth" about extraterrestrials, the presumed truth my experience would have convinced me that they must be hiding. I also became convinced that the altered state I experienced was a critical factor in many UFO encounters. Anyway, whatever was ultimately true behind this phenomenon it was not necessarily of this world.

Oh, by the way, later the next evening – it happened again. This time however I was ready for it and was fascinated to see where the experience might take me. I felt reassured by the fact that this was apparently not happening in the strictly physical world. This made me feel a lot safer. I also was emboldened by the fact that the so-called Close Encounter had stopped when I demanded that it stop. With my fear gone I relaxed and watched the process with intense interest. I hadn't actually been expecting another experience of this kind but just went with it when it happened again. This time the ship I saw in my mind was dramatically larger than the others I'd seen the day before and it appeared to be sitting some five miles above the surface of the Earth. The Mother Ship, I guess? I seemed to understand that this was my last chance to go with them. Whether this meant going for a classic abduction and return scenario or something else I wasn't quite sure. Then the mind probe sensation started up again. I could tell that they were in direct communication with some larger part of my being, a part of me that my regular self is not normally aware of. I strained to hear or comprehend what was being discussed.

My greater self and these beings, whoever or whatever they were, were debating if I should go to the ship with them. A note of concern hit me. Could whatever part of me was talking with them make such a decision for me? I decided I would not allow this to be the case. The conversation came to an abrupt end as I heard the pronouncement, "He's not ready yet." At that moment everything stopped and went back to normal. I got up, a little unsteadily, and looked around. During the entire experience my mother had been in the hallway outside my door folding laundry. I could hear her singing to herself and see her shadow moving in my doorway throughout the entire event. I went and gave her the details of what had just occurred. I figured correctly that she hadn't been aware of anything unusual going on, just as my brother hadn't seen or sensed anything the night before.

Anyway, once that second night's trance ended a flood of memories and understanding rushed through my mind. I remembered a television show I'd seen a couple of years earlier about a supposedly true UFO abduction that happened to a married couple in New Hampshire. It was later made into a movie starring actors James Earl Jones and Estelle Parsons. That show had inspired me to study the phenomenon and caused me to read every book I could find on the subject. I'd even done a term paper on the UFO phenomenon in the eighth grade. As I considered these past events I recognized that a part of me had wanted to understand more about these stories and so, I believe, I had drawn the UFO-type contacts to me for closer examination. Once my psyche had set me up for the apparent opportunity to experience a full-fledged onboard abduction, whether such an experience would have existed only in my mind or on the astral planes or whatever, my resistance got the better of me. Mind you, I'm not suggesting I would have gone physically onboard a physical space ship existing in this dimension of reality, simply that I would probably have experienced myself as having done so. That is after all how many of these supposed encounters seem to work.

As I examined the experiences further and more objectively I noted that the paralysis part of the experience was completely consistent with my being in my astral body and therefore unable to work the physical body until my consciousness was once again grounded back inside it. I had long since become accustomed to returning to my physical body after my astral travels but had not been consciously doing so very often since the night of my extreme fright at the great gray wall and the unknown dimension it apparently led to, a couple of years before the UFO scenario unfolded. I replayed the steps that led me from normal awareness to being in the astral. I saw that as I had lain down each night in bed my awareness had shifted just slightly out of the physical and into the astral. Generally I was used to my mind taking flight with my astral body and leaving the physical far behind.

Sometimes, of course, we all slip away in the middle of the day, going on automatic pilot in the physical. Later we find ourselves wondering what we've been doing for the past ten minutes or two hours? "How could I have spaced out like that?" we ask ourselves. And with no memory of where our psyche went off to while it was gone we're left to shake our heads, amazed that we could have lost that much time. Many long distance truckers and traveling salespeople know the phenomenon of going on autopilot while driving, only to come back and realize they've managed to drive fifty miles or more past their exit.

Not surprisingly, a number of UFO abduction reports are said to have taken place during just such "lost time" experiences while people are driving around late at night or when they're very sleepy. They zone out into the astral and suddenly there's a strange light in the air before them, or a ship appears, or strange men are standing in the road and so it goes. Anyone who's had a telepathic link with other people know such UFO dream/experiences can be shared with others in the car with us. Note that nobody ever seems to get "abducted" in the middle of rush hour traffic. It's always when they're out in the middle of nowhere late at night or lost in their imaginations.

The same rule seems to hold true for at home abductions. Read the accounts and one after another you'll see the people claim they were sitting in a comfy chair, watching TV, reading a good book, or asleep in bed before the altered state of consciousness abduction experience happened to them. I've personally not seen any accounts of somebody who's been wide-awake, completely sober, and in the middle of making dinner for their family when they got whisked away by aliens into a spaceship. Those who do claim to have been taken away in the middle of something such as making dinner for their family have experienced returning to essentially the exact same moment in time when they apparently left, which kind of proves my point that it didn't happen in this reality.

In what I believe may a related phenomenon, in cases of major trauma such as a car accident or a violent assault, the conscious awareness can sometimes abandon the body. In such cases we don't always come back right away because the physical or emotional trauma has been so great. This can result in a long-term separation of the astral mind from the physical brain. Such a state is medically referred to as a coma. In extreme cases so much physical damage has been done to the brain tissue or emotional damage to the psyche that the consciousness cannot effectively re-inhabit the physical brain and body and the person's mind never returns. Medicine would declare such a person brain dead.

Back to my own experiences, while I was mentally replaying how I had gone from normal reality to the UFO scenario I saw that I had slipped just slightly out of my normal consciousness and into the astral without making any significant spatial separation from my physical body. The UFO altered state had kicked in at the precise instant my astral self had started to disengage from my physical, which would normally result in my physical body falling asleep for the night and my conscious psyche flying away. The shift into this altered state of awareness however had been so instantaneous that I hadn't noticed that I was already out of my body. With my mind focused on the apparent UFO experience I was suddenly having I had spent the entirety of each night's event slightly out of phase with my dense physical form, not having the time or spare attention to notice that I was caught between the worlds where the physical and the astral merged into one.

Although I don't claim to have any kind of complete explanation for why the entire UFO phenomenon exists in the first place, I feel certain I was given this experience so that I could help others understand that their own abduction or UFO contact experiences may not have been exactly what they thought they were. These people need to understand that they're not crazy, nor were they in any actual physical danger or necessarily in the physical circumstances they may have felt themselves in. It's important to note that these sorts of experiences are usually super-real and hyper-intense. They often burn themselves into our memories. This can make them become seemingly more real to us than anything that we've experienced in our regular daily lives.

But just as my childhood visit from Santa Claus did not actually happen in this reality, even though all my senses tell me it did, neither are these UFO experiences likely happening in the regular world of normal consciousness, no matter how convincingly our senses may tell us they are. At least that's what all my inquiry has led me to conclude.

A tricky point to make is that there are individuals in the world who've had profound mystical experiences that have forever changed their lives who are essentially in the same category as many UFO abductees. The difference is that they realize that the transformative experience they've endured was part of an inner event in an altered state or other reality. For a fascinating and intriguing parallel check out my story of an apparent visit from Santa Claus when I was four year old given earlier in this book. You'll find an example of this same sort of experience. To see how strikingly similar the two otherworldly encounters really are just try replacing the word "Santa" with "Aliens" and the phrase "Santa's sleigh" with "space ship" and it quickly starts to look very much like the same phenomenon, don't you think?

CHAPTER SIXTEEN
My Future Wife Appears On The TV

On a particular day in 1973 I heard a voice say, "Turn on the television to channel four, now." I turned on the set and found talk show host Mike Douglas talking with comedian Georgie Jessell. Georgie was telling Mike he'd just met this beautiful woman named Rhonda and that he was going to take her to Hollywood and make her a star. They called for Rhonda to come on stage and this beautiful 23-year-old woman comes awkwardly on the stage, virtually pushed into the lights by the backstage crew, saying, "No, no, no! I can't go to Hollywood and become a star! I'm a mother! I have to look after my daughter! No, no, no!" With this the woman walked off the stage, disappearing behind the curtains and leaving the host and his guest stumbling to recover. I found myself asking, "What the hell was that?" Yet, my inner guidance told me I had seen what I was supposed to see.

Twenty-eight years later I showed up for a meeting at a beach house in Malibu, California to meet with the manager of author Jess Stearn about the possibility of my adapting Jess' most famous subject psychic Edgar Cayce's life for the big screen. The author's representative Rhonda and I hit it off at once. We talked for hours while the producer who'd brought us together sat quietly at the table. We traded stories of our lives, with Rhonda telling me how she'd come to show business after turning down the chance so many years before when she was friends with Ed McMahon of NBC's Tonight Show fame. Then she launched into this funny story about when she was a single mom and was driving stars from the airport to be guests on the Mike Douglas Show. She said she was called on stage by guest Georgie Jessell, who declared he was going to take her to Hollywood and make her a star. She'd been afraid that pursuing the opportunity would not create the right life for her four-year-old daughter Tammy so she ran off stage, refusing to have any part of Georgie's plan.

What is the nature of time and destiny that I should have been shown my future wife decades before we were to meet in the physical world? Rhonda and I became a couple soon after we met and have since married and become each other's spiritual partners in life. Rhonda was a widow when we met and I had never married during all those years.

CHAPTER SEVENTEEN

Jim & Dave & The Monte Carlo

Not surprisingly my mother and I were not the only ones in the house born with natural mystical sensitivity. My Dad was mostly an absentee father, but when I really needed him he'd be waiting at the door asking straight out what was going on. Even after I was living on my own he'd show up on my doorstep just at my moment of need. "I saw a vision of you in church yesterday," he would tell me matter-of-factly.

One of my favorite such stories involved my youngest brothers David and Jim. Dave was a teenage boy with a driver's license. Dave was a wild boy in those days and had started drag racing with our Dad's brand new Monte Carlo. One night as we watched TV the lights dimmed momentarily. "What was that?" I said. "Oh, that was Dave," said our youngest brother Jim, "he just hit the electric power lines down by the Town Hall. But don't worry, he'll be alright." At that, Jim got up and walked to the telephone in the front hallway and held his hand expectantly over the receiver waiting for it to ring. I followed him with fascination. "How do you know what happened?" I asked. "Dave's been racing Dad's car around the tight curve at the Town Hall for weeks," Jim said. "I've told David I've been having a dream that he was going to take the turn too hard and hit the power lines if he didn't stop."

I asked him if he had other dreams that came true. "Sure," he said as if it were the most natural thing in the world. Three minutes later the phone rang. Jim's hand dropped down to the receiver and picked it up. "Hey, Dave. You hit the power lines at the Town Hall, didn't you?" Jim said without bothering to say hello or to be sure it really was our brother calling. This was decades before the invention of Caller ID. "I told you to stop racing Dad's car before it was too late." As Jim had predicted, David had walked away from the crash with barely a scratch. The heavy-duty Monte Carlo was not so lucky. The car had taken out a row of pylons and hit both an electric light pole, the source of the our lights momentarily dimming, and an Oak tree, bending the car practically in half in the process.

CHAPTER EIGHTEEN

Living In The Here & Now

By age nineteen, I'd read books on spiritual, religious, psychic, and psychological reality. Some of the more interesting ones included: Autobiography of a Yogi by Hindu yogi Paramahansa Yogananda; The Roots of Consciousness, a doctoral thesis by Jeffery Mishlove; Sun Signs and Love Signs by American astrologer Linda Goodman; Seth Speaks by channel/author Jane Roberts; The Book of Mormon and The Pearl of Great Price, the scared books of the Church of Jesus Christ of Latter-Day Saints; The Jerusalem Bible, an ecumenical translation; The Late Great Planet Earth by evangelical Christian Hal Lindsey about how Jesus was going to return by the year 2000 after Satan ruled the world as the head of the United Nations – the popular Left Behind series of novels are the same material rehashed; Space, Time, And Beyond by Bob Toben, exploring the theories of quantum physics; and There Is A River by Thomas Sugrue, about American psychic Edgar Cayce.

Of all the books I read, the most influential one didn't really impact me until I read it a second time at age twenty. After the second reading I understood that for me the book's most valuable lesson was its simple three-word title of Be Here Now. It was written by American intellectual turned hippie Dick Alpert, who got thrown out of Harvard along with professor Timothy Leary for giving LSD to his graduate students. Alpert left the U.S. for a while, spending time in India, doing lots of mind-altering drugs, and seeking religious experience. He eventually found himself in the company of an extraordinary mystic who taught him drugs were not the answer, that meditation was key, and that over-identification with personal ego obscured the greater truth and clarity of the soul. Alpert would take his lessons back to the West and become a famous spiritual teacher using the name Ram Das, which means "Servant of God" in Sanskrit. I heard him speak on several occasions and shared dinner with him one time. For all the fame he'd gained as a guru I found him modest, and humanly accessible. But the simple lesson that got me was the dictate to "be here now."

The teaching was simple: Stop living on past laurels. Cease taking self-worth from titles, possessions, or worldly accomplishments. Stop trying to fill the space with idle talk or dreams of the future and just allow your awareness to be focused in the here and now. In short, allow yourself to simply be. In the midst of my second reading of <u>Be Here Now</u> I decided to try it out for myself. I monitored my thought processes and each time I found my mind focused somewhere other than in the present I would say, "be here now" to bring myself back to the moment. To my amazement I found that I was almost never focused in the here and now. I was always thinking of things other than what I was doing at the time.

Over the course of two weeks I had to work to bring myself back to the present time and place dozens of times a day. Virtually every time I asked myself, "Am I being in the here and now?" I found that I was not. And then it happened. A shift of my consciousness took place and I found that I had successfully reoriented myself to the present. My life has never been the same. In Zen Buddhism, a specialized Japanese variation of Buddhist discipline, there is the dictate to "Chop wood. Carry water." What this deceptively simple phrase means is to be focused in the here and now. If you're chopping wood to heat your house be completely focused there for that chore. If you're carrying water from the well to your home keep your attention on the task at hand. These are excellent object lessons to illustrate the value of remaining in the present. For example the consequences of not staying focused while you're chopping wood could result in the loss of one of your legs. In the martial arts and military disciplines of the world soldiers are taught pretty much the same thing. "Give everything of yourself to what you're doing," if you want to survive. In business, social activism, politics, and athletics it's, "Keep your eyes on the prize."

Since that transformative two weeks at age twenty I've learned that a single day can have a greater richness and fullness than an entire year of just barely being emotionally and mentally present for one's life. "Always live life to its fullest," was the lesson for me, "for the very next moment may be your last." For those of you who are thinking, "Hey, that story wasn't about a mystical experience!" my response to you would be, "Try actually living fully in the here and now for yourself and see if you can say your personal world hasn't changed practically beyond recognition." Such experience qualifies as pretty mystical stuff in my book.

CHAPTER NINETEEN

The Day I Couldn't Put Down The Phone

It was a few weeks before my twenty-first birthday. I was living in a cooperative vegetarian household northwest of Boston. I had long hair, managed a natural foods store, and completely avoided the drug scene. I mention this because some of the experiences I've had are similar to what people report under the influence of psychedelic drugs such as LSD and peyote. The mystical states many sought through mind-altering drugs came naturally to me and I didn't want to mix my natural mystical experiences with an artificially induced kind. An even stronger motivation for me was that I always knew I'd one day be telling the story of my otherworldly journeys to the world and I wanted to be able to say, "No, I didn't do drugs." I've seen too many minds destroyed by the downside of chemicals and don't want to promote them. If you really want to open up to the mystical side of life I would highly recommend simply paying more attention to the subtle mystical signs and signals that are all around you all the time.

One day the phone rang in our hippie kitchen. As I lifted the receiver I felt a powerful flow, like electricity, course through my entire body. "Hello?" I said into the phone, wondering who or what might be on the other end of this energy connection. It was a woman named Patricia calling for my housemate Bonnie. The pulsing energy continued. I explained that Bonnie wasn't home and took down the woman's phone number. The conversation was over, but I wasn't ready for it to be. My mind still wanted desperately to understand what was going on with this powerful energy link between us and so I tried to keep the woman on the line a little longer. Patricia seemed mildly annoyed at my attempt and said a polite goodbye and hung up.

Afterwards, I stood like a fool in the kitchen with the message for Bonnie still in my hand. I couldn't put it down. Something profound was happening and it was somehow connected to this female stranger. I just knew it. Finally, unwilling to let the scrap of paper go, I made a copy for Bonnie and kept the original for myself. As I stored the precious memento in the top drawer of my clothes dresser I said to myself, "You've got to be crazy. What are you going to do, call this woman on the phone and say 'Hey remember me, the guy who answered the phone?'" As it happened, two days later and a hundred fifty miles away I would meet the woman from the phone in person.

My housemate Bonnie was involved in a place called Birdsong Farm in southern Maine. The farm was a retreat and workshop center for woman's issues and spirituality. That weekend, Bonnie invited me to join her and a few dozen others in sprucing up the place for the coming workshop season. I was the only male in attendance.

On Friday we drove to Maine. That evening as we gathered in a common room to share stories and tell the others about ourselves two women arriving late from Cambridge, Massachusetts walked into the room. Suddenly it was happening again. A powerful surge of electricity ran through my entire body. I recognized it was connected to the shorter of the two Cambridge women. "What the heck is going on here?" I wondered again. I found myself staring at the shorter woman. I couldn't keep my eyes off her. When it came time for her to share about herself she said her name was Patricia and I realized she was the woman from the phone call.

The next morning at breakfast I staked out the kitchen, waiting for her to walk in. I engaged her in conversation the first moment I could. I announced to her that I was Thomas, the one who'd answered the phone when she'd called for Bonnie. I waited for the profundity of the truth that obviously connected our souls together to set in. Surely she must have felt the spiritual energy too and would be as excited as me to learn its deeper purpose. This was after all a center for spiritual seeking and understanding. Patricia seemed a bit put off by my intensity and politely left the room. The workday passed, but I knew Patricia was wondering about me too. I felt her doing so. Later that night we found ourselves together and talked the night away, finally parted company as the sun was rising. Within weeks Patricia had introduced me to an entire world of mystics, psychics, healers, trance mediums, religious leaders, and a mystical community of people that I could finally feel a part of. From then on I would no longer be alone in this mystical journey. I had friends to share it with. Thanks again, Patricia, for coming into my life just when I needed you.

CHAPTER TWENTY

The Healing Circle

Her name was Ellen Fritz. She was quite famous in psychic circles, divorced from an even more famous husband on the cutting edge of the self-transformation movement of the day. My new girlfriend Patricia had set it up. It would be my first reading with a professional psychic.

I'd met psychics before, though the ones I'd met before Ellen were of the gypsy/hustler/con-artist type. It wasn't that these hustlers didn't have psychic ability; it was that their abilities were used to con you out of your money or get you dependent on them for guidance. One such psychic approached me in a health foods store when I was a teenager and told me that she could "psychically see" I was sexually frustrated, a designation that describes most teenaged boys, whether or not they have girlfriends. I was not impressed and politely declined her offer to tell me even more amazing things about myself for cash money.

Ellen was different. She was a smart, honest, fresh-faced Mid-Western gal who at one point had hosted a TV cooking show. But the most important difference between Ellen and the psychic hustlers was that Ellen was sincerely dedicated to helping her fellow human beings and living a life of spiritual service.

When I arrived at her home Ellen simply said "hi" and offered me herbal tea and cookies. She was about as unpretentious as she could be and her warmth and humor were both comforting and disarming. Ellen Fritz worked like many of the professional psychics I came to meet over the years. She'd focus and quiet her mind and then proceed to tell me whatever it was that she felt guided to tell me first. After she had said what she felt most spiritually moved to communicate she offered to answer any questions I might have of my own.

Ellen was accurate on virtually everything she said concerning my past and present. Some of what she told me, I'd never related to anyone. Ellen also offered me her visions of my likely future. One of her more captivating predictions was of a town in the mountains full of conifer trees, lakes, and streams. She saw me moving to these mountains and being very happy there for a time. The houses were warm and friendly and inside the homes were very special people. People like me. Less than a year after this reading I would meet an extraordinary healer and psychic woman, leading to my being invited to join the staff of a new healing and spiritual center that was being founded in the mountains of Western Massachusetts. A few months after moving to those mountains I recalled Ellen's prediction and realized that the place I was now living in was exactly as she had described in her reading. But there are a few other stories to tell before we get there.

Upon the completion of my first psychic reading, Ellen invited me to join a weekly prayer group and healing circle that happened at her home. The folks who came to the group each week were from all walks of life, but what bound us together were the mystical life, a love of service, and a sense of being part of a Divine Plan much greater than ourselves. Each week would begin with a prayer or invocation, asking for protection and guidance from the Divine Source, God by any other name, and making the declaration that only those spiritual forces who were working for greatest good would be allowed to join us. The group prayer we spoke was the same each week and about six weeks into attending the group Ellen asked me if I wanted to lead the group in the prayer that evening. I felt more than ready and already knew the minute-long benediction by heart.

I sat in the center of the group. The others were on chairs or cushions around me. "Strap yourself in and hold on tight, Thomas!" Ellen joked. I thought it a bit dramatic to say such a thing for a simple prayer recitation, but I was determined to do a great job and inspire the group. The group did what it did every week and focused their positive energy on the person in the chair at the center, who was myself in this case.

As I dutifully lead the group in our positive affirmation, I felt a force of energy growing inside my body and all around me with surprising speed. An intense electrical pressure was building at the top of my head and a compression of energy seemed to be filling my spinal column. "Only a few more words left and the prayer will be finished," I told myself. I could hold on until then. As I finished the last sentence, I heard a loud "snap" at the back of my neck as my consciousness was catapulted out of my body and into the night sky above the house. So this is what Ellen had meant when she told me to strap in and hold on tight.

For an instant, I thought to explore the neighborhood and the landscape around me, as I had so many times in my childhood when out-of-body, but my consciousness was on its way to a predetermined destination. I lost awareness of my physical body and the room I'd left behind as I soared in another dimension of beauty and power and healing grace, a realm of angels and of light. I have no idea how much time passed, for where I went existed outside of time and space, but eventually I heard Ellen's playful voice calling from somewhere faraway, "It's time to come back, Thomas! We have work to do! Time to come back to your body!" I was so far away that I had to make a slight effort to re-locate my physical form. Ellen instructed the group to help bring me back so we could get on with the work of the evening. When I returned, Ellen gave me a big smile and said, "Did you enjoy your trip?"

Each week our healing circle would get together and pray for anyone who asked for prayers or who had prayers requested for them by family or friends. The more intuitive and psychic members of our group would offer any visions or inspiration they got as we focused the positive healing energy on the individual or the problem at hand.

One week, we had a couple of folks attend who'd come to ask for prayer help for a friend. Their friend's problem was apparent spirit possession by an evil entity. The story they shared was of a man who had terrible visions combined with a supposed evil spirit speaking through him. His case, we were told, was under study by more than one research group, in part because the man's face would turn black and blue as he choked and thrashed around during these supposed evil spirit possession events.

As I focused on this man's problem, I saw a jungle river scene that I was told by spirit was of this same man's soul in another life. In the vision this man and another man were heads of a very cruel tribe of people who loved to capture and torture people who strayed into their territory. Their camp was decorated with human heads impaled on sticks. I watched the vision as they strangled their victims to death, the unfortunate men's faces turning black and blue in the process. When we asked spirit/God what we could do to help this man let go of this past so that he could be relieved of the evils of this past life we realized that the man had become addicted to his current life affliction.

Before these symptoms had shown up, this man had lived an obscure life with nobody paying him much attention. Since the bizarre seizures and their associated manifestations he'd become a celebrity of sorts in the parapsychological community with groups of doctors studying him and papers being written about him. In order for him to be healed and released of his torment he would have to be willing to become just a regular man again. The so-called possessing spirit appeared to be the spirit of the other man who had been his partner in the atrocities committed in that other life. Finally, it was the general consensus of the healing group that this man was not yet ready to let go of his unique fame and have a healing from his dramatic condition.

I attended this group for the next year and a half before moving out of the area to the healing center in Western Massachusetts. The types of healings and conditions we prayed for were as varied as the members of the human family.

CHAPTER TWENTY-ONE

A Death In The Family

My uncle John Hogan, one of my mother's younger brothers, was very much a part of our family when I was growing up. John was the closest male relative we had after our Dad and in many ways felt to me like a second father. I loved John and his wife Rita. Their four children were our closest cousins when we were kids and the news that we were going to visit the Hogan's always brought happiness to our family. As an added bonus, we also got to see our aunt Alice and her mother, our "Nana" and our only living grandparent, on some of those visits.

When we got the news that John had a brain tumor we were all devastated. Not having John in our family was almost inconceivable. His death was a great loss to the entire Hogan clan.

In 1979, I was privileged to spend a critical night in the hospital at my beloved uncle's bedside. John had what turned out to be the worst night of his hospital stay and I was blessed to be able to be there with him and for him during those difficult hours. When I came to visit him John was fading in and out of this reality, seeing and talking with people who weren't physically present with us in the hospital room and apparently visiting different times and ages of significance throughout his life. I suppose I was uniquely qualified to be in the company of someone whose consciousness was traveling out of the confines of normal time and space. As far as I could tell John's spirit was preparing him for the transition of death into the next world. A few years later, I would work in a nursing home for the very ill and the elderly and recognize patients there going through the same process of disassociating from their bodies and tripping through time as they sorted out their lives towards the end of them.

People who don't understand this important process can get very unnerved in the presence of someone in this state, but I was perfectly at peace with it. Each time I felt John was becoming too upset or too stressed out by what he was going through I'd just touch his arm and gently call him back to the world his body was still living in. At one point, when John was talking to someone only he could see, a nurse came in and asked with great concern, "Does he even know who you are?" To reassure her I said, "John? Do you know who I am?" He immediately said, "Of course. You're Tommy Lyons. Trudy's boy," and then went back to his conversation with the invisible participant.

John Hogan died a month before his forty-sixth birthday. As I write this about him I am now forty-six myself and I am struck by just how young John was and how great a tragedy his death was for his family. John was a teacher who taught advanced mathematics to high school students. He was also a carpenter, a great storyteller, and an unusually devoted family man. Family was the most important thing in John's life. Even as he died so young, leaving behind a wife and four children still in school, John provided for his family and for their futures. He'd built their home with his own hands and then he designed, worked on, and supervised the building of four duplex apartment houses. He worked for years on these projects, using his nights, weekends, and summers off from his teaching job to accomplish these tasks. The income from those apartments would provide steady, dependable financial security for his wife and children long after his early passing. "Patience is a virtue," it is said and John had the patience, the discipline, and the determination to leave this legacy for his family. But what is most striking to me is that John had envisioned building his beautiful home and the four rental income properties to provide for his family years before he was even married.

John's father, my maternal grandfather, had also suffered from an inoperative brain tumor as a relatively young man and had left a wife and several children behind when he died. My grandfather's death had been devastating to his family in more ways than one. The medical prognosis for my grandfather's brain tumor had been that he would be a bedridden invalid for the remainder of his life and a burden on his family. He'd soon lose all his mental faculties and become "a vegetable" they'd told him. When my grandfather died by his own hand, rather than live his final days in a bedridden coma, his wife was forced to go out and find a way to support herself and the three teenage sons still under her care. I'm convinced that some part of John knew his fate, an early death from a brain tumor like his father, decades before it became a reality. But the additional grief and financial hardship his father's untimely death had caused his mother and his siblings would not be the kind of legacy John would leave behind for his own family.

My experiences have caused me to believe that our souls, the part of each of us that exists outside of time and space, know the plan laid out for our lives long before certain elements of those lives are lived. Some apparently follow that life plan fairly closely, while others veer off from the course laid out for us at some other level of our being.

~

After John's funeral, as the Hogan family stood by and watched John's body lowered into the ground in its coffin I looked over and saw John's spirit standing by his family. He looked to my eyes as he had in his better days, but his face was graver and sadder than I'd ever seen it in life. Even as our hearts were breaking for him I felt his heart breaking for his family. I felt his spirit around his family and friends, but it was only when he was standing with his wife Rita and their children that I saw his astral body materialized before me. In particular, John's spirit spent a lot of time with his wife Rita and with their oldest son Bill. I felt John giving all the strength he could to Bill, as Bill was now to be the man of the house upon John's demise. John and his own brothers had been in the same circumstances after their father's death and I'm sure John knew the weighty responsibility his oldest son was feeling.

Of all the deaths we've born over the years, the loss of my uncle John and of my sister Kathy's father Buddy are the ones that still touch us the deepest in my family. They were two very good men, taken so young from a world filled with more than a few people that we all might do better without. Why do so many good people die so young? Perhaps we'll learn the answer to such mysteries at some point in our soul's journeys. In the meantime, let's remember to share all the love and goodness that we have to offer with those still in our lives. We will all of us be gone someday, but I believe it's the part of us we leave behind, that determines whether or not our lives have been worth the living.

CHAPTER TWENTY-TWO

The Waterfall Spirit & The Talking Tree

After high school, I briefly majored in film and theatre at college but my teenage thoughts of becoming an actor paled against my desire to delve into the mysteries of life and spirit. Instead, I dialoged with Native American medicine men, Indian swamis, Western mystics, and hung out with graduate students at major divinity schools.

I remember attending a workshop on mysticism lead by a member of Scotland's Findhorn Community at a retreat center near Amherst, Massachusetts. I was warned upon arrival that the two Siamese cats in residence hated men and that they would bite and scratch any male who got too close. But my heart was so filled with joy and love at that point that the supposedly vicious cats followed me everywhere and even slept with me under the covers of my bed at night.

As I sat in meditation on my second day at the conference I saw a vision of a beautiful thirty-foot high waterfall surrounded by trees and flowering plants. The energy of the place was so beautiful that I wished to go there and experience it in the physical. All morning as we sat in classes I kept feeling the waterfall spirit calling and reaching out to me. In my mind I could see the graceful water dancing down the rocky wall. I could feel it in my heart. I knew I had to find it, no matter how far away it might be. At lunch break, I grabbed some food and quickly headed into the local woods. I just kept going in the direction I felt the waterfall calling me from. After a while, I heard the sound of running water faintly in the distance. I ran in that direction with the sound growing louder as I got closer to the source. Finally there it was before me in all its flowing glory. The waterfall felt alive to me as if it too had a spirit, a conscious soul, whose body of incarnation was the very waterfall itself. I felt it was happy I had come and that it loved to share its beauty and joy.

A few months later I met Patricia and entered the world of mystical and religious inquiry that was so strong in her life. At the time she was about to enter a graduate program at Harvard's Divinity School. Patricia had grown up in Connecticut, the daughter of an Irish father and an Italian mother. Although both were nominally Catholic,

Patricia's father was fascinated by the mystical and many spirit séances and the like were held in their house as she was growing up. As an adult Patricia had chosen the socially activist Society of Friends, commonly known as the Quakers, as her group. On our way from Boston's Quaker Meeting House one Sunday Patricia and I stopped to sit on the grass of the Boston Common, a park in the center of the city. We ultimately sat in the shade of one of the 200-year-old oak trees.

As we approached the grand majestic tree of our choice, I sensed this tremendous presence rooted in the ground before me. I felt its noble spirit and a self-awareness whose body was apparently this great tree. I was humbled in its presence and suddenly uncertain if we should sit down at all. Out of respect for this spirit, we decided to ask for permission to do so. After a moment's pause, I felt the elder earth spirit concede to our request. We sat reverently at the base of its massive roots, feeling more like we were still in church than in a public park.

Later when we arose to leave we stopped and thanked the tree for its comforting shade. As we started to go I felt the spirit of the tree reach out to me. It wanted something in return. For a moment my mind went blank in disbelief. "What could a tree spirit possibly want from us?" I wondered. I approached the tree uncertainly, praying for guidance. I felt spirit guide me to the other side of this great tree, which was some twenty feet in circumference. I was drawn to the thick aboveground roots, but couldn't see anything to do once I got there. Then my eyes were drawn to a dark spot between two root stems. It was a hole that ran deep underneath the base of the tree, probably dug by an animal. The tree seemed to want me to reach inside. I hesitated, thinking a creature might be in there, but the tree spirit persisted.

I knelt down and cautiously felt under the giant roots. Then my hand touched something familiar. It was an aluminum soda can. I searched around but found nothing else inside the hole. I grasped the can and pulled it out. As I did so, I felt the metal object disengage from the interference it had been causing in the energy field of the tree's flow of life force. With the offending object gone, the ancient tree seemed to heave a great sigh of relief. Its peace and dignity had been restored. From that day on I would never again think of plants as simply background in this world of ours. This planet is their home too.

CHAPTER TWENTY-THREE

A Lost Soul Asks For My Help

After a couple of years away I would spend two months back at my parents' home before taking a new job and renting an apartment in a nearby city. Not wanting to be in the way, I slept on the living room floor and commuted to a job I had thirty miles of country roads away. I continued with the healing circle at Ellen Fritz's place, with her playing my mentor and teacher. Patricia and I had stopped being a couple, but would remain friends for years to come.

One evening as I was meditating in my folks' living room I saw the shadowy gray form of a man standing in a corner of the room. Even with all the things I'd seen and experienced since early childhood the appearance of an unknown spirit in the shadows scared the crap out of me. I knew this was the real ghost of someone who'd gotten lost between the worlds, the astral remains of a stranger who had come to me for some reason and I had absolutely no idea what to do about it.

I looked away, hoping it would disappear. I was so freaked out by the feeling of death and despair I felt around it that I sadly couldn't see its underlying humanity. I knew it was a man's ghost, but I couldn't stop thinking of him as "it." I looked back to the corner hoping he'd gone, but he was still there. In fact this time I was able to see him more clearly than before. As I looked at him he looked back and reached towards me as if he wanted to communicate. The whole experience was too much for me at that moment so I hurried out of the room, refusing to look back. I slept across the hall in the den that night.

The next day I called Ellen and told her what had happened. She explained that the ghost had been drawn to me because of my growing spiritual light, which could be seen on the astral planes where he was trapped. She gave me instructions in how to pray for angels to assist me so I could help set him free from his astral prison. When I returned from work, I did as she suggested. After my prayers and healing ceremony for this lost soul I never saw that particular ghost again.

Months later I was approached by another ghost in a city park, but this time I wasn't afraid, as I felt I knew how to handle the situation.

CHAPTER TWENTY-FOUR

Don't Forget Your Muffler

This was truly the strangest and most surreal experience I'd ever had, up until that time anyway. The entire thing was like an episode out of The Twilight Zone. If I hadn't come to understand it within the larger context of everyday miracles and the inner connectedness that underlies the events of normal reality I never would have told another soul about this one. Taken out of context, hell, even in context this one was just plain weird and pretty mind-bending to endure. This cosmic lesson came my way while I briefly stayed at my folks' house at age twenty-one. I'd taken a new job as warehouse manager of a large East Coast natural foods distributing company. That new job was twenty miles to the west and I was on the road a lot for a few weeks.

One day I felt strongly drawn to take a highway route I'd rarely been on. My experience with such strong feelings was that there was a lesson to be learned, a person to meet, or something that I needed to interact with waiting for me on that different route. I drove several miles, keeping alert for whatever might be in store for me. Finally my eyes were drawn to a muffler and tailpipe assembly that had apparently fallen off of somebody's car. For some reason this seemed to be what I was supposed to see. I pulled onto the shoulder of the highway and walked over to the lost muffler. There was nothing unusual about it as far as I could see. "Maybe I'm supposed to head down the road, find the motorist who lost it, and help them reattach it to their car?" I wondered at first. But that didn't seem to be the right answer. "Perhaps it needs to be moved farther from the road so as to prevent a potential road accident?" I pulled the exhaust assembly a good ten feet onto the sloping hill of the roadside and left it there. Nothing. No feeling that I'd accomplished what the Universe wanted me to do. I waited another minute for some kind of spiritual guidance, then got in my car and went on my way.

Two days later I came upon another muffler on a completely different road. Again, I felt it was supposed to mean something. I looked it over, but saw nothing special. Not surprisingly, it was from a different car. Two days after that I came upon another lost exhaust system on the same highway, but miles closer to my parents' home where I was still staying. "That's funny," I thought. "Each one of these mufflers brings me a little closer to home."

Another two days went by and yet another muffler system appeared just off that highway, taking this strange series of car parts another few miles closer to my folks' place. "Okay, let's be rational," I told myself. "This all has to be simply a weird coincidence. How could it possibly mean anything?" And yet intuition told me that it did. The rest of that day and during all of my driving the next day I visually searched the roadsides, as I drove my commute, for any other damaged exhaust systems. "Mufflers fall off people's cars all the time," I reasoned, "surely there will be others." But my search turned up no other such automobile debris.

After an additional two days another muffler appeared on the street, noticeably closer again to my parents' home. At this point I had to prove to myself that this was all simply unrelated coincidence or else I was going to drive myself crazy. I drove as slow as I felt safe in doing, with my hazard lights flashing, and kept my eyes sharp for at least one other exhaust system assembly. It took me a long time to get home this way, but I got there without success. No other exhaust parts. I absolutely refused to accept defeat on the matter and continued driving for miles in a different direction. I kept driving around that day until the sun finally went down and I was completely out of daylight. I had driven down every road I could think of yet hadn't found another muffler assembly lying on or even near any of the roadways I drove on. The most annoying thing was that it still seemed like it was supposed to mean something and I couldn't figure out what! "Could somebody be playing a joke on me?" my mind searched for other explanations. Impossible. No one knew my routes, which varied from day to day, and I hadn't told anyone about this weird experience.

At the next two-day interval I was determined not to see another muffler system left on any roadside. When intuition told me to go left, I went right. When spirit seemed to direct me onto one highway, I avoided that highway and went on a completely different route. With this willful avoidance technique, I managed to keep from seeing another muffler system for an entire six days. But my actions to get me to this bizarre goal had become plainly insane. "This is no way to live one's life," I finally told myself. I'd added at least an hour or two to my commute each day in order to avoid seeing lost exhaust systems I

MODERN DAY MYSTIC

intuitively knew where out there. Whereas I'd physically examined the ones I had seen, before I started trying to avoid seeing them, I knew they were really there and not visions or illusions of the mind.

After those six days of avoidance, I decided to cease this approach. It was plainly ridiculous. "Besides," I told myself, "even though this seems completely real, what the heck am I afraid of?" It wasn't like the metal piping was going to come alive and attack my car or something. "As much as this strange apparent spiritual lesson has come to seem like a weird horror movie sequence it is still happening in real life," I reassured myself. "Just because I can't understand it doesn't mean I have to run away from it." As soon as I stopped using my intuition to avoid coming across another muffler system the next one appeared almost immediately. This muffler appeared just four miles down the same street that my folks lived on. "Okay," I thought. "So what?"

Two days later, I came home to find an exhaust assembly had been deposited at the very edge of my parent's front lawn. I parked the car in the driveway, walked over to the metal exhaust assembly, and carried it to my parents' garage. I broke the assembly into smaller sections and put it with the rest of our trash for the next trip to the town dump. A final two days after that I got all the way home without seeing a single muffler system lying by the roadside. "Whatever that was about," I decided, "it must be over." I parked the car, went inside, and took a shower. When I got out of the shower I made myself something to eat and then watched a little TV. After a bit, I got up to make a phone call in the front hallway of our Victorian home. The front door was open and a friendly breeze was blowing in. I opened the screen door to look at the beautiful sunny sky and there it was.

During the hour or so that I'd been home, an entire automobile exhaust system had apparently fallen off somebody's car and landed exactly at the entrance to our driveway. I literally froze in the doorway when I saw it, as a chill went up my spine. My mind went completely blank at this point, as I still couldn't understand what was happening. The whole thing seemed so bizarre that I actually felt a little afraid to leave the house and face this additional hunk of metal. But I had to, or somebody had to. The muffler system had landed dead in the center of our driveway's entrance. Any car coming in or out was at risk of driving over it and getting their vehicle seriously damaged.

62

I walked across the front lawn and dragged the metal monster out of harm's way and tossed it into the field next door, away from our property. I would deal with it later and no one would see it buried in the high brown grass for now. Mystical lesson or not, I'd had it. I asked the Universe to make this stop. I clearly hadn't understood the message, if there was one, and the entire thing was just freaking me out way too much. I waited to be shown a sign, but there wasn't any.

Two weeks later the entire muffler system fell off my car on the highway without any audible warning or banging about beforehand. By the time I drove back to retrieve the assembly, with my engine jugging loudly, it had already been crushed by a passing truck and had become completely useless. I stared at the wrecked metal assembly in utter disbelief. "Was all this insanity just my spirit trying to warn me that my muffler system was in danger of coming loose from my car?" I asked myself. "Was I simply supposed to have gotten under the car and tightened up some clamps? Could that be what all this incredible series of strange coincidences has been about?"

I flashed on the theories of one of the fathers of modern psychology, those of the famous European psychologist Carl Jung. In his work, Jung had suggested that all life and consciousness was connected at the subconscious or unconscious levels. Jung had posited the idea of meaningful coincidence, known popularly as *synchronicity*. Jung had insisted that we were all connected to a deeper flow of consciousness that brought all of us together in a kind of great dance. Through following the flow of that great dance we all wound up at just the right place at just the right time to connect with whomever and whatever we had agreed to connect with at some other level of our consciousness. "There are no coincidences," is the pop culture phrase that remembers Jung's theories. Or rather, "There are no meaningless coincidences." Everything in fact is connected to everything else at some level of the Divine Mind. Science now agrees that this holds true for the entire physical Universe as well.

What was the mystical explanation for this strange series of muffler encounters? In an apparently elaborate display of this principal of synchronicity, about a dozen different motorists, who were each about to lose their automobile exhaust systems for their own reasons, unconsciously *cooperated* in losing them at just the right place, at just the right time, for me to encounter them. All this apparently for the unconsciously agreed upon purpose of driving the truth of this very mystical, magical, psychological idea home to me in a way that I could not avoid noticing. In the regular course of the events in our normal lives we all get those funny feelings that something we just saw or heard or thought about out-of-the-blue *means something* and that it's something we ought to pay attention to. A typical example of those funny intuitive feelings communicating with us might be when something reminds us of our mother and so we call her only to hear her say, "Oh, I was hoping so much that you'd call today. I tried everyone, but no one knew where you were and I really need your help!"

Another example of our intuition talking to us and us *not* listening might be when we keep noticing snow shovels in newspaper ads, people's barns, and in store windows and we think to ourselves, "I should buy one of those new snow shovels." But we don't buy one because we know we've already got a perfectly good one out in the tool shed. Then later when a big snow storm hits we find out our younger brother borrowed the shovel, without asking to, and that snow shovel is now ten miles away in the trunk of our brother's car on the morning we need to dig our vehicle out of a three-foot snow drift in order to get to an important appointment on time. Damn it!" we say to ourselves. "I *knew* I should've bought a new snow shovel when I had the chance! I just knew it!" And some part of us *did* know it.

How did we know the shovel wasn't there when we had no conscious reason to suspect it wasn't? The same way we know there's something not right about a seemingly friendly person we encounter in a store, at a local event, or simply when we see them walking by. Intuition. Intuition, God, Goddess, spirit guides, guardian angels, the collective unconscious, telepathy. Take your pick of terminology. Choose the explanation that works best for you. But recognize that, at some level, we are all part of a greater whole. Each of us is connected to everyone else and everything else. We all depend upon each other.

I apparently needed to step into The Twilight Zone in order to fully get this concept at a level I would never forget. You do not. A word to the wise; take great care in not getting too caught up in this sort of experimental mind-twisting scenario in your own lives. This is definitely the sort of thing that could make you unnecessarily paranoid and very possibly real world crazy. "Tune in next week when a man will be followed around by a grilled cheese sandwich!" Or maybe not.

CHAPTER TWENTY-FIVE

The Chelas & Their Master

Once direct access to the mystics of the world and their respective traditions opened up for me I wasted no time in learning from as many of them as possible. Some seemed to have true wisdom to offer and real integrity. Others were just hacks doing the best they could. A few were hustlers, some were merely self-deluded, and a couple of these supposed wise people were, as best I could, tell just plain nuts. Happily, the more I immersed myself in mystical learning and altered states of consciousness the more in the flow of life I naturally became.

One lazy afternoon I was reading some mystical treatise while my girlfriend Diana sat a few feet away playing gentle classical pieces on a baby grand piano. We hadn't spoken for well over an hour at that point, as we were both lost in our own worlds of thought and introspection. In the midst of my reading, I found myself fantasizing about traveling across the United States and seeking out the company of Native American shamans and medicine men like the mystical character of Don Juan from the popular books by Carlos Castaneda. Then in my imaginative wanderings I looked down and saw my girlfriend Diana's cat boldly going with me on my journeys. "Wait a second," I said to myself, "This isn't my daydream, this is Diana's daydream." Diana was a major fan of the works of Carlos Castaneda and was planning to move to the American Southwest later that year in order to study alternative medicine at a college in New Mexico. Her cat would be going along. I realized that we had become so close in the few months we'd been together that the normal psychic walls between people had, at least temporarily, come down between us. "Traveling across the country to the Southwest. Don Juan and strong kitties." I said out loud with a twinkle in my eye. Diana's hands stopped on the piano keyboard with a thud. The shock of my reading her mind so completely had taken her out of her musical trance. "You know, Thomas, sometimes you really scare me," was all she managed to say.

One of the more enlightening experiences I had during this period involved my brief contact with one of the more bizarre religious cults operating in the United States. This group is still very influential today with a prolific and successful publishing house that puts out books on many areas of mysticism, but focuses on the *Ascended Masters* of the world's great religions. Mind you, it is my experience that some of the Great Souls and Spiritual Masters of the world's religious traditions do continue to work with us here on Earth, but that doesn't mean that any given self-proclaimed prophet or so-called holy person is the personal spokesperson of the Ascended Masters, just because they claim to be.

It all started one day as Patricia and I were walking on the campus of Harvard. We were no longer a couple by this time, but had remained friends. As we strolled we came upon a poster with the photograph of a middle-aged white woman declaring: "I'm Stumping For The Coming Revolution In Higher Consciousness!" We both thought this was wonderfully bold and decided to check out this woman's lecture, which was scheduled in a rented hall at the University.

When we arrived for the free presentation we were informed that no one would be allowed in without revealing his or her full name, address, and home phone number and writing the info down on a note card. Patricia baulked at this and was ready to walk away, but I got us in by writing down my own correct info and then making up a fake card for Patricia. The lecture only drew a small crowd and it turned out the woman on the poster was not actually going to be there. Instead, a man stepped up to the podium and announced that he was the woman's top *chela* or disciple. He told us of his years as a minister in a particular church and of his knowing that that group held the ultimate truth. He said that after years of service he came upon another church and recognized that this other church was the one that actually held the ultimate truth. "Finally!" he triumphantly told us, after years of dedication and his final disillusionment with this new source of all truth he met this woman prophet, the one from the posters, and recognized that it was "she who held the ultimate truth!" Patricia and I looked at each other and wondered if this disciple of the great prophet had any idea just how poor an argument he was making for his own powers of discernment in the matter of who did and did not hold the ultimate truth of the Universe. Whereas, by his own admission, he'd already been dead wrong at least twice.

After a rather strange short movie of the great prophet in the elaborate robes of a high priestess was shown we were told that there would be a follow-up meeting at a major hotel. I was intrigued to learn more about the inner workings of this quirky religious cult. Patricia was not.

I arrived at the follow-up meeting, two nights later, at what I thought was to be another public presentation by this same religious cult. The event was held in a conference room at a Hyatt Hotel just across the Charles River from Boston. Patricia declined to join me, so I went alone. As I approached the open door to the meeting, the entire room turned blood red before my eyes. In the vision, I saw what might best be described as psychic tentacles in the air throughout the room, as if lurking in the astral realm to capture unsuspecting prey. The word "WARNING" flashed so large and insistently over the scene that I had to stop in my tracks in the hotel hallway for I literally couldn't see anything except the blood red tentacles and the psychic warning sign in my mind's eye before me. Obviously my higher self, or whatever part of the Divine it is that looks after us down here on Earth, was telling me that I was walking into trouble. I remembered a technique that Ellen Fritz had taught me to use in such cases, so in my mind I surrounded myself with white light for spiritual protection. Confident that I'd taken the necessary precautions, I entered the conference room.

The people were welcoming and seemed normal enough, although maybe a little too friendly for comfort. I made the rounds before things got started, chatting with each person in order to learn what I could about the cult and its members. As it turned out, they were all in the cult. I was the only outsider who had shown up. "No problem," I thought to myself. "This is a major hotel, after all, and not some secret basement somewhere. Besides, if any of them actually turn out to be dangerous I'm big enough to take on anyone in the room, if I have to." They weren't exactly a bunch of professional wrestlers. Someone walked up to me with a Polaroid camera and took my photograph. It was explained to me that my picture and all my personal information would be sent to the mother church so that the great prophet could link her energy to mine and bless me. "That sounds nice," I thought to myself. But something about it didn't feel very nice.

The evening began benignly enough. As we all sat in a circle, the male and female heads of the cult's local chapter reminded everybody how great the woman prophet was, about how much wisdom she had, and how honored we all were to be a part of her great work. After this, members of the group turned to me and asked me some questions about myself and answered the ones I had for them, although I felt as if the group leaders were carefully monitoring their members' answers. Generally, everyone assured me that being part of the group was the best thing in their lives. Then it happened, the group chanting. I'd been a part of group chants and religious choruses before and had always been very uplifted by the experience. This was different. The very instant the droning chanting began I felt a psychic terror rush through my body. I found myself nearly paralyzed with irrational fear. It felt like the very cells of my body were being violated by the manipulative power of the energy being generated by this invocative ceremony. I was definitely under a type of psychic attack, and I knew it.

As part of the chanting, the group ritualistically invoked the name of one famous Saint, Master, and Archangel after another. But although they were calling out the names of these supposedly Great Beings and Ascended Masters, I could see all the energy and life force of the group was being sent to the mother of their cult, the great high priestess prophet they all worshiped. This local group, knowingly or unknowingly, was performing a type of ritual magick. But this was not the positive, healing kind of magic we all do when we open ourselves up in loving prayer. This was what is called, in some circles, *evil sorcery* or *black magick*. Not black as in a person's skin color, but that which is not of the light of the Holy Spirit.

It was clear to me, by the powerful flow of energy going out of the group to their far-away female prophet, that the high priestess of this cult knew exactly what she was doing. The entire ritual was designed to direct all of the power, energy, will, and life force of the participants to empower and enrich her, their leader. I cleared my mind and looked around the room to the now closed entry door. The manipulative energy was so intense that I stood up for a moment just to prove to myself that I could leave if I wanted to. It felt as if the giant blood red tentacles I'd psychically seen earlier had wrapped themselves tightly around me. It actually took an effort of will to overcome the extraordinary force that was willing me to stay and submit with the rest of them. Reassured that I was stronger than the manipulative force that had so completely co-opted the group members, I settled back into my chair. I decided to see this thing through to the end for whatever other lessons might there to be learned. But I also decided that I was ready to head for the door if things got even a little bit weirder.

When the droning invocations finally stopped I silently thanked God, my angels, and any spirit guides that might be looking after me for their protection and support. I looked around the room again. All the cult followers seemed lost in another world. Their auras all looked dirty and distorted and incestuously swirling together. They clearly felt the power of this lower vibrational magickal connection and it was intoxicating to them. I wondered if they understood that this was a negative force and not a positive one that they were all participating in. I wondered how many would care, if they did understand. Their leader was a wealthy charismatic speaker with a grandiose vision of reality and of herself, who packed a powerful psychic wallop, to boot. She taught that she personally was the highest incarnation on the planet. The group members were obviously addicted to their drug and their drug was their prophet and all the tales of wonders she wove for them.

As the cult members slowly rose to their feet, I went to the male and female leaders to say goodbye so that I could then politely get the hell out of there. A shock went through my entire system when my eyes met those of the male group leader. His eyes looked like a black empty void. His entire personal will seemed to have been drained from him. Shaking hands with him felt like shaking hands with a corpse. I was momentarily shaken by this brief encounter, but also intrigued. I courteously made the rounds, saying my official goodbyes and intentionally looking directly into the eyes of every person there. They all had those same dead eyes. They looked liked the walking zombies from the *Night of the Living Dead* movies, completely under the spell of the sorcerer. Once again, I was seriously creeped-out.

I'd had enough. I was done with being pleasant and composed. I made a beeline for the door and headed down the hallway as fast as I could. A couple of the cult members called for me to join them for a bite to eat, but I didn't even stop to acknowledge what they were saying. I got out of the hotel and into my car, without stopping to use the men's room. I headed north to Mass. Ave., took a left at M.I.T., and drove until I found a phone booth. It was after 10 PM. I called Patricia and she immediately sensed I was upset. Even though we were no longer seeing each other, I didn't hesitate to invite myself over. She was a good friend who'd understand what I'd just been through and I needed to talk to someone about it.

When I got to her place, Patricia had made tea and offered me food. I told her everything from start to finish. "I did warn you not to go," she reminded me good-naturedly. When I told Patricia about the Polaroid photograph taken of me she looked concerned. She explained to me that many cultures have used things such as hair, clothing, or personal objects to make a psychic energy connection to people at a distance. Healers can also use such things, to better tune into the life force of a needy stranger, but people bent on doing harm may use the same connecting objects to help them in their efforts to inflict psychic harm. The infamous voodoo dolls are made with such principles in mind. Think of a time when you had very bad blood between you and somebody else. Couldn't you sometimes just *feel* the hate and animosity coming from them, even when you weren't around them? This is the kind of stuff we're talking about, except with the intentional use of objects that carry the vibration of the other person. "Photographs are simply a more modern way to help make such magickal connections," Patricia finished explaining. "You should try to get the photo of you back, if you can." I resolved to do just that in the morning.

The next morning, I went to Harvard Square and used a public phone booth to call the only contact number I had for the group. The phone number was for getting directions to the previous night's hotel meeting. The fellow who answered the phone was very friendly and immediately invited me to attend another of their meetings. I told him as politely as I could that I wasn't interested and explained that I wanted to be taken off any mailing list they'd put my name on and that I didn't want my picture sent to their national headquarters. He ignored my request and proceeded to ask me about myself and about my beliefs. He assured me that his group could show me things about the spiritual worlds that I could never imagine. I assured him that I *could* imagine such things and asked if I could stop by his office and talk with him personally about the matter. He responded by slyly suggesting that he didn't feel comfortable telling me where he was. It was clear that he was enjoying his position of power in this dynamic.

At that point, I would have loved a face to face with this pompous fellow, but this was only a phone call and I didn't even know the guy's name. If I was going to get him to do what I was requesting I was going to have to do it over the phone. I prayed silently in the public phone booth, asking God and any guides who might be available to help me get this done. I didn't know how, but I wasn't going to let go until I got what I had every right to get from this smug bastard. I politely asked again to be taken off their lists and to get my picture back. He refused. I suggested that he had no moral right to keep me on this list against my will and insisted that a truly spiritual person would honor my request and respect my privacy. At this the guy actually laughed at me, with a noticeable measure of distain in his voice. Losing my patience I exclaimed, "I demand that you give me that picture!" "No!" he yelled back. "You're never getting this picture back! We have your name, address, and phone number and there's nothing you can do about it!" he said with both finality and nastiness in his voice. I could now feel that he was about to hang up on me.

"Help me, Universe," I said inside my head. "Show me what do to." My mind flashed on the night before when the group repeatedly called upon famous saints, angels, and Biblical figures by name. I realized that the video of the woman prophet had shown her doing the same thing over and over in front of her followers. "In the name of Jesus the Christ, I demand that you take me off your lists and destroy all photos and information about me!" I shouted into the receiver. Stunned silence reached me from the other end of the phone. I was clearly on the right track. "In the name of the Archangel Michael, I demand that you personally see to it that all evidence and all records of me be removed from your files and destroyed immediately!" I insisted.

The local cult leader began babbling incoherently on the other end of the phone at this point. I was definitely getting the hang of this. I threw in another couple of saints and archangels for good measure, repeating my firm demands that he do what I "commanded" him to do, while trying to sound as ominous as I could. "Yes! Yes! I'll do whatever you say! I'll do it immediately!" He blurted into the phone. "I'll destroy the picture of you and there'll be no record left of you! I'll see to it myself!" The guy had not only lost all of his bravado and arrogance, he actually sounded scared. "I'm sorry that you don't want to be a part of our group," he said, sounding like he was in tears, "I have no choice but to do as you demand. Of course, I will carry out your will!"

I understood what had just gone on. His pseudo-spiritual black magick cult used the names of saints, angels, and ascended masters as a way of doing magickal spells and affirmations. They believed completely in the power of such declarations and felt the force of these great souls would be behind their words and demands. By using the same *ritual keys* against them I had been able to trump them at their own game. Once I'd called in the Big Guns (Jesus and various Saints, Masters, and Angels), this local cult member was actually afraid of the magickal repercussions of not doing what I demanded of him.

I was fascinated by the prospect of studying this group some more, but I'm smart enough to learn from my experiences and realized that I would be taking on a formidable enemy by choosing to mess with this so-called female prophet's power base. So I let it go. Plus, with my task officially completed, I was now thinking more of having a nice lunch, checking out the bookstores, and seeing a movie before leaving the city and going home. Happily, the phone booth I was in was just yards from one of my favorite restaurants. "I had better never here from you people again!" I threatened one last time, feeling a little badly now for the guy because he was so weak and lost in this major mind-control group. "You won't," the local cult leader whimpered into the phone. And I never did.

CHAPTER TWENTY-SIX

A Brief Interlude
With Me Playing The Wise Man

My experience with the so-called prophet's followers helped me better understand how a friend's son got sucked into a very controlling cult, led by a Korean-born businessman who claims to be Jesus returned. Any of us who've lost a loved one to a cult or to some charismatic leader have wondered how these people and their ideas could have taken such a hold on the good person that we knew. Well, often it's that they provide that sense of belonging to something greater than one's self, but sometimes it's that the leader demonstrates some kind of unusual psychic abilities. In the world of mystical experience, it's easy to become mesmerized by something out of the ordinary, especially since most of us were raised to believe that such events are either imaginary or something that only happens to God's chosen ones. When somebody discovers mystical experiences are real it can completely throw them off center and cause great confusion concerning everything they've known to be true.

Even those who live immersed in the mystical can fall prey to these uncertainties and self-doubts. I knew a gifted psychic, long ago, who couldn't tell when he was being accurate and when he was just making it up. I remember a supposedly celibate yogi who kept several women on the side, a Roman Catholic priest who didn't believe in Catholicism, and an Eastern holy man who was so afraid that any actions he might take could create *future karma* that would bind him to this Earth for additional lifetimes that he refused to help anyone in any way. At the end of the day we are all just human, no matter how impressive our abilities in the mystic arts might be. None of these amazing people are gods, even if they think they are, for the wisest sage on Earth may only have an inkling of the totality of the Great Mystery. Sometimes, the wisest of them all are the humblest and the least likely to assume grand titles. Those who focus on service to others and not service to their own claims of greatness are the ones most aligned to the Highest Purpose. Or so my sometimes less than humble opinion goes…

CHAPTER TWENTY-SEVEN

Ready For The Rocking Chair

In my early twenties, I got involved with a very cool Unitarian Church whose congregants included eighty-year-old social activists, left-wing political intellectuals, yoga and meditation teachers, Native American shamans, Quakers, divinity school students, and followers of some of the more prominent Eastern gurus of the period. The church was having a charity raffle to raise money, so I decided I'd do the supportive thing and buy a ticket or two. The top prizes were a really nice bentwood rocking chair and a beautiful handmade afghan. Hundreds of tickets were sold. As I was paying for my raffle ticket, I saw in a flash that I was going to win the rocking chair. "No!" I said to the spiritual powers that be, "I don't have room for a rocker in my tiny apartment, I've already got too much furniture. Let me win the afghan!" A very firm energetic response came back at me, "You're going to win the rocking chair." In another mini-vision, I saw that the rocker wasn't actually intended for me, but that I would, in effect, be holding onto to it for someone until they were ready to receive it.

Weeks passed until it was time to give out the prizes at the annual holiday party. As I walked in the door, the ticket-taker playfully asked me, "So what do you think? You think you'll get lucky and win something this year?" "I'm going to win the rocking chair," I said matter-of-factly, as I went inside the church hall. It was a great holiday party and the place was packed with families and people of all ages. All the prizes in the raffle had been donated, so there were many things to win including homemade pies, garden tools, winter mittens, and other wonderful things. As they were announcing the top prizes, the guy next to me asked if I thought I had a chance of winning. "I'm going to win the rocking chair," I informed him. When they announced me as the winner of the rocker, I saw a woman in the crowd across the way go crestfallen. She looked as if not winning the rocking chair had been a real blow to her. Even though it was a very crowded room, I'd felt her deep disappointment from the other side of the hall.

A couple of weeks later, I was standing in the doorway of the church when I overheard a woman sadly talking of how much she had "wanted to win that rocking chair." She told our fellow churchgoer about how poor they were and how she'd "prayed so hard for that chair" using special *visualization techniques* to see it in her home. "I'd even picked out the exact spot for it," she lamented. I studied her for a moment and realized she was the same woman I'd seen so crestfallen when the chair was given to me at the holiday party. "Excuse me," I said and went on to tell her the story I just told you. Spirit offered me the words and I allowed them to flow through me to her. I told her exactly what spirit was telling me. "Even though you prayed so hard to win the rocking chair and did all your magical visualizations the part of you that didn't *believe* you'd ever win put out a kind of 'psychic dampening field' that blocked you from winning that night," I said to her. I continued to explain that our two higher selves had cooperated on another level of consciousness for me to take possession of the rocker and hold it for her until she was ready to receive it.

She was so thrilled and so thankful when I told her I was giving her the rocker that she could barely contain her happiness. For my own part, I was a little sad to see the rocker go. Even though I'd had to cram it into an already crowded corner of my two-room apartment, I had grown quite fond of this beautiful bentwood rocker, but I knew it wasn't right for me to keep it. It clearly meant so much to her that I could never take pleasure in it while knowing I had stolen her joy. I smiled gladly that the Christmas gift she had so wanted for her home was now hers. I knew that spirit had chosen me for the task because I had a good heart and would do the right thing when the time came.

CHAPTER TWENTY-EIGHT

I Get Publicly Snubbed By A Famous Swami

Working at the natural foods company introduced me to an entire community of people who cared about saving the environment, natural healing, and seeking mystical truth. One of the rising stars in that community was Reverend Rick, a young minister. The son of a Methodist minister, Rick had gone in a much less traditional direction. Rick had a guru. Rick's guru was a famous swami from India who used a very potent form of *kundalini yoga* to stimulate the energy centers in the bodies of his followers. The kundalini is said to be the primordial energy of life as it expresses itself in our animal bodies, an energy that lies coiled at the base of our spines. The stimulation and release of that energy can introduce powerful creative forces into our lives with the potential to open our consciousnesses to the realization of the greater mysteries, in other words to achieve spiritual enlightenment.

The Christian evangelical minister who touches believers on the forehead and causes them to experience a "slaying in the spirit by the Holy Ghost" is using the same energy of the kundalini to stimulate a release of that primordial energy. Many traditional Indian yogis and swamis, the ones who possess such spiritual abilities, also use the tips of their fingers or the palms of their hands to send a rush of that energy to their followers. These powerful rushes of energy, not generally understood by the common person, can serve to convince the subject that the swami, minister, guru, shaman, priest, or priestess is an agent of a higher power, which in a sense they actually are. Having such an experience can result in the affected person choosing to join a church, temple or ashram, or to take up as a follower of whoever brought them this experience. "If this person can bring such a profound energy to me," we quite understandably think, "they must have the truth!"

The release of this cosmic energy of life, a force most of us never even imagined might exist, can cause a significant shift in the individual's view of reality. Many become so overwhelmed by the energy rush, and by the utter surprise and awe that they're having such an experience in the first place, that they fall down unconscious as if they've gone temporarily dead to this world. This is the origin of the term, "slaying in the spirit" in evangelical Christian circles. The more sensitive among us can even be affected by such energies just by being in the same room with a person who's moving the fires of the kundalini. Some spiritual traditions teach specific exercises for the nurturing and holding of such energies, although just the regular use of these energies for healing or meditation can increase our ability to use them over time, just like practicing any other skill or craft.

Anyway, back to Reverend Rick and his famous guru. Guru, by the way, is a Sanskrit word that means essentially teacher of wisdom. Sanskrit is the foundation of Hindi, one of the principal languages of India, just as Latin is the foundation language of Italian and Spanish. I had a talk with Rick one day about the Swami's worldview. Rick told me of the Swami's psychic and telepathic powers and his ability to open and stimulate the body's *chakras*, the centers of specific life energies in the body, with his power. This sounded interesting. As it turned out, the globe-traveling Swami was due in Boston in a few weeks. Rick invited me to have *darshan*, an audience and blessing, like with the Pope, at his master's Boston *ashram*. The ashram (monastery) was technically an old mansion donated to the Swami by a person from a very famous and wealthy American family. No, not the Kennedy's. Rick told me that the Swami was, "the most advanced spiritual being on the planet." The followers of the female prophet's cult had told me the same thing about their golden girl. "Compared to Swami," Rick declared boldly, "Jesus was nothing!" This from a minister's son.

As my girlfriend Diana and I walked down the ashram's driveway on the big day a woman in a silk *sari* bowed to us and gave the traditional greeting of *namasté*. Namasté roughly translates to: "I acknowledge the Divine within you." Diana, unfamiliar with the greeting "namasté," bowed and responded to the words she thought she'd heard. "And you *have a nice day*," she said every so seriously Once inside, Diana and I made the rounds, greeting the Swami's followers that we knew. I struck up a conversation with the master's top ordained disciple. He too was a swami, though not of the same rank and stature as the famous Swami we'd all come to see. I asked him to explain the basics of their religious teachings. "What do you guys believe is reality?" I asked. He explained with a religious fable that essentially said, in the beginning was the Divine Godhead and that Being was All That Was. This was essentially a lonely state, so this Great Consciousness created all of the manifest realities in all levels of Universe. "All life is like a great dance of energy," he finished. "The Divine dancing with Itself."

After snacking on sweet cookies, sweet candies, sweet milk, and sweet yogurt, I was hungry and there wasn't anything set out to eat that wasn't sweet, we settled on pillows on the floor and readied ourselves to receive the famous Swami. The great man appeared, wearing a heavy reddish-orange robe, the colors of his religious order, and one of his famous wool hats. Boston's a lot colder than Bombay. His smile was friendly, though he looked like he was in a type of trance or deep meditation. After an inspirational talk about the spiritual path and the nature of God, the part of the ceremony most were thrilled to be there for began. We were one by one to be blessed by the Swami, who delivered a kundalini rush, sometimes called *shaktiput*, to his followers on such special occasions.

The scene was a Hindu version of its Christian counterpart. Whereas the Christian evangelists usually walk by a long line of believers to deliver the energy blessing, the Hindu line filed up to the Swami while he sat on a cushioned chair. Both swamis and evangelists typically deliver the energy blessing to their followers' head or some other body center by using their hands or fingertips. Some use an object of some sort. This particular swami was famous for using a long bird feather. As the line reached the Swami, he would deliver the energy the evangelists would call the Holy Spirit to those who'd come for it. Some passed out from the experience, though most had more familiarity with energies. Unlike some evangelists, the swamis don't have their subjects fall over with people waiting to catch them from behind. Instead, the subject sits or kneels on a pillow, so that if they go unconscious they're closer to the floor with soft rugs and pillows all around to protect them.

As I got closer to the front of the cue I felt very happy. I was grateful for this experience. Many of the faithful, Western and Hindu alike, treated this and other believed holy men and women as if they were veritable gods, so more than a few of the faithful prostrated themselves on the floor before "the master." When I came eye to eye with the Swami, I smiled and thanked him for the graciousness of his house. I patiently waited for his blessing, but then I saw that he was waiting for something, too. I looked deep into his eyes and I saw that he wanted me to bow down to him as if I were an inferior soul. His eyes let me know that only then would I be blessed before the watching crowd of his followers. I smiled and bowed politely, but not as an inferior. This took him by surprise. He was, after all, used to being treated as a god. For a moment he seemed uncertain as to what to do next. Then he turned away with a dramatic look of distain, a show for the onlookers, lest anyone else think they could pretend to be his equal.

I couldn't help but smile broadly as I looked into his angry eyes. He looked to me like a spoiled child who had just been told that there were other children who wanted to play with the toys too, and he didn't want to share. "How sad," I thought to myself. I glanced around the room and saw many faces filled with fear that the great master might turn them down, too. The more experienced ones looked at me with pity. In their belief I had to "surrender my ego" to the great master in order to receive the spiritual light. What they didn't recognize was that their great guru was stuck in his own ego trip.

Over the next decade or so, I would meet several people who had also had contact with the great Swami. My friend Elias told me that an old girlfriend of his had lived in one of the Swami's ashrams as a child and that it was widely known in these inner circles that the old man liked to have sex with little girls. In traditional Hindu fashion the unmarried male and female ashram residents would sleep in large dormitory rooms, separated from each other. This particular Swami was known for slipping into the girls' dormitory late at night and reaching under the bedclothes of his favorite girls. The Swami reportedly claimed to be "checking their virginity."

A few years after my being snubbed by the famous Swami, a popular spirituality magazine published an exposé about the less-than-spiritual goings on in the Swami's ashrams. Charges of child molestation and illegal weapons violations were among the accusations. Further, the spiritual master, believed by his followers possess the powers of a god, was known to be in generally poor health, including a severe case of diabetes. The thick glasses he wore were because he was nearly blind and was he reportedly diagnosed with syphilis.

Those of us seeking a closer relationship with the Divine need to remember that simply having a few impressive psychic tricks in your bag doesn't necessarily make you superhuman or a great soul beyond all compare. Sometimes it just makes you a sad person with a few impressive tricks in your bag and not much else to offer.

CHAPTER TWENTY-NINE

A Meditation On "Enlightenment"

Spiritual enlightenment is an interesting concept, one that means different things to different peoples, though what it ultimately means can only be known through direct experience. One who has direct knowledge of spiritual realities might say what an enlightened state of consciousness is *like*, but until we've had a direct experience of our own, we can never really know for certain what is so. Or so they say.

Patricia and I were no longer seeing other, but we still stayed in touch. One evening I called her on the spur of the moment from my new apartment in Fitchburg. We hadn't communicated in several weeks. The moment she picked up the phone, I saw him. He was a nice looking guy, a little bit older than myself, with a gentle, intelligent face, short brown hair, and matching mustache. I *knew* immediately that this was the new man in her life. Patricia felt awkward and asked if she could call me back in a few minutes. When she called back she asked playfully, "Okay, what do you know?"

I told her I'd seen a man standing behind her. Then I described him correctly. I said I knew he was the new man in her life. My phone call had been unconsciously prompted by the fact that she had brought him back to her place for the very first time. Our psychic connection had sent me the information via the mental radio waves where we all stay in touch with our friends and loved ones. I told Patricia that I really liked this guy's vibration and that I saw that they could have a good life together. When I spoke to her by phone in 2003, she and Dave had two teenage girls and had been together over twenty years.

Soon after that phone call years ago, I was in Cambridge and shared breakfast with Patricia and her new man Dave, at their invitation. He looked just like I'd seen him in the phone vision and I liked him even more after having had a chance to talk with him. When they went off to their respective graduate schools, Patricia to Harvard and Dave to M.I.T, I was invited to hang out in the apartment. I used the time to do a deep meditation. The meditation I started turned into a teaching vision for me about the nature of spiritual reality. I knew that I was being shown this cosmic movie for a reason so I paid close attention.

In the magic movie that played before my eyes I saw a soul come to this world from another world far away and establish itself in the physical bodies of our Earth's dimensions. Eons of time passed as that soul experienced all manner of physical life, learning many things and making many mistakes in the world of men and women.

Over the centuries this soul in human clothing learned to bring more and more of its larger consciousness into this three-dimensional realm and with that accomplishment acquired wisdom and learned to rise above the worst callings of the animal bodies we all reside in.

Over many lives lived, in many cultures, this soul developed a passion for learning and, with that deeper learning of the lessons of this physical dimension, a true compassion for other souls in the physical.

Finally, that deep spiritual impulse caused this soul to increasingly seek only the higher expressions of human consciousness. Life after life was lived in the various religious orders and mystical disciplines of the human family until the soul's larger existence broke through to ultimately enlighten the human brain and mind.

Awareness of these higher truths caused this particular soul to grieve for those still so deeply lost in the struggle of life in these three dimensions.

This being now chose to return to this world again and again, each time having to bring the soul's awareness back to its latest vehicle so that it may be of service to the lost souls still in the darkness of ignorance.

After additional centuries of lives lived in the service of others (some in obscurity, some with more public notoriety) total freedom from the illusion of the physical worlds was attained and the veil of mystery forever thrown aside.

This Greater Being was freed to wander the cosmos at will and when it was time to leave this realm behind (perhaps until the end of the dance of time itself) this Being knew it would do so in full awareness as it returned to the Source of All Being, of All That Is.

Cosmic diploma in hand, this Great Spiritual Knower rose up into the heavens above all Earthly clouds of falseness and once again became One with the Godhead, separate no more.

This illusion lasted for a few eons, until the Soul was ready to learn the next lesson.

Then, the Great Sage, risen from the lower worlds of coarse reality, found Itself in motion, moving towards a destination unknown and unimagined. It was amazed to discover there was still more. The All Knowing Wise One had not known that there could be more.

In vast wonderment, it soared through infinite undefined possibilities until It found Itself on a New Path. As the Redeemed One took its rightful place on the Path to the Final Mystery It shivered with anticipation of the unexpected final completion before it.

Gradually the Path defined itself more clearly, a path at once new and yet totally familiar. As the One settled into a steady rhythm, moving ever forward, it glimpsed Another just ahead of itself, and then Another and Another until the One was stationed in the back of a very long line, cued up to reach the next point of departure.

Others came up behind the One. They wore the religious costumes and faces of many peoples from many centuries across existence. They too had realized the Final Truth.

~

As the One Self reached the Destination, a Clerk matter-of-factly handed the One Self a series of forms to fill out and some literature to familiarize Itself with for its next baby step in the Eternal Dance.

"Next!" shouted the Cosmic Clerk, after it had given the All Knowing its paperwork. With this final shock, The All Knowing One began to develop just a tiny inkling in its Awareness of just how little It actually knew of the "All That Is."

82

CHAPTER THIRTY

Pedestrian Signs & Running On Faith

It was 1979 and people were already talking a great deal about how the world was going to end in either the year 2000 or 2001. One very nice guy named Paul called me aside to share the profound numerological truth he believed he'd uncovered. To illustrate this truth, he wrote the number 666 on a piece of paper. This infamous number is taken from the writings of a man called John in the Christian New Testament. It is generally believed that he used the number as a code to refer to an individual. The references to this "number of his name," along with descriptions of visions from an elaborate series of dreams, are recorded in a book entitled the Apocalypse of John or John's Revelation. This number is believed by some "End Times" or Doomsday Cult Christians to be connected to a future evil figure. Many scholars believe it refers to a Roman Emperor long since dead. See the chapter "What's In A Name?" at the end of this book for more on this subject.

Continuing to illustrate his profound discovery, Paul wrote the number 666 a second and then a third time. Finally, after pausing for dramatic affect, he added the three sets of three 6s together:

$$666$$
$$666$$
$$+666$$
$$1998$$

Paul nodding knowingly at the obvious truth he'd just revealed to me: 1998 was the year the great prophesies of the End would come to pass!

Today, we can comfortably laugh at his folly, but many people held their breath for decades waiting for the dreaded year to arrive. Millions more waited in terror for the years 2000 and 2001, just as they had for the years 1900, 1000, 999, 666, 500, and others on the Western calendar. One of my favorite and amusing 666 revelations was one I found written on a men's room wall back in the mid 1980s. The full legal name of the then U.S. President, Ronald Wilson Reagan, was underscored by the counting of the "numbers of the letters of his name." (6+6+6)

83

The way the bathroom graffitist had laid it out was as follows:

RONALD WILSON REAGAN = 666
   6   6   6

Presumably, the anonymous graffiti artist responsible had supported a different candidate for the office of the U.S. Presidency.

Great anticipation for the year 1998 had also been generated by Jess Stearn's famous book Edgar Cayce, The Sleeping Prophet. Jess, an old newspaper man who knew a good story when he heard one, had distorted the psychic predictions of Edgar Cayce for dramatic effect and declared that Cayce saw his terrifying visions of major changes on the Earth's surface coming about by the year 1998. Actually, Cayce, who died back in 1945, had predicted that the significant changes in the Earth's weather patterns leading ultimately to major changes in the topographical map of the planet would *begin* somewhere between the years 1958 and 1998, and that the realization of these anticipated Earth changes might take 150 years to complete.

By the way, the next big year anticipated by growing numbers across the West for something absolutely terrible or absolutely wonderful to occur on a global scale is the year 2012. This year is said to be the end of the Mayan calendar, among other things. Actually, the event of December 21, 2012, the Winter Solstice, ends a *particular phase* of the larger cosmic cycle represented in the Mayan Calendar. There are also some major shifts in Western astrological terms, including the planet Neptune entering its own sign of Pisces in the Tropical Zodiac. Some claim this date will herald the birth of a New Age of love and peace for humanity, while others are suggesting the reversal of the magnetic poles of the Earth may occur, creating massive death and physical catastrophes beyond any in recorded history. We shall see, I suppose.

But back in the late 1970s I would live in an amazing place and share life with some fascinating people, all because one of those people felt her repeated coincidental meetings with me were a sign that I should be invited to join her. Her name was Eva, and she and her husband were two of the most beloved mystics and healers in the U.S. for at least a decade. Eva had grown up as a Mormon around Salt Lake City, Utah. A traditional wife, Eva was the mother to twelve children by the time I met her. I believe it was during the birth of her sixth or seventh

84

child that Eva's life was to be forever transformed by a series of profound spiritual revelations. The birth had been a tough one and Eva had not been expected to survive it. During it all she went through a classic near-death experience. For her, this included a visitation by an angelic spiritual being, one that would come to her again and again for more than a year of her life, teaching her the ways of natural healing.

After that experience, Eva became such an accomplished psychic and hands-on healer, according to the story she told me, that she became a thorn in the side of the male-dominated Mormon culture and was finally branded a "witch" for challenging male Church authority. As Eva told it, after the death of her first husband certain extremist elements within the Mormon community decided she should be put to death per the Old Testament Biblical dictate from Exodus, Chapter 22, Verse 18, "Thou shalt not suffer a witch to live." Eva further offended the extremist elements by getting re-married to a non-Mormon. At the urgings of friends and family, Eva and her new husband left their home in the middle of the night, taking their children with them. They laid low for years thereafter, traveling in secrecy and living in safe houses for fear that Eva would be murdered.

I met Eva and her husband Gene at one of their healing workshops in Boston. They had collected a number of students over the years that traveled with them in order to learn whatever they could from Eva as she worked to heal a seemingly endless line of good people in need. Eva and Gene said they were in the process of acquiring a large property in the Berkshire Mountains of Western Massachusetts to be used as a healing center. I walked away from that first meeting privately telling my friends that I was going to live at that healing center with them. I had seen it.

Over the next nine months Eva and I would cross each other's paths in different parts of Massachusetts. On one occasion I felt so inspired, I put all the money I had on me in a church donation box, only to find that the gas gauge on my car was reading dead empty. This was in the days before ATMs and Mega-Banks with branches everywhere. Nevertheless I felt so uplifted, I was convinced I could "pray my way home" without the additional gas. Curiously, it didn't occur to me to simply pray for additional money to buy the additional gas I needed. Pretty much on faith alone, I drove ninety miles on the highway in my old heavy duty Plymouth station wagon and then an additional thirty miles on lesser roads, with the tank reading "empty" almost the entire way. I just kept praying with all my might the entire time until I made it home safe. Once before that day, I had watched the gas gauge on my Plymouth wagon merely reach the empty mark and promptly run out of fuel. These days most carmakers give their new automobiles a hidden reserve to keep this event from happening.

As a test, during the week after the magic gas tank incident, I let the car run down to the empty mark to see just how far it would go before running out of fuel. The car ran less than ten miles before failing. I'd bought a spare gas can for the test and brought it with me. To offer a less fantastical explanation than answered prayers, I could suggest that perhaps the fuel gauge had somehow gotten stuck on empty for the trip home. However I still find it curious that it never got stuck any other time during the two years I owned the car. But, I digress.

It had been a good four months since I'd seen or heard from Eva, when she drove up in a station wagon to pick up a load of organic food at the natural foods warehouse that I was, by then, managing. Eva's eyes opened wide as saucers when she saw me standing there. She told me she'd kept feeling like I belonged at her new healing center and had repeatedly thought she should locate me. Having found me without the conscious effort, she invited me on the spot to come and live at the new healing center for the opening of the first year's summer workshop program. I accepted. My girlfriend Diana was quite impressed at the invitation from Eva, as I'd been telling her for six months that I was going to be invited to join the staff at this new place to be called the Center of the Light. Even though I had no obvious skills to offer and had only spoken briefly with the founders on a few occasions *spirit* had shown me that I would be living there and that I had something important to offer. That had been good enough for me. A couple of months after bumping into Eva at the loading dock of my natural foods company job, I headed west to the mountains of Western Massachusetts. Diana headed to college in the American Southwest.

P.S. – I don't recommend trying to "pray your way home" from work today, instead of stopping to fill up at a gas station. It was truly a pretty foolhardy thing to do, especially when I could have just asked somebody for help. My pride and ego at the time prevented me from doing so. Still, it makes for a great story…

CHAPTER THIRTY-ONE

The Center Of The Light

When I moved to the Center of the Light in the spring of 1980, I was about to turn twenty-two. Over the next three years I would study such things as energy healing, natural and herbal medicines, massage, meditation, dream interpretation, and the power of prayer. I would also meet many leaders of the New Age movement and a variety of Eastern and Western mystics who came to teach and visit.

I remember one particular Swami who arrived in reddish orange robes. He'd just arrived in the United States and had seen a photograph of the Center when his devotees took him to a Manhattan health food store. "Take me to this holy place," he was reported to have said. This Swami had a significant entourage with him when he arrived at the Center and packed quite a psychic wallop of spiritual power. But then again, so did Eva. It was fun watching as the two of them wordlessly sparred on the beautiful grounds of this new healing center. At the time Eva, who had extraordinary healing abilities, had not been able to help one of her twelve kids with a major head cold. When the Swami learned that the sick boy was Eva's son, he walked up to the child, placed his hands on the boy's head, and knocked the sickness right out of him. We were all very impressed. Not to be outdone, when Eva learned one of the Swami's entourage was also ill and that the Swami had not been able to help that individual she wasted no time in relieving the devotee of his ailment, in plain view of the Swami and his other followers.

My time in the Center would be a truly magical part of my young life. One time, I decided to hitchhike about 120 miles to the Boston area to visit a friend for the weekend. I got a quick lift to the highway onramp and then prayed to God for a ride to take me as close as possible to my friend's apartment. After about forty minutes, a car stopped. The driver said he was heading towards Boston. I was actually going to Cambridge, the next city over from Boston, but he *felt* like the right guy, so I got in. When we got about twenty-five miles outside Boston he said he had to get off the highway to make a quick stopover and that he would be at least an hour. I prayed it would be quick, because I really wanted to be at my friend's place before it got too late. As it turned out, the man's quick stopover was at the building directly across the street from my friend's apartment, literally thirty yards from my destination. Things would go that way for me for a while.

One time Eva said *spirit* had told her that I needed the healing power of the Yarrow plant. I was to pray and let the spirit of the flowers know I was coming to cut them so that they could pull in some of their life force and minimize the shock. I was then to cut some of the flowers from the fields on the property and make a tea with them. It was also suggested that I soak in a yarrow flower bath in order to allow the specific vibration of the flower to merge with my own energy field. I followed these instructions for about two weeks, but really didn't feel any improvement. At that point, I coincidentally found myself in an experimental class on the healing power of flower essences. At the end of the class, we were told to close our eyes and see if we could tell one bottle of liquid flower essence from another by its vibration. My partner didn't want any peeking, so we put a blindfold on me as well. I got different feelings off the different small bottles placed in my hands and then finally the energy of one of them really blew me away. The power was so strong that I felt everything about me change inside for the better. I asked what flower it was from, but my skeptical partner said she'd tell me later and continued the experiment. I got the identical feeling off of two other bottles she would place in my hands before we were done. At the end my partner told me that all three bottles that I had felt so strongly about had been from the same plant. Yarrow.

I was fascinated to learn that the flower Eva had felt guided to prescribe for me felt so powerful in this bottled form. I wondered why the fresh flower itself hadn't had any noticeable effect when I had cut and used it repeatedly. When I told one of Eva's top students of my odd experience, she asked me to show her the flowers I'd been cutting. When I brought her to the field, she had my answer for me. I had been picking the wrong flower, Queen Anne's Lace, instead of Yarrow. She took me a few yards away and showed me the correct flower. To my untrained eye the two flowers had looked identical. But once I had them to compare against each other it was clear that they were completely different plants. I would go on to use the right flowers and those treatments felt wonderful and very healing to me.

While at the Center my psychic visions would continue to pop in from time to time, with an interesting mix of subject matter. One time I awoke late at night with a vision of what looked like a monster on the property. I saw that the monstrous form was an astral manifestation of the growing hostilities between two of Eva's top students, both of whom had been studying with her for years. The next day, I learned the two women in question had been arguing outdoors that same night and had been frightened out of their wits by this giant monstrous *spirit entity* that appeared before them as they screamed at each other. I successfully described the monster of their vision and explained that they had created it themselves as an energetic manifestation of their animosity. From that day on they put their differences aside.

Another sort of monster would also come out of the Center, but it would come in the form of a novel to be published by a visitor. I happened to be standing in the Center's parking lot entrance when this very pleasant fellow pulled up and started asking questions about the Center. He identified himself as a writer who was planning a book on dreams and said he'd heard that he could learn about dreams at the Center. I directed him to Eva and her students Linda and Mary Kate. This guy came by almost every day for a couple of weeks as the staff worked to teach him everything they could about the dream world.

About a year later, a new book arrived in the mail from this same author. It was a novel about dreams, based in part on the extensive research he'd done on dreams at the Center. The book was called Nightmare On Elm Street and was about a vicious child molester who terrorized people in their dreams. Eva and the staff were horrified to read the sick story that the seemingly nice fellow had spun out of all the assistance they had given him. If you can find a copy of the original novel (not the novel written based on the movie script) you'll see that in the novel's Dedication he thanks Eva, Linda, Mary Kate, and other members of the Center of the Light staff for their time and kind assistance. The original book, of course, went on to spawn the series of vicious horror movies with the star murderous character of Freddy Krueger. We all found it sad that a place called the Center of the Light, a place dedicated to helping and healing the members of the human family, was used to create something so ugly, sick and hateful.

Note: Years later, the Center of the Light would go down a very different road than the vision Eva had for the property and its work and would eventually cease to exist. Eva also went down a different road, abandoning the mystical life she'd been living for a more traditional Christian approach to God. My blessings to her and her family.

CHAPTER THIRTY-TWO

Angels Among Us?

Can our eternal souls truly know more than one form of existence? Do our spirits really continue beyond this solitary lifetime, appearing in different places and in forms other than the ones we know as our physical selves? Virtually every culture in the world says yes. Some Eastern ideas about reincarnation, for example, suggest that our consciousnesses may continue to take new physical forms over time; male and female; tall and short; Asian, African, European; etc. Some of those philosophies also suggest that our souls can experience lives other than human. With this view, the so-called *sacred cows* of India are treated by many of the Hindu peoples as human souls who are currently incarnated as cattle. That these souls are not human in this life does not diminish the sacredness of those lives for many Hindus.

Even most self-described conservative forms of Christianity tell us that God created our souls at some distant point in the past and that they exist in some otherworldly dimension until the time of God's choosing for them to be born into this world. After death, the belief goes, our souls are then sent to either Heaven or Hell. This traditional approach allows our souls at least four different locales in which to exist and experience being. Those possibilities are: 1.) Pre-Physical Existence, 2.) Earthly Life, 3.) Eternity in Heaven, and 4.) Banishment to Hell. Furthermore, certain of the evangelical Christian churches insist that, at a critical juncture in the future, the true believers living on Earth will be brought into a special safe place up in the heavens with Jesus and the angels and then later deposited onto a New Earth once their anticipated battle of Armageddon and a Tribulation period is over. This sky dwelling place and the New Earth give the Christian evangelicals at least two additional places in which to exist and experience as reality. That's a possible five or more locations per soul. Then there are the evangelicals that insist they will go on to rule the Universe along with God, some believing they will be assigned actual planets across the Universe to lord over. The potential number of worlds for the soul to experience becomes staggering in this scenario. Roman Catholics don't focus on this idea of a safety zone in the sky at Armageddon, but they do offer us: Pre-existence; Earth; Heaven; Hell; Purgatory (a place between Heaven and Hell); and Limbo (a dwelling place for un-baptized babies.) This allows Roman Catholic souls to experience three or four out of a possible six localities per soul.

Who offers our souls the greatest number of possible experiences of different realities? Perhaps surprisingly, it is the physicists of the mechanical sciences who far surpass the Buddhists, Hindus, and all other major belief systems. The more classical physicists tell us that "energy can neither be created nor destroyed" and that every atom, every molecule, and every subatomic particle may ultimately have the opportunity to be a part of everything else in existence. "We are made up of the stuff of stars," goes the saying in these scientific circles. That is, the matter in our bodies was once a part of the great stars in the Universe and may one day again be a part of these massive worlds of burning fire in the heavens. Then of course, there are the theoretical physicists of quantum mechanics. Let's just say we haven't got the time or the space to count all the worlds of probability in all the levels of Universe that these folks believe our consciousnesses may exist in.

Can a soul choose to experience reality as an animal, or as a plant, or even as an inanimate object? Why not? Is it possible for a soul to experience reality as a human here on Earth as well as an alien on another world or in another dimension? What's stopping it from doing so except our own preconceived notions of our souls' limitations? I've wondered sometimes about the passion many people feel about the idea of aliens from other worlds secretly living amongst us. Is there some *deeper knowing* in our psyches that informs us that a variation on this scenario may actually exist? Like the characters from *Star Wars* perhaps we too travel across great distances over expanses of space and time. But rather than traveling in spaceships, maybe we make our journeys through the vehicle of our own soul's consciousness?

Hey, wait a minute! Wasn't this chapter entitled: Angels Among Us? Well, yes. The reason I prefaced this segment with many theories and religious teachings concerning how and where our souls may or may not incarnate is because the idea of angels living amongst us may fit nicely into the same conversation. Although the term re-incarnation means taking a new form in the flesh, it can be stretched to allow us to set aside the necessity of a worldly physical body when talking about incarnating. As for the existence of Angels in physical form, on occasion I've had the experience of seeing what appear to be angels in the classic form of ethereal beings that move with wings of light or energy. In each case they were performing some act of service. Then one day I met a woman who appeared to possess such ethereal wings of her own. She was a beautiful and loving soul, who's spent her life giving to others. We'd been spending a lot of time together helping others. One evening, as we were sitting in a semi-lit room, I turned to see the silhouette of a large pair of what looked like *wings of light* directly behind her, appearing to extend out of her back. I was taken by surprise at this mystical vision, but recovered myself quickly and told her that I could "see her wings," which I knew of course didn't exist in this dense physical reality. She smiled at me with gentle twinkling eyes and merely said; "Now you know who I really am. Most people will never know." She told me that, years earlier, she had learned her soul had come to Earth from a dimension that we call the realm of angels.

Over the years, I would encounter a few other people, both men and women, who appeared to me psychically as *angels among us*, living in human bodies. There was an *angel of love* who seemed to magically bring people together everywhere she went. She was a free spirit who was always in need of a place to stay, a free meal, and a few bucks sent her way. But in return, before moving on, she would somehow manage to bring soulmates together and people around her would manage to find the person they'd always hoped for to share their lives with. There was one you might call an *avenging angel* who would come to the aid of good people who'd been done terrible wrongs by others. This avenging angel would go to bat for abused women against their former mates who refused to allow the women to live their lives in safety and peace. This apparent angel would first attempt to turn the abusers away from their victims. If the abuser refused to listen to reason, something terrible would invariably happen to the abuser soon after. I don't mean someone would come and break their legs or something like that. I mean these people would slip on the ice one day and fall and hit their head and die or their financial lives would suddenly come to ruin and they would have to completely shift to dealing with those problems or they would learn they were dying of cancer. It was as if the *life force* of this apparently angelic intercessor had been able to shield the abuse victim from further harm and all that evil abusive energy would turn back on the individual who had created it, doing the same kind of damage of ruining their lives as it had been doing in the lives of the abuser's victims. I know it all sounds like a fun fantasy movie plot, but energy apparently can work that way. I think at some level of understanding we all know that evil can and sometimes does get turned back on the evildoers and that's why we love such stories in film and literature. Even though these possible angels in human form were as distinctly different from each other as any other members of the general population, each one of them had a softness and a *radiance* about them that could change in an instant to a powerful countenance when angered or when encountering injustice. Some seemed to know the mystical truth about themselves and some did not. There also seem to be those of this apparent angelic vibration, like in any other group of souls, who choose the evil over the good in their worldly interactions.

As for the woman whose *ethereal wings* I was blessed to see one night? Well, I can say that every time I'd go somewhere with her people seemed to stop what they were doing just to watch her pass. There was just something about her presence that brought warm smiles to even hard and weary faces. Babies and small children in particular would call to other children and point her out. Their eyes and tiny faces lit up with wonder when they looked her way. When she smiled back, the blissful looks that came over their faces were a joy to behold.

I've learned that I'm not the only person who's apparently seen classic angels with wings of light. There are some very popular books that explore angels in the world today, written by a woman named Doreen Virtue and available at http://www.AngelTherapy.com. Also popular is a Christian-oriented Guideposts publication called *Angels On Earth* magazine touting "True Stories of Everyday Miracles."

Are these images just our minds translating certain qualities into the classic cultural images of angels that so many of us have been raised to imagine? Is it just that there's some indefinable thing at the core of these rare souls that calls to mind the concept of an angel better than any other type of classification or description? That certainly sounds like a perfectly reasonable and plausible explanation to me. But what if one of the many varied groups of souls living amongst us on this extraordinary world of ours actually dwells, at another level of reality, in what we've historically called the realm of the angels? It's certainly a lovely thought, don't you think?

CHAPTER THIRTY-THREE

I Float Away Up Into The Sky

My early months of living at the Center of the Light and the next three years of living nearby were often times of great wonder and learning. They were also a time of some very hard lessons about life. But before the hard lessons came my way I would learn many fascinating things and learn to see the world of the spirit in much broader and more universal terms than my upbringing as a Roman Catholic had ever allowed for. True, I'd learned a great deal from the sporadic mystical experiences I'd been having since I was an infant, but there's definitely a lot to be said for sharing knowledge and experience with others, each of who may have their own unique perspective to offer.

Some of my newly expanded perspective came through reading such alternative spiritual writings as The Secret Doctrine; A Course In Miracles; The Aquarian Gospel; The Essene Gospel of Peace; The Lost Books of the Bible; and the esoteric writings and teachings of Alice Bailey; Helena Roerich, author of the Agni Yogi series; and Roberto Assagioli, the creator of the spiritual psychological model known as Psychosynthesis. Without needing to embrace or reject any of these various tomes or philosophies, I allowed these books to help me open my mind to a world of possibility that I hadn't had the opportunity to even consider before.

In my more personal world, I took my vegetarian lifestyle to a new level and became a totally raw foods vegan. This would prove to be an interesting experiment for a number of reasons. The first thing I noticed upon taking to eating only raw vegetables, fruits, nuts, and seeds was that I started losing weight quite rapidly. My reason for later stopping this diet was that I spent most of my day chewing just to get enough calories in me to keep up my strength and energy during the long cold New England winter. A lot of new recipe books and approaches to raw foods living have evolved since those days. Another interesting side effect of this new way of eating was that I also became much lighter. By lighter, I mean more filled with light. My entire vibration was raised to an extraordinary level. I started to see and hear things in the mystical realms all of the time. The only problem with that was that I was becoming so spacey and ethereal that I could barely function in normal reality and I had a job to go to and bills to pay. On a pure raw foods diet my body became so light and non-encumbering that I barely paid it any attention.

Things finally came to a head one day as I was walking the grounds of the Center of the Light, vaguely aware of the various public events going on around me. As I looked up into the sky, I was drawn to the beauty and clarity of its clear blue glory. I felt myself becoming *one with the sky* and all that it embraced, above and below. As I floated away up through the sky, I occasionally looked down at my body wandering around with all the other people down below.

After some time, my friend Roseanne came up to my vacated body and tried to engage it in conversation, only to find that nobody was home. Roseanne knew I was on a raw foods diet and that I was also severely hypoglycemic. She determined I needed rescuing before I seriously hurt myself. It took a while for Roseanne's voice to finally reach me from somewhere down below. "Thomas, come back!" Roseanne called from far away. "Thomas, you have to come back to your body now!" Over and over she called until I looked down to see her staring up at my astral body floating around in the sky. When I did so, our eyes met. (Her physical eyes and my astral ones.) "Thomas, please come back!"

Roseanne was a concerned friend and I didn't want to scare her, so with heavy effort I made my way back down to the earth and re-entered my body. "Hi Roseanne," I said. Roseanne appeared greatly relieved that I had returned. I told her not to worry, that I was fine and could return to my body at will. We laughed over the incident and promised to visit with each other later. I hadn't really noticed, until she let go, that Roseanne had been holding my hands the entire time we'd been communing. When she'd realized I was gone, she'd taken hold of me and had been using her own body to help ground me and pull me back down to earth. The moment she turned away and let go, I floated right out of my body again and headed back up into the sky.

I hadn't actually intended to go back up, but this was the first time I'd been brought back to my body with somebody else's help. I hadn't realized I wasn't grounded by my own power, but only by proxy through Roseanne. I called to Roseanne for assistance, but she was walking away from my physical form and couldn't hear my astral call for help. I started to tell myself that I ought not to vacate my weak, spacey physical body at that moment, but the sky looked so inviting…

The next time I was aware of my physical body, Roseanne was holding onto it again and calling her fiancé Paul for his assistance in getting me back down again. It was nice to see Paul's warm friendly face. At first he looked at bit concerned, but soon we all laughed once we agreed that I hadn't suffered any permanent physical or mental damage. In a time when so many young people were experimenting with psychedelic drugs, we all knew of somebody who'd gone too far away and hadn't ever fully come back. Some of those lost kids, decades later, are still around today, wandering the streets in dirty clothes and mumbling to themselves or sitting in cells in psychiatric wards of hospitals and prisons. As an experiment, both Roseanne and Paul let go of me for a moment and, of course, away I went. They took hold of me immediately and agreed that one or both of them would hold onto me and keep grounding me until I was able to do it again for myself.

There was some kind of big event happening on the stage in the performance hall, so Paul and Roseanne brought me with them, holding onto my hands like parents with a small child or a beloved pet on a short leash. My urge to go flying about was so strong that I would still float away the moment only one of them let go. It was taking both of them to keep me grounded at that point. After a while, they let me float away to a certain degree, but not too far away, while they fed my body solid food and liquids to help with the grounding process. I can still remember looking down at Paul with his bushy beard and laughing face looking back up at me floating near the vaulted ceiling of the expansive performance hall. I felt like I was a balloon on a string. I have absolutely no recall of what was going on onstage that afternoon, only that there were a lot of people sitting in the audience and having a good time. Thanks again, Paul and Roseanne. It's nice to have good friends who understand this mystical life of ours.

CHAPTER THIRTY-FOUR

Benjamin Crème & The Lord Maitreya

Following a guru, teacher, or any kind of spiritual leader can be a very interesting adventure. Happily, I've had some wonderful teachers and mentors who have helped me invaluably over the years and for whom I will always be grateful. That being said, they ain't all shining jewels of wisdom and enlightened purity.

The town of Great Barrington, Massachusetts was the next town over from the Center of the Light. While living there I came across a few different traveling gurus and local spiritual teachers who offered to make me their student. One guru from the East invited me to be his disciple, but said that I would have to stop all of the healing work, energy work, meditation, and astrological study I'd been doing and thereafter do only exactly what he told me to do and eat only what he said I could eat. Now, I'm certain he had real and valuable mystical lessons to offer me and other potential students, but whereas I'd already lived as a child for the first eighteen years of my life I decided to pass on his kind offer to dictate my every move. One teacher I began studying with quickly found herself so uncertain of her superior knowledge that she kept asking me for my knowledge and input on each and every topic. That would have been fine, except that she was charging me for the cost of each class. After six classes with her and her other students, I politely bowed out and went my way.

One of my favorite stories was of this American guy who'd spent some time in India with some very interesting spiritual masters and had come back to the United States truly believing he'd experienced "enlightenment." A very relative term, to be sure. The folks who worked at a local bakery/café had become his spiritual students. I casually watched this group as they slowly but surely learned what their supposedly enlightened master did and did not have to teach them. After a couple of years they reached a turning point where the entire ashram came to an end. They took charge of their own destinies and their guru, now without a group to support him and pay him homage, went off to graduate school. I thought this was a wonderful ending. They realized he didn't know everything just because he'd had some profound mystical experiences in India, and he realized it too.

There were many other fascinating people I checked out during that time. One of the most interesting was a guy who raised quite a stir as a public spiritual figure in the early 1980s. He was a British-born artist and concert pianist who became, for a time, the most listened to mystic of the 20th century. His name was and remains Benjamin Crème. In April 1982, Ben Crème took out full-page ads in major newspapers around the globe, including the *New York Times*, *Los Angeles Times*, and papers in London, Tokyo, Sidney, and others announcing:

"THE CHRIST IS NOW HERE"

Not surprisingly, this got him a lot of media attention for a while.

I first heard of Benjamin Crème back in 1980. His just-published book entitled, <u>The Reappearance of the Christ and the Masters of Wisdom</u> had become the book that everybody in the alternative spiritual and New Age circles was talking about. The born-again Christians were talking about it too, but saying it was the work of the Devil. Two years earlier I'd read some of the mystical writings of the former Christian missionary Alice A. Bailey, including one called <u>The Reappearance of the Christ</u>, published in 1948, and correctly guessed that Ben Crème's new book was related to that work. The basic premise of Crème's book was that the hoped-for World Teacher (know as *Messiah* to the Jews, *Maitreya* to the Buddhists, *Krishna* to the Hindus, the *Imam Mahdi* to Muslims, and *Christ* to the Christians) had come at last and was soon to reveal His Presence to the world for the sake of bringing about Universal Peace and Harmony. This was and certainly is a wonderful idea and a very appealing alternative to global thermonuclear war and the total annihilation of all life here on planet Earth. But was there any truth to his grand and hopeful claim, I wondered?

Ben Crème was traveling the globe with his message of hope for the world and some friends of mine and I eventually went to hear him speak at a university in Connecticut. The auditorium had about 400 seats and everyone one of them was filled that night, with an overflow crowd huddled in the large hallway just outside the main entry doors. I sat with a group of my mystical friends, although the man on my immediate left was a stranger. As we waited for the evening's presentation to begin, the fellow on my left turned to me and spontaneously launched into an elaborate discourse on what I gathered was one of his favorite topics: "How to become a *breatharian*."

Breatharianism, by the way, is the theoretical postulate that because everything is made up of energy it might be possible to live on air alone - i.e. *breath* - if one's system could extract all its needed energy from the surrounding air and the cosmic ethers. This fellow had clearly read all about it and was now choosing to share this profound occult wisdom with me. I looked over this skinny, meek, middle-aged man and wondered if this was his standard line of conversation to everyone? I suspected it might have been. At the time I didn't think much about his frail, slender body. Thinking back on it now, it occurs to me that his extreme thinness may have been because he himself was attempting to become a breatharian.

Anyway, his instructions for becoming a breatharian went something like this: One had to start by purifying one's body by becoming a vegetarian and eating only healthy whole grain and organic foods. This pure, cleansing, preparatory diet should last a full seven years before moving on to the next phase. Clearly, this impromptu lecture wasn't going to offer me a shortcut to achieving breatharianism. For the next seven years, he explained, one must eliminate all cooked foods and only eat fresh vegetables, fruits, nuts, etc. Essentially, one must become a raw foods vegan. The short version is that every seven years you were to refine your diet even more: seven years of fruit only; seven years of liquids only; etc. until one's vibration was so subtle and refined that one could exist by taking life force strictly from the pure air that surrounds us. Oh, it also required going somewhere the air is still pure. Now, here's the kicker: He ended his treatise by solemnly stating that, "If at any time during the entire forty-nine year process of cleansing, purifying, and raising your vibration to the level of breatharianism you experience even one negative thought or one negative emotion it will *break the cycle* and you'll have to start the entire forty-nine year process of purification over again." Having shared what he thought was great occult knowledge with me, the man sagely turned away from my gaze and put himself into a meditative state for the rest of the evening. I politely said nothing.

To date, a small handful of people around the globe continue to attempt breatharianism as a path to spiritual purity and enlightenment. One Australian businesswoman claims to have successfully achieved breatharianism in the mid 1990s and supposedly continues to take in "liquid light" as her only food from the cosmos to this very day. On the downside, at least six people are believed to have starved themselves to death in an attempt to duplicate her reported achievement.

The auditorium finally quieted, the lights dimmed, and British occultist Benjamin Crème was introduced to the audience of more than 400 individuals. He played a delightful piece of music on a grand piano set on the stage for that purpose and then he introduced himself. He told us about his spiritual life and how he came to be *psychically linked* to the New World Teacher known as "Lord Maitreya." Maitreya, according to Crème, regularly communicates with him telepathically, though on occasions such as on that night's public display Maitreya metaphysically *overshadows* Crème's own person. Crème, in turn, then speaks for Maitreya to the audience. With this explanation behind him, Crème focused himself and said that he was about to be overshadowed by Maitreya and that in a moment he would be speaking for the "promised World Teacher." What happened next is where it got interesting for me. Crème took a deep breath and then everything seemed to change in an instant. I psychically saw the aura of energy around Crème's body expand enormously and fill the entire room with a beautiful and very powerful energy. As he began to give his address, supposedly from Maitreya, I took note of a very distinctive type of energy vibration that resonated throughout the room. It was similar, in a way, to a very specific series of multi-leveled musical tones played all at once. Over the years, I would experience such vibrational tones in other organized mystical orders and energy disciplines. Just as you and I can recognize a friend's voice over the phone the instant we hear it, group energies can have a specific identifiable quality, too.

Crème talked for under an hour, but by the time Maitreya's/Crème's message of a world of love and peace was completed I was honestly very deeply moved. And I wasn't the only one. All around me, people were holding each other and crying, speaking in hushed tones of wonderment and questioning whether or not this could be real. Over the next few days, I was forced to ponder what it might mean. Crème had written in his book and repeated onstage that we should all look inside ourselves and see if we felt inwardly moved to take up this cause and join him in getting out his message that the New World Teacher had arrived. He suggested we should only take such action if we got that "yes" from our innermost selves. As deeply moving as his performance and its message of hope had been, when I looked inside myself I did *not* get a yes that told me to join this guy and his movement. As powerful as the energy Crème brought into the room had been, my intuition and my own inner voice reminded me that it still was not proof that his beliefs were correct and his message true.

More than a year later, on April 25, 1982, some of the most influential newspapers in the world carried Ben Crème's full-page ads announcing Maitreya's imminent revealing of himself as the World Teacher for the New Age that was supposedly upon us. When the Lord Maitreya did not "simultaneously reveal himself telepathically to the world on every television screen and in the native tongue of every one on the planet" as predicted Mr. Crème explained that the World Teacher could not "according to the cosmic law of free will" reveal himself until enough people truly wanted him to in their spiritual hearts and minds. At this writing, nearly a quarter of a century after Mr. Crème proclaimed Maitreya's imminent magical introduction to the world, a small number of his followers around the globe continue to wait for the rest of us to catch up with them so that their hopeful prophecy may finally be revealed.

There is more to this story and it's a very interesting one for a number of historical and religious reasons, but telling it is not my purpose here. I simply relate it to help people understand that even a profound magical and mystical experience such as the one many of us had in that auditorium in Connecticut in and of itself does not constitute proof that the message being delivered along with all that wonderful and impressive energetic fanfare is the truth. The revelations of the mysteries of life and the laws of the Universe are, for whatever reason, apparently a bit more complicated than that.

Back in 1980, I had another unusual experience around the same time I first heard Ben Crème speak. I was working in a general store when a new song by John Lennon came over the radio. Upon hearing the song I heard *my spirit* say, "What are you doing? Your work is done. You're not supposed to be here any longer." I realized that my spirit had recognized John's spirit and was saying that he was supposed to have left this Earth by then. I was shocked by this strange revelation, yet it felt like I had been shown a mystical truth. A few weeks later, the news came that John Lennon, the spiritual inspiration for a generation of young people, had been shot to death on the streets of New York City. It was apparently his time to go, at least according to the spiritual vision I received weeks earlier, and yet we all wish he was still with us. In a way, his spirit and his message through his music still are.

CHAPTER THIRTY-FIVE

The Deerfly Spirit & The Miracle Of Life

The Center of the Light was surrounded by acres of trees, rolling hills, ponds, and streams. It had two large houses, a couple of smaller ones, a large barn that had been converted to a musical performance hall, and many smaller dwellings for guests stay in. It was a beautiful place where you could be close to nature and still have a roof over your head at night. We had deer and other wild animals that could be spotted on the land, especially in the early morning hours. The Center also played host to a large number of native bugs and flying insects. It was one of those insects that brought me this particular story. The Deerfly.

Deerflies and horseflies are basically the same flying critter. They look rather like a large, muscular, elongated housefly, but have a wicked temperament and an extremely painful bite. They are famous for going after large mammals, such as horses and deer. They're also notorious for attacking and biting people, like me. It was the height of deerfly season and these flying predators were so bad that year that a lot of people preferred to stay indoors rather than make the trek across the property from one building to another. Until the deerfly onslaught hit that first season, I'd felt there was no place on Earth that was as serene and as peaceful as the Center of the Light. It was a dream come true, a sanctuary where I truly felt at one with nature and in harmony with all beings. Now, at mealtimes, a lot of people attending classes had begun asking anyone who was going that way to bring a meal for them so they could escape the attacks by the vicious deerfly population.

One beautiful day, a large deerfly swooped out of the sky and made a dive at my head. I waved it away and sped up my pace as the flying monster came at me again and again. It moved with dizzying speed, attacking from behind me, above me, at my legs, and at my arms. It was so fast it seemed to be coming from almost every direction at once. I was amazed to observe that my attacker was a solitary predator and not a small swarm. Just when I thought it had spun around to my right, it bit me hard on my left arm. The pain was so sharp that I instinctively whacked the bug so hard with my right hand that the swat from my hand to my arm hurt almost as much as the bite itself.

The energy of the flying monster had seemed so angry to me and now I was also furious. I had moved my spirit into such a loving and peaceful place in my short time at this healing retreat that bringing such angry emotions and pain to me seemed like an especially cruel assault on my happiness. I looked down at the recently mown lawn under my feet and furiously searched for the body of the deerfly that had attacked me. There it was on the ground, a mangled lifeless body that seconds before had been so relentless in its attempt to feed on my flesh. I picked up the twisted deerfly carcass and stared hard at the lifeless bug in my hand. "How dare you attack me and take away the peace and joy I've worked so hard to find!" I demanded inside my head as if, somehow, this oversized insect was conscious and could understand me. "What did I ever do to you?" I raged on some more. I continued to focus my accusatory thoughts on the apparently dead deerfly in my hand. I was so upset that I felt emotionally unable to drop the matter and leave it alone. As my mind continued to demand some kind of response, an extraordinary apparition appeared directly before me. It came in the form of a nine-foot-tall Deerfly Spirit.

The vision of the giant Deerfly Spirit loomed angrily above me, its hind legs rested on the ground while its body stood erect like a giant man or an oversized bear reared for attack. Its multiple-faceted eyes stared at me menacingly as its consciousness declared to me in a flat and unflinching denunciation, "Humans are evil!" He looked at me coldly, with a manner of utter distain. I realized that I wasn't actually addressing the spirit of the individual deerfly that lay twisted in my hand, but rather what could be called the Oversoul of the Deerfly species, the consciousness of the greater being whose body of physical incarnation were the swarms of deerfly that came around us year after year. I was stunned, not so much by this massive presence before me, though that was quite an extraordinary sight, but rather by this entity's sharp denunciation of the entire human family. "We're evil?" I said in my mind. "You're the ones who relentlessly attack the innocent creatures of nature that have done you no harm! What have humans ever done to you?"

"Humans are evil," It said again. "You destroy everything in your path! You have no respect for any life that is not of your own kind! You poison the air! You poison the ground! You take from every place without giving back! You treat all other lives with disrespect, as if you were all that mattered! You are a plague upon this earth!"

I couldn't help but see the Deerfly Spirit's point. A part of me wanted to counter the Deerfly about its own species' predatory actions, but I recognized that this was a rare chance to communicate with such a being. And, to be fair, deerflies don't selfishly kill and destroy everything on the planet like we do. I asked the Deerfly Spirit to look at all of the caring human souls at the Center of the Light who were dedicated to healing the planet and bringing harmony back to *all the kingdoms* of the natural and spirit worlds. I asked it to acknowledge the other such places sprouting up across the globe and the millions working to restore the environment. I could see I had made my point. The Deerfly Spirit's demeanor now showed its grudging acceptance of the truth I had just spoken. Its energy toward me softened ever so slightly, though its fierceness and fiery nature never mellowed. I knew not to expect it to. That untamed fury was a part of its essence. Not everything in nature is gentle and kind. The Deerfly, like us, has its place in the circle of life and death.

Our interaction completed, the giant apparition of the Deerfly Oversoul slowly faded from my vision and I was left standing alone with the mangled body of the deerfly I'd swatted earlier still cradled in my hand. I knew I should go and lay the little body to rest in the bushes and let nature take its course of returning it back to the earth, but I couldn't bring myself to just toss it away. My brief brush with the larger spirit essence of this tiny creature had awakened in me a great respect for the sacredness of its life, even though its place in the world of nature was one that most of us large land mammals don't generally appreciate. I deeply wanted for the entire violent incident between it and me to have never happened. I wanted to *heal it*, to bring it back to life, and in that moment I refused to accept that it wasn't possible. I wanted it to *live*.

I cupped its crumpled body in my left hand and placed my right hand gently over it. I prayed to God and to all the powers of good and healing in the Universe. "Let this creature live," I prayed over and over again. "Let this being be healed and live." I felt a force of energy begin to flow through me. It moved from the top of my head into my hands. I prayed harder and focused all my will for this healing to occur. I kept this up for at least an hour. Then I slowly opened my hand to see if the little critter had stirred. Nothing. It looked the same as before. Something inside me still refused to let it go. "I won't give up," I thought to myself. "It will be healed if I only have faith." I gently closed my hand again over the deerfly and returned to prayer and invoking healing energy and power from the Universe. "God will let this happen," I told myself. "I will not abandon this creature."

Hours went by and eventually I got hungry. I had missed lunch and it was now closing on dinnertime. I gingerly made my way down to the dining area and carefully got myself some food, using my free hand to serve myself. Eva, the extraordinary healer of this Center, asked me what I was doing. She'd noted that I was keeping one hand closed and using the other. Thinking back, I wonder if she had also seen or felt the energy that I continued running through me and had been running for hours. I told her the story in brief and let her know I was going to keep praying until this little bug was healed. I opened my hand for a few seconds to show her, as I had every hour to check for any progress, and then closed my hand again. Eva smiled at me with the deepest appreciation of the purity of my intention. "Keep at it," she encouraged me, "and let me know how it turns out." Then she went on her way.

Although Eva had left my sight, I got the feeling that she had somehow added some of her own quite extraordinary healing energy and will to the process. I felt her invisible support, though I knew that the task was mine to see through to the end. I had to remain committed and focused without breaking the flow. Another hour passed. I checked for signs of life. Nothing had changed. I returned my focus and will absolutely and totally to sending life force to this creature. "Let it live," I prayed to God again and again. "Let it live." A few minutes after my renewed efforts, I felt a sudden flash of energy in my closed hand. Energetically, I saw it had been infused with a pure white light. I knew in that moment that it had happened. Slowly I opened my hand and saw that the crumpled, twisted deerfly I'd been holding for over five hours was no longer crumpled or twisted. It looked whole again. I knew my faithful prayers had been rewarded. This creature would live. There wasn't any movement yet or any signs of life but the little flying bug I'd swatted so hard hours ago had been put back together by the powers of the Divine Spirit.

I kept praying. Forty-five minutes later, I saw it move. The creature started to slowly stir to life; much like a cat or a dog might stir from a very deep sleep. It moved slowly, groggily for another ten or fifteen minutes. Finally I sensed it was ready. I held my hand out, fully open. The deerfly stood, steadied itself, and then ever so slowly flew away.

Now, I know how all this sounds, but this is exactly as I experienced it. I have no explanation as to precisely what happened or how it happened. I'm not even suggesting that this little deerfly was actually dead and brought back to life. All I know is that its life force had left it and then its life force had finally returned. From that day forth, I was never again bothered by a deerfly. For the rest of the deerfly season, people who had not heard my story about the Deerfly Spirit would see me happily strolling across the broad field or down the long gravel driveways and question, "Why don't these little monsters bite him?" Workshop goers asked me if I was using some kind of special deerfly repellant or if I had a natural deterrent like garlic or an herbal mixture. I didn't want to freak them out so I didn't tell them what I thought, but in my heart I knew I had made peace with the spirit of the Deerfly and they had made peace with me.

Whether it's just unrelated coincidence or whether it's something more I don't know, but I can report that although I've been occasionally bitten or stung by other flying things over the past twenty-five years, I've yet to be bitten, or even bothered, by another deerfly or horsefly since the day that this seemingly miraculous event took place. In fact, wasps, bees, and other like creatures seem to leave me alone. I believe it may be because I understand that their lives are sacred too and I treat them as fellow travelers in this life.

Of course not all flying critters or crawling bugs are so civil, in particular the fire ants found in the deserts of the American Southwest. More often than not, though, I'm able to collect a critter that's unwelcome in our home and carry it to safety outside the house. My wife and I now have a young cat Alexander who we got from a local animal shelter. Since his arrival, the problem we'd been having with crickets invading our home has been greatly reduced. Not only had the crickets been defecating everywhere, the "chirping" sound made by even one of them rubbing their legs together can be so loud and grating on the nerves that it can be close to impossible to fall asleep some nights.

After writing all day, and working lastly on this chapter, I settled in for sleep sometime after midnight. As I did so, a couple of crickets started up with an incredible racket in the bathroom, immediately off the master bedroom. I went to investigate and they stopped their noise. Psychically I told them I would go after them if they started up again on this night. I went back to bed and they started up again within moments. Even turning the TV volume up loud couldn't drown them out. I'd given them a chance, but their instinct had gotten the better of them. With our cats sound asleep, I went to the bathroom and swatted them dead.

After that I couldn't sleep, so I went back to work. I made another attempt to sleep around 2 AM. There was one cricket making a terrible racket somewhere in our bedroom. The last thing I wanted to do was hunt down and kill another cricket. Inspired by the memory of my visit with the Deerfly Spirit and the general truce I've had with most such critters since then I decided to try and communicate with it. Quietly I reached out with my mind into the dark room and found the cricket. I silently touched its essence. At that moment of psychic contact it hesitated in its chirping sounds for an instant. Then it started up again. I knew I had made a connection. I opened my heart chakra, the place of universal love in the center of the chest, and sent out a wave of love to the noisemaking insect. "Please stop," I said with my mind and open heart. "Please stop, please stop, please stop." After the fourth time I silently asked it to stop, the cricket faltered in its noisemaking. "Please stop," I thought again and sent it another wave of love. The cricket settled down with what I swear sounded like a friendly little chirp. It took me about a half hour to slip off to sleep. The cricket never made another sound. A year and a half later, as I am fixing a few typos and doing some minor revisions to this already published book, they've yet to bother us again.

CHAPTER THIRTY-SIX

Astrology Practices East & West

A year after that summer at the Center of the Light I'd already made some of my first painful mistakes in the world of young adulthood. Friends Steve and Dara, kind neighbors David and Penelope, and mentors at the Center had each come to my rescue at different times. By my twenty-third birthday, I'd gone from being in love with life to feeling like a complete failure as a human being. I was an idealist who'd discovered I was far from perfect and the reality of this was crushing to my young ego. Another kind couple offered me a job, renovating an old Victorian house they'd just bought. I accepted. Christian and Johanna were both serious students of astrology and their home by Smith College quickly became the place to come to for good company, fine Spanish wine, and hours of discussion about all things astrological. They were wonderful people and very gracious hosts.

But before my time with the astrologers in Northampton, I spent time with a fascinating and exceptional American named Barbara Cameron. Barbara's husband was a diplomat with the American Foreign Service and they had spent over twenty years on assignment in the Orient. Barbara had become an avid student of Eastern mysticism during those years, eventually learning the astrologies of both India, known as *Jyotish*, and of the Buddhist monks of Burma, called *Mahabote*. One Buddhist nun, a woman named Daw Hla Than, who had spent years in a Burmese prison for civil disobedience to the country's famously repressive regime, was to take Barbara as a student.

After returning to the States, Barbara, with her husband and children, settled into a beautiful old home in Great Barrington, Massachusetts. Barbara continued her practice of Oriental astrology, learning Western Astrology to compliment her Eastern techniques. I became a student of Barbara's, although I was more interested in her life experiences than in mastering the various astrology systems of the Orient. My study of mystical systems at that age had generally been to afford myself an in-depth understanding of the inner workings and mechanisms of the spiritual worlds rather than to turn myself into an academic expert on any given subject. Burmese astrology and *Jyotish* (Vedic astrology) were no different for me in that regard.

Barbara's husband had always winked at her practice of astrology, but had never taken it seriously. On March 30, 1981 – the day of the attempted assassination of American President Ronald Reagan – all that was to change. The attempt on President Reagan's life was caught live on television as he was leaving a speaking engagement at the Hilton Hotel in Washington, D.C. The time was approximately 2:30 PM Eastern Standard Time. The TV happened to be on at Barbara's home when it happened, so she rushed to her computer to calculate an astrology chart for the precise time of the assassination attempt.

The major astrologies of India and Europe believe every place has a unique energy that has no exact counterpart anywhere else and that every moment in time is unlike any other. The very foundation of these astrologies is the study and charting of the cycles and complex mathematical relationships between multiple celestial positions. All of these observations are designed with the aim of reading the Hidden Divine Language encoded in each unique moment of space and time. That being said, these two systems are quite different in a number of significant ways. I'm not an expert, but I'll give you the basics.

The standard Western astrological model follows the apparent seasonal path of the Sun through the Equatorial or Tropical regions of the Earth and uses the precise geometric relationships, drawn inside the mathematical circle of 360°, of each of the major physical bodies in our Solar System (Sun, Moon, Planets, Planetoids, Large Asteroids, etc.) to each of the other large bodies using numerous geometric angles, including 0°; 45°; 90°; 120°; 180°; and so on.

Jyotish, the astrology of India, on the other hand is a Moon or Lunar based system. It uses an elaborate system of predetermined relationships of each planet's classically determined influences and considers how each of those planetary energies works with or against each other. Although to the uninitiated the terminology may sound pretty much the same, they're as different as apples and oranges in application and practice. When Western astrology refers to the Sun being in Libra they are referring to the Sun's position from the exact moment of the Fall Equinox continuing until the Sun appears to have moved exactly 30° of arc beyond that position. When a Jyotish astrological chart shows the Sun in Libra it is showing that the Sun appeared against the backdrop of the astronomical constellation of Libra in the sky, which is not directly related to the Sun's apparent movement across the Earth's equator as read by Western astrology.

The reason for the similarities in the terms is that the two systems came from the same source over twenty centuries ago, but have since gone in very different directions. The Western branch continued to use the same names for their Tropical Zodiac as it followed the apparent movements of the Sun and planets across the equator and to the points on the global map known as the Tropic of Cancer and the Tropic of Capricorn. The astrologers of India, however, continued to use the *fixed star* groupings of the Sidereal Zodiac, the same ones used by scientific astronomers today, as a backdrop for their own very unique system for deciphering the secrets of life as displayed in the sky. Western Geocentric Astrology places the planets into twelve houses of varying sizes, depending on which *house system* is used, with the Sun as a key figure in the overall delineation of that chart. The astrologers of India usually divide their charts into twenty-seven or twenty-eight different houses, called *nakshatras* or Lunar Mansions, using the Moon as the key figure instead of the Sun for reading the mysteries hidden in its astrological charts.

So if somebody tells you you're "a Cancer Sun in Western Astrology" and "a Gemini Sun in India's Astrology," don't fret. The two meanings really have nothing directly to do with each other, as they mean very different things. Just as with other languages, a word in modern English and a similar or identical word in modern French or Spanish doesn't necessarily mean the same thing just because, centuries before, those words came to us through the same common Latin ancestor. Spoken languages evolve over time, just as the astrologies of East and West have evolved. Sidereal, Geocentric, Uranian, Chinese, Burmese, Heliocentric, Native American, etc. are all unique astrological systems for seeking to uncover the hidden meanings believed by so many peoples to be encoded in all of creation. On this point, there are those who have tried to discredit Western Astrology by claiming that the division of the sky into twelve equal parts is totally arbitrary and that, by this logic, the sky might just as well be divided into thirteen equal parts or fourteen equal parts and so on. Actually, most modern astrologers would not argue against this. In fact, there are astrological researchers who regularly experiment with such alternative divisions of the sky in order to view astrology from less traditional perspectives and to increase their understanding. This study is called *harmonics* and divides the sky up into many possible mathematically equal slices.

Getting back to the attempted assassination of Ronald Reagan in 1981, Barbara calculated a *horary chart*, as opposed to a natal (birth) chart, for the exact time and place of the incident and compared it with the known birth information of President Reagan himself. "Reagan's been shot," Barbara told her husband. "The horary chart indicates violence and internal bleeding for the President, as shown by the conjunction of Mars to the Sun in the eighth house and the opposition from Saturn, but mitigating factors from Venus and Jupiter tell me that he'll be okay and that he'll have a rapid recovery." Barbara's husband's first reaction was that she had gone mad. The TV news programs were continuously showing the assassination attempt, as captured on video, and it was believed by all at that time that the President himself had escaped injury. In fact, even President Reagan himself didn't know, at first, that he'd been shot.

Reagan's official website says that when the first gun shots were heard he was thrown into the back seat of his bullet-resistant limousine by a Secret Service agent, who then threw himself on top of the President to protect him. The President felt a deep pain in his chest cavity and told the agent to get off him, mistakenly thinking that the Secret Service agent had broken one of his ribs by jumping on him so forcefully. Even when the President discovered blood coming from his mouth he guessed incorrectly that his lung had been punctured by the broken rib he still imagined was caused by the Secret Service agent. It would be two hours after the assassination attempt before the general public was informed that the President had indeed been shot after all. The media finally reported that the President's body had been pierced by a bullet that ricocheted off of his bulletproof limousine before entering his body under his armpit. This was why there was no outer chest wound to suggest that there was a bullet inside him.

Before anyone else knew the truth, master astrologer Barbara Cameron made the correct determination of President Reagan's condition within three minutes of the attack using an astrological computer program and her vast knowledge of astrology. Just as Barbara had predicted only minutes after the attack, the elderly President was not incapacitated for long and was back at the White House a mere twelve days later.

Barbara Cameron was to become both a mentor and a dear friend to me. Less than five years after this famous incident, Barbara herself would be dead from cancer. She had told me early on that she knew from Jyotish calculations when she was most likely to die. To my knowledge, she was right on the money concerning her own demise. Her family, friends, and the world lost a Great Soul to death that day. A fate that all of us must face, sooner or later. During her lifetime, Barbara was the only Westerner to be a regular contributor to *Raman's Journal*, a prestigious astrological publication in India. Barbara also became a master of the Burmese astrological art of Mahabote, disproving the traditional belief by the Burmese people that no one outside of Burma could use the system.

Before her death, Barbara Cameron published three books:

Mahabote: The Little Key
Predictive Planetary Periods: The Hindu Dasas
Turning The Tables: A Mitigation Manual For Adverse Influences

Her books were published by the American Federation of Astrologers and can be found online at their website http://www.Astrologers.com.

There was so much that I could have learned from Barbara Cameron, had I accepted her offer to become her spiritual chela and *Jyotish* astrological protégée, but my destiny had other places to take me. And so I moved on, as I felt I must. *Namasté* to your beautiful soul, Barbara, and blessings to your family.

CHAPTER THIRTY-SEVEN

The Shawnee Prophet & Chief Tecumseh's Curse

There's a famous "curse" that's still talked about by astrologers and others interested in such things that dates back to the 1840s. The so-called curse is generally said to have been placed on the future U.S. President William Henry Harrison by a Native Shawnee Indian Chief called Tecumseh after the famous battle at Tippecanoe. Other sources say the curse was made years later and by the Prophet Tenskwatawa. Warrior Chief Tecumseh and the Shawnee Prophet Tenskwatawa worked for years to stop the army of the U.S. Government from taking over any more of the North American continent than they and the European settler/invaders before them had already taken. For a brief few years, Tecumseh succeeded in creating a union of several Native American peoples, based in part on the model used by the American colonies to unite against the British in their war for independence. He developed military alliances between the Native peoples of the South, the Northwest, and areas east of the Mississippi River, with his own people in Ohio and Indiana, against the advancing American forces.

In 1810, thirty years before Harrison became the U.S. President, Tecumseh delivered a speech to Harrison, who was at the time the Governor of the Indiana Territory: "Brother...I want to speak to you about promises that the Americans have made...the Jesus Indians of the Delawares...had confidence in...promises of friendship...yet the Americans murdered all the men, women, and children, even as they prayed to Jesus...The same promises were made to the Shawnee...I mean to bring all tribes together, in spite of you...Sell a country! Why not sell the air, the clouds, and the Great Sea, as well as the earth? Did not the Great Good Spirit make them all for the use of his children?...I am Shawnee! I am a warrior...I am the maker of my own destiny! And of that I might make the destiny of my red people, of our nation, as great as I conceive to in my mind, when I think of *Weshemoneto*, who Rules this Universe..."

The movement to protect themselves from the abuses of the American government was a sweeping one that believed the only way for the Native Peoples to survive the white man's continuous onslaught was to say "no further" to American land grabs and expansionism and to reject white American culture and all of its trappings. After a long bout with alcoholism from the whiskey the white men brought to the Native Peoples the man who was to become known by the spiritual name of *Tenskwatawa* (He-Who-Opens-The-Door) fell seriously ill. When he awoke, he was released from his addiction to the bottle and with a great clarity of spirit offered a vision and a message for his people: "My brothers! My sisters! I have been given a great power. I have been told by Our Creator to use this power to save you. My name is Tenskwatawa...I died and went to the World Above..."

The collective faith in the warrior spirit of Chief Tecumseh's Native unification movement and in their spiritual leader Tenskwatawa was broken in 1811 during an attack on the forces of General Harrison lead by Tenskwatawa, the Shawnee Prophet, while Tecumseh was out of the camp. That was the famous the battle of Tippecanoe. The Sage and Prophet who was believed to have powers to foretell the future, who had successfully foreseen an eclipse coming in 1806 and predicted an earthquake in 1811, had promised his followers a victory in battle against Harrison's forces and that victory did not come. After the disheartening loss at Tippecanoe Tecumseh is said to have sent a message, via the release of American prisoners captured in the battle, to his enemy on the battlefield, General William Henry Harrison. The message is said to have been a grave prophecy that has come to be called "Tecumseh's Curse." Another version of the story says that it was Tenskwatawa, the Shawnee Prophet, who made the prediction decades later, shortly before Harrison was to make his first run for the U.S. Presidency against the sitting Vice President Martin Van Buren.

Either way, the generally agreed upon gist of the prophecy or curse is this: "Harrison will not win this year to be the great chief [the U.S. President], but will win next time. If he does...he will not finish his term. He will die in office. And after him, every great chief chosen every twenty years thereafter will die. And when each one dies, let everyone remember the death of our people." For Harrison's part, his reputation with the American public was made on his breaking the back of the Native American resistance at the battle of Tippecanoe. Twenty-eight to twenty-nine years after the battle of Tippecanoe during the 1839-1840 campaign for the U.S. Presidency Harrison ran as the Whig Party candidate (later to become the Republican Party) for the second time. This time, however, he ran on the strength of his war record against the Indian uprising and chose John Tyler, the popular former Virginia Governor, as his running mate. His political slogan, used in banners and put to song, was "Tippecanoe and Tyler too!"

Harrison won the Presidency this time and then died of pneumonia two and a half months after taking office. He was the first U.S. President ever to die in office. Whether due to a Native American curse, or just by a mathematically extraordinarily unlikely coincidence, every U.S. President elected in a "0" calendar year, a twenty-year cycle from 1840 until 1980, died in office either by illness or assassination. Whether it was their first term, second term, or (in the case of Franklin Delano Roosevelt) a third term, every President elected every 20 years has died in office. Furthermore, of the eight Presidents to date who've died in office, seven of them were elected in that twenty-year cycle. The only U.S. President to die in office who was not a part of that twenty-year election/death cycle was Zachary Taylor. Taylor was elected in 1848, not a "0" year, and died from cholera in 1850.

Elected in:

1840 – William Henry Harrison died of pneumonia in 1841
1860 – Abraham Lincoln died by assassination in 1865 (his 2nd term)
1880 – James Garfield died by assassination in 1881
1900 – William McKinley by assassination in 1901
1920 – Warren G. Harding died of food poisoning in 1923
1940 – Franklin D. Roosevelt died of a stroke in 1945 (his 4th term)
1960 – John F. Kennedy died by assassination in 1963

Most astrologers point to a major astronomical conjunction that happens in the heavens roughly every twenty years as the trigger or timing device for this strange and sad event. That astronomical event is the periodic conjunction of the transiting planets of Jupiter and Saturn. Each conjunction occurred with those two planets moving through the Earth Signs of Taurus, Virgo, or Capricorn. Some say this is symbolic of the battle with the Native peoples of the Earth over the very rights to the earth (the land) itself. When Ronald Reagan was elected to the U.S. Presidency in 1980, the next "0" year of the apparent death-in-office cycle, many astrologers debated whether or not the "curse" was going to make its mark on U.S. history again. What made the 1980 election different, astrologically speaking, was that this was the first time in 140 years that Jupiter and Saturn would conjoin in an Air Sign (Libra), rather than in an Earth Sign. Many suggested that the cycle, whether a curse or not, might be broken by the change in the elemental energy from Earth to Air.

1980 – Ronald Reagan survives an assassination attempt in 1981

Did Ronald Reagan, the only modern U.S. President known to have been guided by astrologers, via his wife Nancy, break "Tecumseh's Curse" by not dying in office? The next few years should decide the issue once and for all for those who believe in such things. At this writing in early 2005, the sitting President, George W. Bush, has just been elected to a second term. Bush's first ascendancy to the office took place after the 2000 election, with the Jupiter/Saturn conjunction back in an Earth Sign (Taurus). That year would be the next "0" year in the death-in-office cycle if that infamous cycle, meaninglessly coincidental or otherwise, continues.

2000 – George W. Bush awarded Presidency via U.S. Supreme Court

Is there or was there ever an effective curse on the U.S. Presidency? Was the curse broken by Ronald Reagan? Or is Tecumseh's Curse back on track with the election of another U.S. President during the Jupiter/Saturn conjunction in the Earth Sign of Taurus? Most astrologers and New Age mystical types seem to agree that the cycle of death has been broken. Others insist it may be back on track with the election cycle returned to an astrological Earth Sign. For my part, I simply find it a fascinating historical drama to take note of.

Another curious bit of statistical death information: Of the first five men to hold the office of the U.S. Presidency {George Washington; John Adams; Thomas Jefferson; James Madison; and James Monroe} three of them died on the 4th of July. Those U.S. Presidents that died on America's birthday were: John Adams (July 4, 1826); Thomas Jefferson (also July 4, 1826); and James Monroe (July 4, 1831).

CHAPTER THIRTY-EIGHT

The Battle Of The Grand Masters Of Reiki

One day in 1980, I had a bad headache and a stranger offered to help. He put his hands on my forehead and immediately I felt this very distinctive sort of low-level electrical current running through me. This unique energy was emanating from the hands of the stranger. "What is that you're doing?" I asked. "It's something called *Reiki*," came his answer, "it's a type of healing energy." After a couple of minutes, my headache was gone. I thanked him for helping me, and that was that.

About two years later, I was deeply immersed in a Healer's Training Course conducted by Eva at the Center of the Light. One of the many people who showed up at the Center was a North American woman of Japanese heritage named Phyllis Lei Furumoto. Phyllis, in a very humble fashion, let it be known that she was the "Grand Master" of a system of energy initiation known as Reiki. I recognized the Japanese word *Reiki*, which roughly translates to Universal Life-Force-Energy. The person who'd helped me with my headache two years before had used that word to describe what he did. I started asking questions.

A couple of weeks later, I received my first energy initiation into Reiki in a very simple ceremony, which consisted of Phyllis placing her hands on a few different spots on my head, hands, heart, etc., and grounding that energy in me so that I could access it at anytime. When the initiation was complete I was delighted to discover the same electrical energy flow I'd felt coming from the hands of both Phyllis and the person who'd first touched me with it was now flowing from my own hands. I was fascinated by my new ability to move this very specific energy through my body for self-healing, for centering, and to help take away other people's pain as well. I soon discovered, however, that not everybody in the world is as sensitive as I am. Some were impressed and amazed when they felt the energy coming from my hands. Others felt little or nothing of this energy vibration. I've learned since that most things subtle or metaphysical in nature went completely over the heads of many people. It can be a bit like being a wine connoisseur and sharing a rare wine with a guest, only to be disappointed when their simple response is, "It tastes like wine to me."

Some experiencing the metaphysical energies of Reiki have had their lives changed forever. Others say it just makes them feel relaxed. But there is also the matter of degree. I've noted the 1st Degree of Reiki Initiation, regardless of who does the initiating, is made stronger and more dynamic with the next level of initiation, 2nd Degree Reiki. Also there is the cause and nature of the healing or emotional crisis being attended to by the Reiki practitioner.

When I've used Reiki for healing, I've found I can sometimes work for an hour to clear out the deeply rooted stresses of a chronic migraine headache and have the energy recipient free of migraines for weeks or months thereafter. The same level of energy sent to a chronic sufferer of sinus headaches can have a much more short-lived effect. This is probably because the sinus headache sufferer continues to eat the same mucous causing foods that caused the sinus blockage in the first place. Energy work, of whatever kind, may seem like magic to the uninitiated, but it exists here in this physical reality and is to some degree subject to those laws. We too exist in this dense physical dimension, regardless of where our consciousnesses and truest selves may ultimately emanate from.

A year or two after taking the 1st degree Reiki energy initiation with Phyllis I underwent the 2nd Degree initiation with Phyllis' student, Linda Keiser. By that time a very private controversy had become a very public one, at least in the alternative healing communities of the day. Another woman was claiming that she, not Phyllis, was the true Grand Master of Reiki.

As these things traditionally go, the Grand Master of any system of knowledge chooses a successor from his or her best and most loyal students to continue the work after they die. The late Grand Master of Reiki in America, a Japanese/Hawaiian woman named Mrs. Hawayo Takata (1900-1980), had trained and initiated a reported 22 students to the level of Reiki Master Teacher by the time of her death. These Reiki Master trainings began around 1975, just five years before her passing.

According to some accounts, Mrs. Takata herself had been at the center of a major storm when the 2nd Grand Master of Reiki, Japanese Dr. Chujiro Hayashi, had chosen Mrs. Takata as his successor to become the 3rd Grand Master of Reiki. Not only was Mrs. Takata a female, but the Hawaiian-born woman was a foreigner as well. This reportedly did not sit well with some of Hayashi's other top Japanese students, or so that version of the story of Mrs. Takata and Reiki goes.

When choosing the next Grand Master from her top 22 students/Reiki Master Teachers, Mrs. Takata chose a woman in her early 30s named Phyllis Lei Furumoto as the inheritor of the mantel of Reiki Grand Master. But, Phyllis was not only one of Takata's elite circle of top 22 students, she was also Takata's granddaughter, first initiated into Reiki when she very young. This choice of a family member did not sit well with one of Takata's other elite students, a woman named Barbara Weber. Weber insisted the title of Grand Master had been promised to her and that Takata had unfairly changed her mind at the end.

Official records show Barbara Weber became a Reiki Master Teacher on September 1st, 1979, while Phyllis took her Reiki Master initiation earlier, in April of 1979. But even though Barbara and Phyllis had been made Reiki Masters in the same year Barbara insisted, after Takata's death, that she had knowledge denied the other 21 students. Around this same time, Weber acquired a Ph.D. and had for some reason decided to change her last name to "Ray." Weber started calling herself Dr. Barbara Weber Ray and set to work teaching the special energy she and her students were calling the "Reiki Ray."

The continued objections by Barbara over the choice of Phyllis as Grand Master led to tensions and division in the developing Reiki community, with some people feeling they had to choose sides as to who to support. A number of people decided they'd rather not be initiated into Reiki, so as not to find themselves in the middle of this controversy. Some turned to other Reiki Masters trained by Takata, including John Gray and Ethel Lombardi. Ethel managed to separate herself by developing a variation of the original Reiki energy that she called "Mari-El." "Mari" was for Mary, the mother of Jesus, and "El" being one of the traditional Hebrew names of God.

Barbara eventually called her work "The Radiance Technique" and announced additional levels of Reiki attunement that neither she nor the other Reiki Masters had mentioned earlier. She also trademarked the terms "Real Reiki" and "Authentic Reiki." Some accused her of doing so in order that no other Reiki Master could say that their initiations were "real" or "authentic." All this dragged on for years.

In the mid 1980s I showed up for a Reiki sharing group near Phoenix, Arizona. There I discovered that Barbara Weber's accusations against Phyllis Furumoto had become the generally accepted "truth" by those who'd read Barbara's book on Reiki and been initiated under Barbara. I asked the group's leader, a very pleasant woman whose name was also Barbara, what she thought of Barbara Weber-Ray's claim that Phyllis couldn't possibly be initiating people into Reiki because she'd never been given the "keys" to the Reiki Ray. This Reiki Master, trained under Barbara's banner, gave me what had become the official party line of The Radiance Technique Reiki faction. "It's true," she confidently told us, "Phyllis doesn't have the keys to the Reiki Ray."

I'd been initiated into 1st Degree Reiki by Phyllis and 2nd Degree by her student Linda Keiser and there was no question that the very distinctive energy vibration of Reiki had been flowing out of my hands since that time. Still, I said nothing for the moment. Instead, I decided to participate with this Reiki faction for their group sharing and see if I could distinguish any difference, either in quality, intensity, or vibration, between my Reiki energy and this groups' Reiki energy. As it happened, they all just assumed I was attuned under Weber-Ray's faction just as I had shown up assuming this was a nonsectarian group of Reiki students and practitioners. The local Arizona-based Barbara divided us up into two groups: Reiki I initiates and Reiki II initiates. She, as the only Reiki Master in the group, would be guiding us all for the evening.

I paid close attention in the Reiki II group, but found no discernable difference between the Reiki energy they were using and the energy I was using. Then something quite remarkable happened. Barbara called all the Reiki I initiates into our Reiki II room and instructed everyone to carefully observe me. "Had I been found out?" I wondered. "Was there something subtly different in my Reiki that this more advanced initiate had picked up on that I couldn't sense?" However, instead of condemnation for my Reiki technique I received glowing praise.

Barbara told everyone to watch closely and to try to "sense the power of the Reiki Ray" that came through my hands. "Thomas is demonstrating the most powerful and dynamic 2nd Degree Reiki energy I've ever experienced from anyone," she declared to the group. She advised the others that they too had the inner potential to do Reiki at this high level if only they'd apply themselves to the degree that I obviously had. She then asked me to share my experience of the Reiki energy, the history of how I came to be attuned, and how I had developed such a powerful expression of Reiki.

"Well, actually, you should all know that I received my Reiki training under Phyllis Furumoto," I politely told the group of Barbara Weber-Ray Reiki followers. For a moment the room went dead silent. I looked directly into local Barbara's eyes for a response or rebuttal. To her credit, she awkwardly attested something to the affect that, "Well, it would seem that Phyllis really *does* have the Reiki keys after all."

As time passed, an entirely new group of Reiki adherents came along. Some jumped into the fray defending Phyllis, others inherited the claim that Barbara should have been Grand Master. Additional Reiki students across the globe embraced one of the Reiki energy variations developed by other Reiki Masters. Some of these Reiki variations are quite dynamic, while others seem more of a weaker, watered-down version of the original Reiki energy. I know of at least thirty-seven different variations of Reiki energy initiations out there these days and I'm sure there are many more. There are also now many differences in structure from one Reiki Master to another. Some initiate their students cautiously over a period of months or years while others offer to give you all of the Reiki initiations in one weekend. Some teach the special hand positions and pattern-clearing techniques while others don't bother. I've even heard of so-called Reiki Masters who leave some of the initiations out because they're not comfortable with them. On the high side, there are those who've gone back to the source in Japan for a purer connection to the Reiki vibration. A few others seem to have managed to directly connect to the source within, just like Reiki's founder Dr. Mikao Usui.

For those who'd prefer to stay away from what may be left of the battle of the Grand Master(s) of Reiki, I would recommend looking into the work of Rosanne Amato. Rosanne is an extraordinary Energy Master living in the United States who has managed to keep her humility intact, her priorities in order, and her head on straight after many years in this field of consciousness and energy initiation. Rosanne is effectively the Grand Master of three distinct systems of initiation: Temple Reiki, The Omega Shakti System, and The Triple Helix. However, her feet-on-the-ground approach to her spiritual work and her conscious avoidance of fancy titles and the glamour that goes along with them cause her to have no interest in making such a grand claim for herself. The Temple Academies teach these systems to able students and can be found on the Internet at http://www.Helix3.com.

I had been interested in becoming a Reiki Master Teacher under Phyllis Furumoto way back when, but in those days becoming a Reiki Master required paying a fee of between ten thousand and twenty thousand dollars and an unpaid apprenticeship period of a year of two, and I just didn't have that kind of cash lying around. After years of experiencing some extraordinary energy initiations in other systems, most notably Omega Shakti and Agni Dhatu Samadhi Yoga, I finally became a Reiki Master under the tutelage of the woman who was to become my wife, Rhonda Clifton Lyons. Rhonda, like several other teachers, had taken her energy opening as a Reiki Master and found doorways to other powerful energy vibrations as well. She now initiates her students in a technique she calls Angelic Life Force, which serves to open up the energy pathways in her students to allow them to connect back to the Source of All Life for personal transformation and growth. She and I now work together performing these initiations.

For those of you who don't run in such circles, you should know that there are many other energy-healing schools and techniques and many different forms of spiritual initiation into expanded states of awareness to learn about. Just to give you the flavor of the possibilities, here is an extremely inadequate list of techniques that are already a regular part of the spiritual lives of millions of people across the globe:

Acupuncture - Angelic Life Force - Angelic Reiki – Shiatsu
Agni Dhatu Samadhi Yoga - Aikido - Barbara Brennan Healing
Bioenergetics - Black Hat Tantric Buddhist Feng Shui
Chi Kung (Qigong) - Do-In - Energetic Bodywork - Faith Healing
Jin Shin Do/Jin Shin Jyutsu - The Johrei Fellowship
Hawaiian Kahuna Healing - Kriya Yoga (a.k.a. Kriyashakti)
Kundalini Yoga - Kung Fu - Magnetic Healing
Native American Cherokee Healing (a.k.a. Eagle Medicine)
The Omega Shakti System - Polarity Therapy - Pranic Healing
Shaktiput - Tai Chi - Temple Reiki - Therapeutic Touch
The Triple Helix

It should be remembered that *any* training might turn out to be only as good or as bad as the person giving that training. These things are not magic, although they may seem that way to the neophyte. At least a few of these systems are caught up with their own share of pomp and ceremony. This focus on the *great lineages*, however honorable they may be, can obscure what may sometimes be the lesser motives in some of those involved in these systems.

~

The Story of Reiki, the extremely short version, is as follows:

Dr. Mikao Usui is said to have discovered the keys to the secret knowledge of the healing energies of Reiki in the mid-to-late 1800s, after years of seeking and a final vision on a sacred mountain in Japan. Reiki means, essentially, Universal Life-Force-Energy. Before Usui's death, he is said to have passed the knowledge and responsibility of Reiki to a retired Japanese Naval Commander, Dr. Chujiro Hayashi, who became the 2nd Grand Master of the Reiki system of healing and spiritual development. As Japan approached its entrance into World War II, Dr. Hayashi, at least in the generally accepted Western version of the story, is said to have chosen Mrs. Takata to be his successor, in part due to his hope that the sacred knowledge of Reiki would be safe from destruction in war by giving it to a foreigner living in a foreign land.

There are various translations of the basic philosophy of Dr. Mikao Usui, the founder of Reiki in Japan, some more structured than others.

My favorite is perhaps the simplest:

Just for today, do not worry.
Just for today, do not anger.
Honor your parents, teachers, and elders.
Earn your living honestly.
Show gratitude to everything.

- Dr. Mikao Usui

CHAPTER THIRTY-NINE

I Happily Spend My Last 20 Bucks

"This too shall pass" is a bit of real wisdom that has made it into pop culture. Those who've never been to the depths of themselves might mistakenly think it's a lightweight thing to say. It is not. Sometimes the only thing we have left to hold onto is the knowledge that our current problems will not likely last forever.

After helping Joanna and Christian with their house, and them helping me through some very rough emotional times, I moved to an apartment complex in the poor part of town. While there, I took any job I could to get money coming in. I removed old fiberglass insulation from buildings, did day labor construction jobs, worked with migrant farm workers, picking green beans, squashes, and apples (if you think your job pays badly, try migrant farm workers' wages for a month and you'll think you're rich), and I mopped floors for minimum wage. I barely made enough to survive, but I was twenty-four and determined not to ask my family for help. I went through one period where there was just nothing out there for me, so I spent my time meditating, reading the Bible, and studying astrology. During that span of time my only food was brown rice, carrots, and water. One evening I looked at the 1½ lbs. of uncooked brown rice and the 2 lbs. of carrots I had left and decided that I'd rather eat nothing than to make rice, carrots, and tap water my third meal of the day.

Each day I had expressed thanks to God for the life that I had and for the fact that I had food to eat, when others in the world did not. Still, on that particular evening, I decided I'd much rather go to my favorite restaurant and have a decent meal for a change. I literally had one $20 bill left, plus a couple of dollars in loose change, and zero prospects for work. Yet, inside, it felt right to take myself out to dinner. I had to change the energy and get off the broken-down path my life had been on recently. I knew sitting around and feeling broke and desperate was not the correct frame of mind for me to be in if I wanted my circumstances to improve. I walked to my favorite restaurant, a reasonably priced health foods place called Paul & Elizabeth's Restaurant in downtown Northampton. I got to the entrance and did another *inner check* on my choice to spend almost every last dollar I had left on one dinner out. It still felt right, and it was definitely what I wanted to do. I had a very nice dinner, enjoying every bite. I even had dessert. Tax and tip brought the total cost to about $16, at 1980s prices. I was glad to pay it. I walked back to my rented room feeling good and positive about my life. My "luck" was about to change, and I knew it.

I went to bed early and woke up before sunrise with a profound feeling of light and energy all around me. I could feel that my soul, my spirit, was guiding my human shell that day, and I knew I had to let it. I was completely at peace and one with the Universe. I saw in a vision that I would need to put on the only suit I owned later that morning, but that I had some time before that would be necessary. I shaved so that I wouldn't have to do it later, laid out my suit, tie, and shoes and then began to meditate. After meditation, I switched to reading my favorite translation of the Bible, the one called The Jerusalem Bible.

Late in the morning, I was told by spirit that it was time to put on the suit and go into the center of Northampton. I knew I needed to get to Amherst, which was two towns away. There was paid employment waiting for me there. I could feel it waiting for me. I went to the bus stop with my remaining $6 and waited for the moment when I would know what to do next. I didn't buy a paper for the employment ads, because it didn't feel like that's where I'd find the job, and with only $6 left to my name, 25¢ was still 25¢.

I'd been at the bus stop for about two minutes before someone called my name. I knew less than ten people in that part of Massachusetts, so I paid it serious attention. The person who called me was Sharon, a fellow student from the Center of the Light, which was located some 60 miles away. I told Sharon I was waiting for a bus to Amherst. As it turned out, she had just left a meeting and was headed back to her job in Amherst. Did I want a lift? I knew that I was to go with her, if only to save the cost of the bus fare, so I said yes. On our ride to Amherst, Sharon mentioned some of the stresses she'd been having at work. She ran a social services office at the University of Massachusetts that provided counseling services for battered women and their families. She had been trying to get approval for months for funds to hire a temporary typist to help get her agency's files in order. She informed me that just that very morning she'd made the decision to hire somebody for cash, off the books. She would sort it out with the budget department later. The work had to be done. "Thomas, do you know anyone who types who might need the job?" she asked.

I arrived at her office already dressed in the appropriate attire, my suit and tie, and ready to go to work. As it happened, I had learned how to type in high school and could accurately type about 42wpm. I worked the rest of the day and then took the bus home. The next day was a Friday and I was concerned that I wouldn't have enough food to get me through the weekend and still have money to pay for bus fare back and forth to my new job. But I said nothing. Towards the end of the day, Sharon apologetically handed me $150 cash. "It's all the petty cash I can spare today. Is it okay if I pay you the rest next week?"

That action of letting go and completely trusting the Universe had set things in motion that would bring me back to my friends and neighbors in the Great Barrington area. A month or so later my lease agreement was up in my rental share and after a few days on Sharon's couch, I got an offer from my friend Grace to share her house in Monterey, Massachusetts, located just one town east of Great Barrington. Grace's husband Jerry had died a couple of years before and she was lonely for company. They'd been avid Theosophists for many years and I was interested in learning more about it, though it would be a while before I really knew what a Theosophist was. We were living in snow country and fall had already begun. Grace had no one to help her with the chores around her place and was concerned about being by herself during the coming winter months. "Could you possibly move in right away?" she asked me. I liked Grace very much and was happy for the chance to return home and to give Sharon back her couch. I said yes.

CHAPTER FORTY

Some Of My Favorite Deaths

I spent that winter at Grace's house in Monterey, Massachusetts, a beautiful town of less than 1000 year-round residents that swelled to three times that population in the tourist seasons. Although Grace insisted I should take life slow and just study my healing and astrology courses, I took a job at a local nursing home to support myself. I also wanted to apply some of the healing skills I'd been learning.

I worked at a nursing home while continuing to study the movements of the planets, comparing what effects I should be witnessing, according to my astrology texts, with what actually was happening in the everyday world around me. One of the more fascinating things I observed was in the area of mundane astrology (the astrology of world events). Barry Lynes had written and self-published a book analyzing the astrology charts for both the United States and the Soviet Union. He'd become fascinated by the obvious and powerful connections the charts for the two separate countries had linking them together. Barry was a friend of Joanna and Christian, so I'd gotten a copy of the book from him before leaving Northampton.

Barry Lynes was a Vietnam veteran whose 1960s friends kept talking to him about the wonders of astrology. He finally decided to study astrology with the intention of proving it was a bunch of nonsense. Instead of disproving astrology, Barry was stunned to find that it could be quite accurate in its depiction of people, places, and events in the real world. Barry became an excellent astrologer and would ultimately write a couple of very insightful books on his studies before turning his attention to other interests. In the middle of the Cold War, Barry spent months researching the history of major events for both the United States and the Soviet Union. With this information he *rectified* the charts of both countries in order to arrive at the precise moment when both of these nations could be said to have come into being, essentially determining each country's birth time.

Rectification in astrology is a process that works with the chart of a person, event, organization, or nation, and compares the suspected start or birth time with actual events in the lives or histories of the subject.

Because the apparent movements of the planets in our skies truly are related to events here on Earth, the correct birth time can yield a predictable pattern of influences in the life of the subject. If the life does not flow along with what the birth/start time predicts it ought to, the experienced astrologer knows that the birth time must be incorrect. The exception would be those souls who don't seem to respond to the influences of astrology, which, according to spiritual law as I understand it, we don't have to. Astrological influences can be like other influences in our lives such as weather, upbringing, personal relationships, etc. We can respond to these influences, and be moved by them, or we can shrug them off and go our own way. Easier said than done, perhaps, but entirely doable as far as I understand it.

Continuing, an experienced astrologer using a rectification technique will then work with a chronicle of the major pivotal events in the life of the subject until they arrive at a birth/start time that yields a chart that does make sense and that lines up consistently with the major pivotal events in the life or entity in question. The final test of such a rectified chart is to see that it consistently and correctly predicts the major future turning points and dates for important events in the life of the subject, whether that subject be a person, a marriage, a business founding, or a country. Chart rectification in astrology, by the way, is a very specialized area, kind of like brain surgery is in medicine. Most astrologers will have had little or no practical experience in rectifying charts. Those who are skilled at it know it can take a great deal of time and effort. The rectified charts Barry Lynes came up with for the two nations mentioned above are: 1.) The United States of America - July 4, 1776 - Philadelphia, Pennsylvania - @ 4:46½ PM; and 2.) The Soviet Union - November 8, 1917 - Petrograd - @ 3:32 AM.]

I watched in amazement during 1982 and 1983 as the planet Neptune slowly transited back and forth over the 4th House cusp of the Soviet Union chart that Barry had calculated. That country lost three elderly leaders in the space of about two years. This sweeping away of the old guard made room for the visionary leadership of the last Soviet leader Mikhail Gorbachev. The 4th House represents the home front. Neptune entering that house suggested a possible spiritual rebirth, as well as a time of great confusion and uncertainty on that nation's home front. Neptune can also represent the end of the cycle of life (death) in preparation for a rebirth. Furthermore, things often happen in three's under Neptune's influence. Neptune passing over this part of the Soviet chart might be seen as an indicator of the passing away of those three elderly leaders in such a short period of time.

During my eighteen months working at the nursing home I also observed a very close relationship between the stationary shifts of the planets Pluto and Saturn and the periodic waves of illness and death of the elderly patients at the nursing home. Each time Pluto or Saturn would appear to slow down and shift directions in the sky (an optical illusion for us here on Earth, caused by the regular change of our orientation in the Solar System as the Earth revolves around the Sun) there would be a distinct rise in serious illness and sudden death in our patient population during those approximately two-week periods. Aside of the fascinating astrological observations, the time I spent at the nursing home was for the most part a rewarding time. While there I got a chance to do a lot of good and help a number of people who were in pretty bad shape. I worked for those residents in the poorest health.

There was a fellow named Joe who'd had a stroke and had lost the power of speech and the ability to use much of one side of his body. When I first came to work there, Joe was known as a holy terror. He was always angry and lashing out at the other nurse's aides. The good-hearted middle-aged women who'd been working there for years as nurse's aides thought he was "just crazy," and unfortunately treated him accordingly. Stroke victim Joe would grouch at them in grunts and the women would ignore him or laugh and jump out of the way when he would get angry at their attitude and take a swipe at them.

One day Joe was really out of control and had hit one of the nurse's aides a good one. Joe was at least six feet two inches tall and had been in the construction trades before his stroke, so he could still hit somebody pretty hard with his remaining good hand. I happened upon the scene and Joe calmed down ever so slightly when he saw this tall, intense young man standing in his doorway. I looked Joe square in the eyes and immediately saw the clarity of thought behind the anger and frustration on his face. I knew then why "Crazy Old Joe" was so pissed off all the time.

When I approached him, I had to physically hold him down because at first he responded to me as he had the other nurse's aides: biting, kicking, scratching, and punching. "Stop it, Joe!" I said firmly. "Cut it out, now!" Joe kept lashing out at me as I used my limbs and body weight to overpower him and settle him down. Once I had this big man pinned, his face filled with fear. "Don't worry, Joe," I said. "I'm not going to hurt you. I just had to stop you from hurting me. I know you understand everything that's going on," I continued, "I can see it in your eyes. But the women don't understand that you didn't lose your mind when you had your stroke. And the way you lash out at them just convinces them you really are crazy." Joe made an annoying series of repetitious sounds that I understood was his way of imitating the upsetting way the female nurse's aides laughed and made fun of him. I assured Joe that they were nice women. They just didn't understand his situation.

I called the women in and explained to them that Joe wasn't crazy. He was just angry and frustrated that he was being treated as if he was. As I made each point, Joe made an emphatic "Yeah, yeah, yeah!" sound that made it clear he supported what I was saying. The women looked in Joe's eyes and finally understood that they'd been unintentionally treating Joe terribly disrespectfully and that his mind was still all there. They sincerely apologized to Joe for their lack of understanding. And Joe accepted their apologies.

From that day on "Crazy Old Joe" became one of the most upbeat and pleasant people we had on our floor. The women went out of their way to talk to him, reading him interesting news from the paper and telling him jokes that made him laugh. We figured out that Joe liked country-western music and so his radio was tuned to the local country station. Before, the aides had tuned the radio to whatever they wanted to hear, much to Joe's annoyance, mistakenly thinking he didn't know the difference. Now Joe happily hummed along to the music all day long.

~

As much as most of us don't like to think about it, death comes to us all. Working around the sickness and death in a nursing home helps to remind you of that every day. Having no real fear of death myself, due to my mystical and otherworldly experiences informing me that I had nothing to fear from death, I became the one on my shift that generally dealt with people's bodies once they had passed on. In the eighteen months I worked at the nursing home, I estimate I prepared about eighteen people's bodies for delivery to the local morgue and funeral homes, or just about one a month. Sometimes the deaths were sudden, sometimes we had ample warning, but we all knew (patients, visitors, and staff alike) that our facility was the last stop in life for almost everybody that came through our doors. There were tragic deaths and peaceful deaths and, as it happened, I also had my favorite deaths. These were the ones where the individual was clear and at peace with the transition of consciousness they were making and those who'd been in such pain for so long that the end of that pain could only be counted as a blessing.

My favorite death of them all happened to my favorite patient of them all. Her name was Alma, a retired local schoolteacher who had been, by all accounts, beloved by generations of local children. And Alma, by her own account to me, had loved being a teacher to each of those kids. Alma had been brought to our facility after suffering a sudden ailment that had left her completely paralyzed from her neck down. The same event had left her with symptoms of Tourette's syndrome, a curious neurological disorder that can cause one to say things that one would not ordinarily say, including the use of obscenities. The Tourette's syndrome caused most of the staff on my shift to be pretty freaked out in Alma's presence. Many of them avoided going into her room if they could possibly help it. I, on the other hand, loved Alma's company and she, mine.

Alma had only been with us a few weeks when the doctors looking over her case came down with their final pronouncement. Alma was going to be paralyzed and plagued with Tourette's syndrome for the rest of her life and there was nothing they could do about it. Alma informed me of the grim pronouncement without any obvious emotional or mental distress. After what had happened to her she really hadn't thought it was likely that the doctor's were going to be able to reverse things for her, anyway. "So now what?" I queried her. "I'm going to die," she told me matter-of-factly, "as soon as I can manage it." "How long do you think it will take you to die?" I asked. "I'm going to give it my best shot tonight," she told me with a determined look on her face. "There's no way I have any intention of living trapped in my body like this for years to come," she continued. "I've lived a good life and I'm more than prepared to leave it."

I offered to stay the night by her side after my shift was over, so that I could be there to help her with her transition to the other side if she needed it. "Oh, that's okay," she said. "I'm not afraid. Besides, I may not succeed right away. It could take me days, even weeks to let go of this old body. You're a young man, but you work hard and you need your sleep. You should go home and get your rest." I wished Alma well and good luck with her efforts to let go of the body that was no longer being of service to her. I hugged her goodbye and she kissed me on the cheek.

The next day, when I showed up to start my shift about 3 PM, all the employees around the nurse's station suddenly went quiet and solemn. One of the nurse's aides came up to me and quietly said, "Alma died last night." They all knew how close I'd gotten to her. "All right! Good for her!" I declared spontaneously, pleased that this strong, wonderful woman had so easily taken charge of her destiny and let go of the body she'd decided to leave behind. Understandably, the nurses and the aides were shocked by my response. Seeing the look of horror on the faces at the nurse's station, I quickly explained, as much as I could, about why I was pleased for Alma and how she had been determined to die that last night and let her consciousness move on to whatever came next for her spirit. I know they didn't quite get it, but we all knew by that time that they also didn't quite get me. The fact that they didn't quite get Alma either, kind of made it all okay.

There were some other very positive passings (deaths) at the nursing home. One of gentlest was of this woman in her mid-to-late 90s who had been bedridden for years, though largely still coherent and alert. It was some kind of family event and her room was filled with supportive family members all the way down to her great-grandchildren. In the middle of this joyous visit, surrounded by her loved ones, and with her favorite music playing on a boom box, she just stopped breathing.

Sally, the nurse on duty, and I politely ushered the family out and closed the door behind them. This was the closest I'd been to someone at the exact time of their death. Generally, we discovered someone had died in the night or at some point between the time we'd brought them dinner and the time we entered the room to say goodnight. In this case, a family member had called us as soon as their grandmother had stopped breathing. Sally and I had been just outside the door, so only a minute or so had passed from the moment she had apparently left her body for good. Sally had just come back to nursing after a twenty to twenty-five year break, during which time she'd raised a family. This was her first death in a quarter century. Sally checked the woman's body over uncertainly and asked me, "What do you think?" "She looks dead to me, Sal." I said in response. Sally broke out in a quiet nervous laugh and I laughed quietly with her. "I gotta be sure about this," she said. "I can't very well tell the family she's gone, only to have her start breathing again a few minutes later." We double-checked all the dead woman's vital signs: pulse, heartbeat, respiration, body temperature, eyelids, etc. The dear old woman was indeed dead. In fact the energy all around her body seemed remarkably peaceful and even happy. Sally and I were glad for her. The old woman had left her earthly shell surrounded by those she loved and by those who loved her. It was a good way to die.

Not all the deaths were so peaceful. Sadly, more than a few people are placed in nursing homes and then ignored by their families. Others go into Alzheimer's and dementia and become completely lost and confused in the physical world their bodies are still a part of. One such lost, confused, and very elderly woman died one night while I was on the evening shift. It fell to me to prepare her body to be taken away.

As I entered the room to prep her now empty shell for removal to the funeral home it was destined for, I saw her *astral body* floating above her dead physical form. Her human mind was apparently still just as confused and disoriented as she had been in the last years of her life. This took me quite by surprise. I had been under the false assumption that somebody's mind would clear once the diseased brain and body were no longer a part of the equation. Yes, I had already dealt with people whose consciousnesses had gotten trapped in between this world and the next, but I had figured it was because they were too attached to this world, in some way, or else were afraid of facing what came next.

As I wrapped her body up in the shroud for transport to the funeral home, I tried talking to her spirit. I looked at her floating astral body and explained to her that her physical body was dead now and that she could move on from this world any time she chose. Although I was persistent, the old woman's ghostly self seemed disinterested in me. Instead, she seemed partly fixated on her now dead body and partly fascinated by her ability to float around the room. Confusion and disorientation, however, seemed to remain her main defining qualities. It was late at night, and the funeral home was close by, so the two men from the funeral home showed up in record time to retrieve her remains. I was left with precious little time to help this woman's consciousness on her way before they hauled her body off. The guys loaded the corpse into a body bag and onto a gurney and then proceeded down the hallway with her. The confused dead woman's spirit left the room and followed the men who had her body. "This is not good," I said to myself. As the body and its former occupant moved down the long hallway towards the elevator, I hastily headed after them, wondering what the heck I was supposed to do now.

I struck up a pointless conversation with the funeral home guys, while silently praying and asking for help. I was stalling for time and hoping for Heavenly assistance. I remembered what my mentor Ellen had taught me four years earlier about dealing with disincarnate spirits. "Call in the angels and ask them to take the lost soul away." In my mind, I called for angels to come and assist me and to take this lost, confused soul away so she wouldn't wind up haunting a funeral home or a graveyard for years to come. Just as we reached the elevators, two angelic beings of shining white light appeared in the air over the body and reached out to the old woman's astral self. She seemed confused for another moment and then a sense of peace and calm came over her. Just as the funeral home guys were wheeling the gurney into the oversized elevator, the woman's spirit turned away from her body and she and the angels moved away together, disappearing from my view. I stopped my walking and talking abruptly, as I'd actually completely lost track of whatever small talk was coming out of my mouth. I was just greatly relieved that I didn't have to follow them down the elevator and halfway to the funeral home.

Nowadays, in retrospect, I know that I could have simply stayed behind and prayed for her spirit to be assisted. I would have focused my prayers and my will on this need until I felt a shift of the energy and received the understanding that all had been taken care of. But, we live and learn. (And, presumably, die and learn as well.)

CHAPTER FORTY-ONE

My Friend Steve & Our Invisible Roommate

On my first couple of days in the Berkshire Mountains, I met a guy my age named Steve Dondoros. We had both come to the Center of the Light to study and learn about all things mystical and spiritual. We became fast friends and have been in and out of each other's lives now for about twenty-five years. He's been kind of like an extra brother. He's also one of the best electric guitarists in the country, so I'm sure you'll be hearing about him before too long, now that he's gotten back in the music game in Boston.

Stephan Chris Dondoros (*Stephanos Christos* to his Greek relatives) is also an unapologetic mystic. The psychic connection between he and I has at times been as strong as any I've had with close friends or family members. When we ended up renting an apartment together, I noticed that Steve constantly answered the questions I was about to ask and responded to the comments I was about to make *before* I even opened my mouth. At first I naturally assumed that he knew of his extraordinary ability and just took it in stride. When I finally joked one day, "You could at least let me say what I'm going to say before you answer me!" he looked at me surprised and said, "You mean you didn't say that?" "No, Steve, I only *thought* it," I laughed. He was such a natural psychic he didn't even know he was reading my mind. After that, when I'd catch him answering before I opened my mouth to say what I was going to say, I would just point to my closed mouth and we would both burst out laughing. We really did have a lot of fun. Steve is a really nice guy and for that reason, I suppose, people have, over the years, taken to giving him a variety of nicknames and other terms of endearment. Steve is rather dark in complexion, being a mix of Turkish and Greek, and with an orange robe and a red dot on his forehead could easily pass for an Indian swami. Furthermore, he has the spiritual depth to merit it. With Steve's propensity for casually making profound and insightful comments, I took to playfully referring to him as *Sri Sri Stevananda*, "the Master of Understatement".

There was another curious thing that started happening after a while. We'd become so immersed in our discussions about life and God and whatever that we'd lose track of who had said what. Literally neither

135

one of us could tell who had spoken or made a given statement. After this happened a few times I implemented a strategy for sorting it out. We would consider what had been said, or merely thought, and examine the sentence structure, choices of vocabulary, etc. in order to determine which one of us had originated what.

A couple of times, back in that same apartment in Great Barrington, Massachusetts I thought I saw Steve walking from one room to another only to find him, seconds later, somewhere else. The first couple of times it happened I shrugged my shoulders and thought, "That's kind of weird." The next time it happened I asked Steve directly if he'd been in that part of the apartment. He hadn't. Concerned that somebody might have somehow gotten into the apartment, we both cautiously searched the place for an intruder. We didn't find one.

Then one day I looked down the hall to my left and I saw the guy walk into the bathroom. For an instant I thought, "It has to be Steve," although the person I saw for an instant seemed to have lighter hair and a different face. In that same instant Steve walked out of his bedroom, which was to the right of the kitchen, where I was standing. I ran down the hallway and into the bathroom. There was no one physically there. Even if there had been time for someone to slip out the bathroom window (there wasn't) the second story window was still locked from the inside. Steve and I checked the rest of the house and found nothing and no way out except through us.

"Enough of this," we decided. We sat down and went into a deep meditation and discovered that the extra roommate we'd been seeing around our apartment for the last few weeks was a young guy, close to our age, who'd died in a car accident. He'd gotten stuck between the worlds and had settled into our place because he liked the vibe. Due to Steve's influence we were kind of a rock 'n' roll household. Steve and I prayed and asked for this young man's spirit to be released from this realm. After about twenty minutes, we felt a shift of energy that signaled his release and we never saw the guy's ghost again. We wished his spirit well. Rock on, dude and enjoy the Light!

CHAPTER FORTY-TWO

I Get Stranded For 16 Months In Albany, NY

My time in the Great Barrington area drew to a close. I'd been working a second job on weekends at a farmer's market in Manhattan selling breads and cheeses from a Biodynamic farm, a farm that uses the techniques of the late German mystic Rudolph Steiner. I loved aspects of my life, including the trips to New York City, but increasingly I felt it was time to move on. I packed up my big chocolate brown station wagon and drove across the state line from Massachusetts to New York to the state capital of Albany, which I mistakenly thought would be more cosmopolitan and progressive than where I'd been living.

As I crossed the state line, I got the strangest sensation that I'd just moved into some kind of an *alternate future* for myself, one that would take me off the path I'd been on. Some thirty-five miles into my fifty-mile trip and the head casket blew on my car, leaving me stranded on the highway with pretty much all of my stuff. Actually my friend Jennifer had the rest of my stuff in her much smaller car and eventually circled back around and got me. The New York City farmer's market gig was Jennifer's main job at the time and I was her part-time assistant. My entire game plan of working more hours with Jennifer had just been torpedoed. Without a car, I couldn't get to the farm to do the gig in Manhattan. Without the job in Manhattan, I couldn't afford to go out and buy another car. Having just put some serious money down and signed a lease for the apartment in Albany, I needed that money for my immediate rent and bills.

I found myself essentially stranded in Albany, New York, scrambling for whatever work I could find before my meager resources ran out. For those of you wondering how a guy who supposedly has such good psychic intuition could have gotten himself into such a silly predicament, the answer is that my intuition had been telling me for months *not* to go to Albany and that I would regret it if I did. Of course I went anyway, because I was young and foolishly in love with an unavailable woman named Dana who was living there. Somehow I'd determined that if I were living there too she'd realize that it was me she loved instead of the more stable guy she'd been with for a couple of years. Such is the power of youthful self-delusion.

So, as I mentioned earlier, I was screwed. The first couple of months were a bit of roller coaster ride. I took jobs painting houses, unloading trucks, and being a substitute typist. When it became clear that my cool apartment with all the modern conveniences was a bit out of my part-time-job price range, the woman who owned the brownstone I'd rented was very sweet about letting me out of the lease early without penalties. I found a more rustic place down the street with industrial windows, vaulted ceilings, and skylights that let the sun and the city in, and went about setting myself up as an astrologer. I'd been studying for about three years at that point and even though I knew I had a great deal more to learn I seemed to have a natural knack for the art of doing readings. Way back during my first months of study, people had already been telling me that I was a much better astrologer than some of the more seasoned professionals they'd been going to for years.

I started by putting up business cards in the local health food stores and vegetarian cafés and by advertising in the local New Age paper. I picked up extra money by selling ad space for the paper and bartered for free advertising space by writing articles for the paper on astrology, Reiki healing, and the like. Word of my astrological services quickly got around my neighborhood of old hippies and young progressives and several folks came to me for readings. Some were excited about it and some just liked me and wanted to help support my new venture. The feedback was generally pretty good and before long word-of-mouth was sending me a steady flow of astrology clients.

Doing paid astrology readings for total strangers was definitely an interesting experience. Being an honorable guy, I gave everything I had to make it worth the money. I spent more than an hour calculating each chart and then double-checking the math. Personal computers and astrology software programs were in their infancy in those days and both were a bit out of my financial reach at the time, anyway. Once the chart was drawn up, I would spend an hour or two studying it before the client arrived so that by the time they walked through my door I had a good idea of who they were, what was going on in their lives, and what important influences were coming up.

As the months went by, I'd have people run up to me on the street to tell me how helpful the reading I'd done for them had been or how right I'd been about everything from their relationships to future events that I'd seen were on the way for them. One interesting side effect of focusing so much on each individual chart was that I found I could actually see the chart *hanging in the air* in front of me as we talked on the street. I'd say, "Oh yes, I remember your chart. You have your Moon in Capricorn in your 11th House with that challenging opposition from Saturn." I wasn't so much remembering their charts as I was reading the charts that my memory had reproduced before my mind's eye. It was a sort of selective photographic memory. The astrology charts had apparently been burned into my brain by my staring at them for hours, months earlier. This allowed my mind to recall them, months later, and allow me to clearly see them in the air before me.

So if astrology is so right on, how come astrologers don't always get it right? The same reason people of every other discipline aren't perfect. They're just people. Some are better than others and some are terrible, just like in every other profession from doctors to lawyers to accountants. Some are very good, a rare few are brilliant, most are okay, and some truly ought to be put in prison for misrepresenting themselves as somebody who knows what the hell they're doing! Such is reality. (This one, anyway.)

One of the biggest problems with astrologers is that most astrologers, myself included, are largely self-taught. And there is zero regulation. Anybody can hang out a shingle and call themselves an astrologer. If you're interested in getting a reading from a psychic or an astrologer, ask around, just like you would for a good restaurant or an honest mechanic. Common sense still applies, even when you're dealing with things that may seem very uncommon. If you don't know anybody you trust who can recommend a qualified astrologer, trust your own gut. If you get a bad feeling, or if you're just unimpressed with the person standing before you, just say, "no thanks." Turn and walk away just like you would to any other situation or person that doesn't feel right.

These days there are a small handful of excellent astrological colleges, as well as numerous teaching programs in the West, though most practitioners still learn what they can from books and from others who are also self-taught. If you want to check out an honest-to-goodness top-notch school of astrology, you should look into Kepler College in the U.S. They're a full four-year college of astrological studies, who graduated their first group of seniors in 2004. You can find out more about their programs at their website http://www.Kepler.edu.

In Britain, the Faculty of Astrological Studies has been the place to go to learn from the best teachers since 1948. You can find them on the web at http://www.Astrology.org.uk. Also of interest: the American College of Vedic Astrology, teaching Jyotish or Vedic astrology, found at http://www.ACVAOnline.com, and The Wisdom School, whose astrological focus delves into the mystical teachings of British-born mystic Alice Bailey and her uniquely esoteric take on astrology. You can find them at http://www.TheWisdomSchool.org.

Another major problem with astrology's reputation is that there's a lot of crap for sale out there that claims to be astrology, but isn't worth the paper it's printed on, or the website space it's taking up. A friend of a friend graduated from journalism school and was hired by a newspaper chain. Being the low person on the ladder she was assigned the lesser task of writing the obituaries. She was also assigned to write the daily astrology column for newspapers in Connecticut, Massachusetts, and New York State. She went to her boss, saying she didn't know anything about astrology. "Don't worry, it's easy," her boss explained. Her superior handed her basic suggestions on how to convincingly make up a phony astrology column each day: "When writing about Leos talk about pride, ego, and generosity," the newspaper's cheat sheet suggested. "When writing about Cancers talk about home, family, fear, and insecurity." And so on it went. "Just make it up," she was told, "It's all just for fun, anyway." She did, and her fake astrology columns were read daily by millions of subscribers until she was assigned a better job at the newspaper chain. At that time, somebody else, just fresh out of journalism school, was assigned to write an astrology column on a subject they knew nothing about.

While in Albany, I coincidentally met a retired typesetter who'd spent forty years working for the two major newspapers in the area. This was in the days before computers took over most of the tasks. He told me that when he took the job, back in the 1940s, he was given several dozen horoscopes, already preset in type, for each of the twelve Western astrology signs. Every day on the job, for the entire forty years, he would simply rotate those same preset so-called horoscopes for the daily and weekend editions of both papers. I'd read the daily newspaper astrology columns when I was a kid and had noticed the same thing. The exact same horoscopes, word for word, appeared again and again over the years. Clearly those so-called astrology columns were a bunch of worthless nonsense.

These days many newspaper horoscopes are written by people who actually know something about astrology, but the better of them know there's often very little, if anything, they can say to $1/12^{th}$ of the world's population (for each sign) that's going to be of any personal value. Astrologers call such columns "astrological weather reports." Unfortunately their attempts can often be like those of a meteorologist trying to give a generalized weather forecast for an entire continent.

Where did all these fake and generalized astrology columns come from? It actually started sometime after the invention of the Gutenberg Press, back in the 1400s. Gutenberg introduced movable type, the same basic technology used by that retired typesetter in upstate New York. Movable type allowed books and journals to be mass-produced on printing presses, instead of being produced one at a time by hand. The Gutenberg Bible was the first mass-produced book ever available to the European world and beyond. With the availability of this new technology, some of the wealthier members of European society, who were generally the only ones who could read and write competently, started producing their own journals in which they could express their opinions on science, history, politics, current events, etc.

As the story goes, there were some amongst this new breed of educated *journalists* that were knowledgeable in the mystical arts, including the ancient art of astrology. Those who wrote well on this fascinating subject of astrological planetary influences quickly found that their journals were the most popular with the reading public. Everybody, it seemed, wanted to read such journals, whether they understood astrology or not, because the idea of the movements of the planets having relevance to our everyday lives was so interesting. And so modern *newspaper astrology* was born. Before long, other wealthy journalists were including astrological commentary and advice in their published *papers* as well, whether or not those writers knew anything about the subject. They just wanted their papers to be popular, too. The average uneducated reader, of course, couldn't tell the difference between honest astrological commentary and someone simply making it up. Frustratingly, this silly and embarrassing trend continues to this day, making legitimate and talented astrologers look like fools, and making daily fools out of millions of the rest of us.

CHAPTER FORTY-THREE

"Grace 'N Vessels" Meets 8-Year-Old Shawn

My friend Sultana lived close to the Sufi retreat center, the Abode of the Message, in upstate New York. *Sultana* was a Sufi name given her by Pir Vilayat Inayat Khan, the now-deceased head of the Sufi Order International. Pir Vilayat's father was Hazrat Inayat Khan, credited with having been a major force in bringing Sufism, that beautiful, mystical, peace-loving aspect of Islam, to the Western world. The famous poet Rumi wrote in that tradition. Sultana was a nice Jewish girl who was also a spiritual seeker, like myself. She split her time among her Sufi life, importing jewelry and religious art from India, and playing single mom to her eight-year-old son Shawn.

One day we got a call from our mutual friend Jenaabi to go and check out a Christian Evangelical Faith Healer known as Grace 'N Vessels. Grace (a.k.a. Pastor Grace James) and her husband Pastor Larry James have a ministry in Connecticut, with outreach to the Appalachians, Street Ministries, and Evangelistic Services held from the Northeast to the Mid-West, according to http://www.GraceNVessels.org.

Jenaabi, Sultana, Sultana's son Shawn, and myself arrived, along with hundreds of Christian faithful and wannabe faithful, to experience a couple of hours with Pastor Grace's ministry at a public auditorium. The highlight of Grace's service was her sharing "the power of the Holy Spirit" of God with the assembled through a technique known to many in evangelical Christian circles as the slaying in the spirit. This "slaying in the spirit" phenomenon is essentially identical to the *shaktiput* energy blessings delivered to the faithful by many Eastern, and a growing number of Western, spiritual teachers, gurus, healers, swamis, and other mystical types. Whether in private or in a large group the person able to access this spiritual energy touches the subject on the forehead, with either the palms of their hands, their fingertips, or some physical object, and sends a strong surge of energy into the subject. The energy surge typically evokes a response in the subject's body, mind, and emotions, often releasing an ecstatic energy rush that can be quite delightful, intoxicating, and very commonly, disorienting. Many subjects are so overwhelmed by this experience, especially during their first time, that this release of primordial spiritual energy (called *kundalini* in some circles) causes them to feel dizzy or even lose consciousness. In Eastern-style ashrams, this tendency for some people to get dizzy and even pass out and fall down is often dealt with by having lots of pillows and thick carpets on the floor. Often devotees, students, and followers of the spiritual leader will be there to help those receiving this strong energy to maintain their balance.

In a number of Christian evangelical ministries, where the preacher delivers such a spiritual energy rush, calling it "the Holy Spirit," they use catchers. These catchers are generally strong men who stand behind the subjects and catch them as they start to lose their balance, caused by going into an altered state from the energy rush. Many Christian evangelicals have made it standard practice to always have catchers behind the subjects. Some even encourage the subjects to let go and fall back into the waiting arms of one or more catchers, so as to more fully experience the Holy Spirit. More than a few critics of such religious rites have suggested that this standard operating procedure adds extra drama to the experience that falsely makes it grander than it might be otherwise. For my part, I'm all for the idea of catchers and soft pillows in these energy delivery sessions. Better safe than sorry.

Grace spent time preaching before moving on to what for many was the main event. Grace told us of having breakfast with her family just a few days before saying, "...and just as my husband passed the milk across the table, do you know what 'the Lord' said to me?" She then went on to tell us what the Lord said. It was clear, like many people with similar abilities, that Grace had both healing abilities and some degree of the psychic abilities of *clairaudience* (the ability to hear spiritually what most others cannot) and of *clairvoyance* (the extrasensory ability to see what others cannot).

Jenaabi, Sultana, and I were tempted to go up and experience the energy transmissions, but were concerned we might cause a disruption for the good folks who really needed to be there. The thing was, we weren't willing to play along by pretending to believe in exactly what she and her followers believed in. If the question of our "faith" were to come up, entirely likely under the circumstances, none of us were willing to become liars. So we stayed put in our chairs and watched. However, we had amongst us someone who didn't have the same moral dilemmas and concerns to deal with, Sultana's eight-year-old son Shawn. Shawn had grown up around Sufi masters, Hindu swamis,

Kung Fu and Aikido teachers, psychics, intuitive healers, Reiki masters, and the like. To him this was just another wonderful expression of the Divine Mystery for him to touch and experience. When he turned to us adults and asked, "Can I go up?" we all said, "Yes, what a great idea!" Shawn could go up with a clear conscience and then report back to us what he'd experienced, without the risk of us making an unhappy scene for Grace 'N Vessels and those who'd come to glimpse this wonder.

Grace went through a long line of adults, one by one, touching them on the forehead and letting them fall back into the arms of the catchers stationed behind them. The Holy Spirit was doing its work for the faithful and we sat by and watched with great interest. When it came time for the children to line up for their energy blessing, Shawn went among them. Grace talked of God and the Holy Spirit as she moved down the line of the children. The kids went down like dominoes, slain in the spirit even faster than the adults. However, when Pastor Grace got to little Shawn, it was a somewhat different story.

As I mentioned, Shawn had grown up experiencing many types of mystical practices and energy techniques, so even a strong shaktiput, Holy Spirit, or kundalini energy surge, was not enough to knock him down and put him out. In fact, instead of going into an altered state and dropping into the waiting arms of one of the catchers, like all the other kids, Shawn just stood there taking all of the Holy Spirit energy blessing Pastor Grace could manage to send him. Grace was clearly taken by surprise at Shawn's ability to take what she was serving up. We watched intently as Pastor Grace James focused her mind and will and delivered the strongest energy she could directly into Shawn's forehead. Shawn remained standing. Finally, she looked for assistance from the body catchers and they collectively pushed and pulled Shawn down to the floor to join the other children, most of whom were still unconscious from the power of the energy surge.

Regaining her command of the situation, Grace moved on down the line with the rest of the children, who were once again dropping like flies. But before she'd gotten to the end of the line of twenty or thirty more kids, Shawn was already back up on his feet and asking enthusiastically, "Can I have some more, please?" The entire audience stared at Shawn and then back at Pastor Grace, as Grace collected herself. "My, my. This child sure does love the Holy Spirit!" she managed to say. Shawn continued to stand in anticipation, so Grace came back his way to finish the job. Grace put her hands on both the front and back of his head and gave it everything she had. Five seconds went by. Shawn seemed unaffected. Ten seconds went by. Shawn started to develop a silly, happy grin on his face. Appearing determined, Pastor Grace kept the energy blast coming on strong. Finally, Shawn's knees started to buckle. Grace and her catchers took that as their cue and quickly moved to gently push and pull Shawn down to the floor to join the children who were actually unconscious. When Shawn returned to us in our row of seats, he was grinning with happiness from ear to ear. "That was great!" he said, looking back over his shoulder as if he wanted to go back and get some more.

My reason for telling this particular story is not, in any way, to embarrass or diminish the legitimate spiritual and healing gifts possessed by Pastor Grace James or those of any other honest Christian evangelical preachers or faith healers out there. I am all too aware that much of the human population is in desperate need of something to hold onto that inspires them to believe in a Higher Power and to hope for a better life. I sincerely bow to all those of faith, throughout the world, who spend their lives in service to bring healing and inspire hope in the masses of people that so deeply crave it. My point with this story is to inform those who have the "ears to hear" and the "eyes to see" that the blessings of the Divine Spirit, God, Goddess, the Great Mystery by any other name, are spread throughout every people and within every sincere faith and heart in the world.

From what I've seen of the woman known as Grace 'N Vessels, she appears to be the real deal, a person to be honored for her kindness and decency and for the sacrifices that she willingly makes for the sake of others each and every day of her life.

Namasté, Pastor Grace, and keep up the good work.

CHAPTER FORTY-FOUR
Jane Roberts & The Seth Material

My friends and I continued on our individual spiritual journeys. John focused on Scotland's mystical Findhorn Community and on his study of the life of Catholic monk Padre Pio, said to have had the *stigmata*; Roseanne and Paul got married and moved away so Roseanne could train as a Waldorf School teacher; Sarah took a job teaching nutrition at the newly founded Kripalu Yoga Institute; and Tina went to Peru.

Tina got back from her time in Peru when I was at the beginning of my time in Albany. Over the phone she told me of these amazing journeys she'd been on, some of them fueled by natural psychotropic drugs the shamans used to help open the participants' consciousness to other realities. (Such drugs, natural or not, are potentially very dangerous, by the way, and not for "partying" purposes.) Tina told me of a run she'd taken through the hills around some of the ancient Incan ruins of Peru in which she was able to see clearly in the pitch darkness as if she had bright lights shining from her eyes, illuminating the path in front of her feet. This was truly a holiday to remember.

Once my finances stabilized, I made the occasional trip south to New York City on the Amtrak commuter train, including a visit with Tina. When I got there, Tina was bustling about her house telling me of this incredibly soothing, yet invigorating, coca leaf tea that she'd gotten in Peru from her shaman. She told me she'd searched for it in every health food and herb store in the greater New York City area, but couldn't find it anywhere. She'd just about run out of the stuff, as she'd been drinking it night and day for months, and needed more. "What kind of tea was it?" I asked, not certain I'd heard her correctly. "Coca leaf tea," she said distractedly. "Tina?" I said, "Coca leaf?" "Yeah, yeah, coca leaf tea. I can't find it anywhere!" Tina continued her constant activity. "Tina," I pressed her, an amused smile growing on my face, "Coca leaf! The same coca leaf that they use to make cocaine?" A look of deep realization slowly dawned on Tina's face. "Oh my God!" she said. "That's why I couldn't find it in any of the health food stores!" Tina, an otherwise very bright and educated professional woman, had so innocently accepted this "herbal tea" from her shaman that she had brought a couple of good-sized bags of the stuff right through Peruvian and American customs, neatly tucked away in her luggage.

The continuation of my own spiritual journey took a more law-abiding direction. While in Albany, I did a number of experiments, inspired by the writings of Asian martial arts and healing arts master Mantak Chia. I also studied the lives and works of various spiritual masters from India and North America and read almost every book by or about the American writer on alternate views of reality, Jane Roberts. Among Roberts' most mind-bending books were those supposedly written through her by a personality called Seth. In a trance state, Roberts would speak as Seth, who explained that his personality was actually from an earlier incarnation of Jane's, when her/his soul was said to be alive as that particular man. Roberts' Oversoul, the greater soul that lives many lives, was said to have chosen the personality of Seth for its communications with the personality of Jane as an interface for the exploration and exchange of ideas and information about the nature of reality. Seth/Jane Roberts claimed that our human consciousnesses exist in a much larger context than most of us have ever imagined. Seth/Roberts' description of reality, in fact, is much closer to the theory of Quantum Mechanics, multiple universes, and infinite levels of probability than anything commonly found in either Western or Eastern mysticism. Seth claims our daily reality is dramatically more flexible and malleable than the classical ideas of the laws of physics could have possibly allowed for. *Mind* is said to be the ultimate participant in the dramas of life and history, with both individual and the collective/mass consciousnesses constantly altering the fabric of reality. According to Seth, all lives cooperate, at a deeper level of awareness, in the moment-to-moment creation of physical reality itself.

Again, these ideas are very much in line with the theories of Quantum Mechanics, developed in the 1920s, and today considered to be the foundation principles of all reality by a growing number of the world's most respected and leading cutting-edge physicists. These updated laws of physics are considered to be actual truths by some of the top minds in the world, who are quietly working away in the most elite and prestigious universities and scientific organizations on the globe. These same explanations concerning reality remain the stuff of science fiction to the mind of the average citizen. The principle difference, as I see it, between these advanced scientific explanations of the laws of physical reality and the ideas put forth in the Seth/Jane Roberts books is that Roberts' books suggest that each of us is capable of taking these ideas out for a test drive and proving the truth of them to ourselves in our everyday lives. She suggests that we can use the understanding of these supposed laws of reality to make our lives more of what we would consciously choose for them to be. Of all of the Jane Roberts/Seth books, the most pivotal one for me and the other people I know who've been profoundly affected by these books is called: The Nature of Personal Reality (published in 1974), followed by The Individual and the Nature of Mass Events (published in 1981).

One of the more curious things that happened for me in this endeavor is that I found myself going into altered states of consciousness while reading the books. Sometimes I would only get a paragraph or two, or even a sentence or two, into the headier volumes before I would start to experience the concepts being laid out in the words on the page. I would also regularly experience the concepts in the books playing themselves out as actual examples in my life, mere hours *before* I would read about them in the Seth books. I'd go through a couple of fascinating days of unusual and highly instructive object lessons concerning the ability of the mind, mine or someone else's, to alter someone's actual real world experience, only to turn the page in the book I'd put down hours or days earlier and find the very next subject directly and specifically describing what I'd just been going through.

Some kind of psychic symbiotic relationship was seemingly going on between my mind and the consciousness expanding ideas laid out in the books. The books claim that all time (past, present, and future) is malleable or flexible. Not only does what we do right now affect the future possibilities that we align ourselves to, but what we do now can have a causal affect on which variation of the past our lives are responding to, according to these teachings. This is theoretically due to the existence of virtually infinite possible variations in time coexisting simultaneously.

Why are so many of us self-proclaimed mystics these days embracing all of this quantum theory stuff? Well, because we've been living these apparent laws described in quantum theory all our lives, so we recognize their seeming validity in our day-to-day reality. While reading one of the Seth books, I found myself struck by an experience I'd had two or three years earlier when I found myself going back in time in my consciousness to when I was a little boy. In that vision I was helping to talk my eight-year-old self out of that suicide attempt on my parent's front lawn. I found myself wondering, "What part of my larger being or Oversoul might be connected to the Master, my spiritual teacher, who used to come to me in visions in times of need as a child?" An interesting mind stretching exercise, to be sure.

One of the more intriguing ideas in the Seth/Jane Roberts books is the suggestion that our souls can live more than one life at the same point in time. In other words, there may be one or more people alive right now who have the same soul as you. Instead of each of us simply possessing other *past lives*, and other future incarnations, Seth/Roberts declared that many of us may also have other *concurrent* lives, other incarnations of our higher selves that are alive and living in the same world we are. Impossible you say, even those of you who are convinced of the reality of reincarnation? Why should our Eternal Souls be limited to one life at a time just because our *minds* are limited to that idea? We could even take this further and consider the postulate that we are all One Being and that any sense of separation from each other is ultimately an illusion. Find these concepts intriguing? Try reading some of the writings of Jane Roberts/Seth and wrapping your mind around the ideas and see how they feel to you. Take them out for a test drive, if you will. If they're too much to take in, try reading some of the more popular books on quantum theory, quantum mechanics, or on the concept of a Holographic Universe. Then see if the ideas of Jane Roberts and Seth don't make a whole lot more sense.

CHAPTER FORTY-FIVE

The Psychic Faire Circuit

After doing astrology readings for a while I was ready for something a little more fun than seeing one person at a time in my home office. I discovered there was a traveling Psychic Faire making an appearance in Albany. I decided to go over and meet the psychics and maybe have a reading with some of them, if they looked interesting. The average psychic faire has anywhere from a handful to a couple dozen psychics, astrologers, tarot readers, and people doing other forms of divination. This one had about fifteen to twenty psychic readers of various stripes doing 15-20 minute readings at $15 a head. The quality of psychic readers and the faires that some of them appear at can vary from very high quality to an absolute waste of time. Far too many so-called psychic faires are filled with readers who are just learning how to do readings. Many of these wannabe readers are taking paid classes with someone who's supposed to be teaching them how to be psychic. To be fair, there is the exceptional teacher who carefully chooses exceptional students and presents only the best of their student crop to the general public in such venues, but this is not the rule as far as I've seen.

On the other hand, there are psychic faire organizations that demand a very high quality of ability from their readers. Those readers either have to come highly recommended or else they have to audition for the faire organizers and prove they know what they're doing. The psychic faire I happened upon that day in Albany was actually the most professional and highly quality group of readers I've ever seen assembled together. When the faire organizer, a professional psychic herself, suggested that I audition for them as an astrologer, I was a little concerned I wouldn't be good enough. Happily, they liked me.

Carol, the local faire organizer, was also a knowledgeable astrologer. She taught me a trick I've used again and again over the years that allowed me to do readings at the faire. She taught me how to do a decent short astrology reading without having a complete and accurate birth chart to read from. The trick? Read from the daily astronomical information available in an *ephemeris*. An astrological ephemeris gives the position of all of the planets in our solar system, as well as the position of the Sun, the Moon, the eclipse points, and some of the larger asteroids for every day of every year. It also details the major geometric angles the celestial bodies are making to each other, as well as the Lunar cycles and other stuff useful to the educated astrologer.

As it happened, the psychic faire I'd happened upon had been so well received that they had long lines of people cued up waiting for their turn to have a reading. Having pleased Carol with my skills, I was thrown immediately into the mix, with a spare ephemeris borrowed from another astrologer. I picked up another useful skill on that first day - speed-reading. I'd spent three years calculating and reading people's birth charts with the utmost attention to detail and intensive study. The average astrology reading I'd given up until then ran from 1½ to 3½ hours. Suddenly, I had just 20 minutes (22 minutes tops) to give the clients something helpful to walk away with and then clear my head for the next one.

My mind quickly became laser-focused as I would meet each new psychic faire client. Occasionally, a client would have a copy of their birth chart with them, but in most cases the only information I had to work with was their birth date. With this I was actually able to learn quite a bit about someone's life, by seeing where the various planets were the day they were born and in what relationship the planets were to each other. Whereas the planets represent specific personality and life qualities in each chart, I could compare what I saw on the printed pages of the ephemeris with the person sitting in front of me and get a pretty quick picture of the individual and their issues. Much more impressive to some was the demonstrated ability to tell people specific and accurate things about people who weren't there with us, by using those people's birth dates, and correctly explaining the positives and negatives between the client and the absent person.

One of the coolest charts I've ever been shown was set before me by a husband and wife couple who were also working the faire as readers. They had apparently come to test my skill. The chart they placed in front of me had no name, no date of birth, and no place of birth. It was just an astrological wheel, house cusps, and planetary positions. The only thing they told me about the chart was that it was for a person, as opposed to a chart for a nation, a business, or an event, and that I would recognize the name. I first noted that Pluto was in mid-Virgo, with Neptune in mid-Scorpio. I was born with both of those planets in the same signs, so I then checked to determine the positions of the other outer planets of Uranus and Saturn to see if their positions were near enough to suggest that the person in question was close to my own age. At a glance, I could see that the other outer planets were completely out of proper orbital range to be near my birth year, letting me know that the chart in question was for someone who had been born at least a few centuries before me, and quite possibly many centuries before me. I started to do the math in my head, knowing the approximate number of Earth years it takes each of the outer planets to make one revolution around the Sun, to determine which century the person of the mystery chart before me had been born into, when the married couple that brought the chart to me stopped me. "Just try reading the chart and see what it says to you," they said. "We don't want you to have any clues."

I took a quick look at the chart, and noted that Sagittarius was rising, with Mars in the 1st house, very close to the Ascendant. After quickly looking at the other relationships to the Mars/Ascendant conjunction I was ready to begin. "This was a deeply religious and passionate person who spoke his mind quite forcefully," I said. [This from the Mars rising in Sagittarius trine Mercury in Aries.] I was already reading the chart as a man, for the chart seemed very masculine in several ways. "But what this person had to say brought him in direct conflict with the religious and governmental powers and authorities of his day," [this from the exact square of Pluto in Virgo, in the 9th house, to the natal Mars] "because the words he spoke were considered radical or even revolutionary by those powers." [This from Uranus in the 3rd house exactly opposing the Pluto and exactly square the Mars.]

I noted the Sun was at the very end of Pisces, exactly conjunct the Nadir, which told me the chart was calculated for midnight. I guessed that the house system being used would support that hypothesis. The Sun was also exactly square Jupiter. Drawing from this information [and from the natal Uranus trine Neptune] I determined, "This person was also deeply spiritual, and someone with a profound mystical knowledge who was probably very psychic and highly intuitive. This person, probably a man, also had a deep warmth and a natural sensuality [Venus in the 2nd house] but could also seem emotionally distant and even mysterious, combined with the ability to demonstrate an almost feminine gentleness." [Venus in Aquarius square Neptune.]

This was clearly a brilliant, multifaceted, and extremely complex person who had the presence of greatness about him. I began to think in terms of the most brilliant and famous souls that had lived in both the European Renaissance and of the great artists, philosophers, scientists, and thinkers of the classical period of Ancient Greece. "Who could this be?" I wondered. "Clearly the message he offered [Mercury] was also his destiny." [Pluto sextile Neptune in an exact yod formation to the Mercury.] Several times I thought the person this chart described sounded a great deal like Jesus of Nazareth, but I knew of no historical evidence for an exact date or time of birth for Jesus. Finally, the couple told me, "It's a chart calculated by an astrologer, from information concerning the birth of Jesus, given in the readings of Edgar Cayce."

I need to say that I personally have no idea what the birth chart of Jesus of Nazareth might be. I only share this story because it made such an impression on me at the time. The fact that the creator of the chart [Alexander Markin] used the psychic readings of Edgar Cayce, combined with the classic Biblical references to the nativity of Jesus, was quite intriguing to me, especially because the resultant chart was so compelling. I did a quick search on the Internet while writing this section and was not surprised to find that a number of others have come up with their own versions of a chart for Jesus, calculated from the sources they've found most convincing and compelling.

Before letting the chart get away, I copied it down for myself. Less than a year later, I went to the Edgar Cayce organization's local office in Phoenix, Arizona and located a copy of this supposed Jesus chart in one of their publications. [The Horoscope of the Nativity by Alexander Markin - The A.R.E. Journal - Volume XIX - May, 1984 - Number 3]

The reason I am so able to recall my original logic from when I first saw the chart is that I write this with the chart from the A.R.E. article sitting in front of me on my desk. Most astrologers have a method that they follow, when first looking at a chart. Mine is to glance quickly over the chart, follow the elements that immediately grab my attention, and then work my way into the rest of the chart from that starting point. This combined with my intense memory of the initial reading made it easy for me to recall and recapitulate my own original logic.

The rationale and method Mr. Markin used in coming up with this Jesus birth chart is laid out in a series of articles in The A.R.E. Journal, with the chart itself printed in the 4th in the series, and would require me reprinting the entire articles to give you all the pieces of the puzzle. If interested, I suggest you contact the folks at A.R.E. for more information. Their official website is http://www.ARE-Cayce.com. For those of you astrologers out there who are just dying to see the chart for yourselves, here are all of the pieces, as I first saw them:

Main Points:
*Sun 28° 43' Pisces – *Moon 7° 31' Gemini – *Mercury 15° 32' Aries
*Venus 12° 50' Aquarius – *Mars 18° 53' Sagittarius
*Jupiter 29° 27' Gemini – *Saturn 2° 18' Taurus
*Uranus 18° 27' Pisces – *Neptune 13° 47'ʀ Scorpio
*Pluto 18° 16'ʀ Virgo – *Vertex 2° 29' Leo

House Cusps:
*1ˢᵗ (Ascendant) 15° 08' Sagittarius
*2ⁿᵈ 19° Capricorn – *3ʳᵈ 27° Aquarius
*4ᵗʰ (Nadir) 28° 43' Pisces – *5ᵗʰ 24° Aries – *6ᵗʰ 18° Taurus
*7ᵗʰ (Descendant) 15° 08' Gemini – *8ᵗʰ 19° Cancer – *9ᵗʰ 27° Leo
*10ᵗʰ (Midheaven) 28° 43' Virgo – *11ᵗʰ 24° Libra – *12ᵗʰ 18° Scorpio

I don't know which house system was used. Birthplace would be the classic Bethlehem. Whereas I feel the Lunar Nodes are critical in any chart, as taught to me by astrologer Barry Lynes, I have looked up their approximate positions, according to the info given above:

True Nodes:
*North Node 23° 32' Aquarius – *South Node 23° 32' Leo

Good luck, and don't forget to wear your seat belt.

~

Happily, we weren't constantly swamped all day and evening long at the Faire, which allowed us to catch our breath, grab a bite to eat, and visit amongst ourselves during the slower times. One of the more entertaining things to do was to do readings for each other. This, in itself, would prove to be a real eye-opener, for reasons other than you might suspect. I'd had at least a half dozen readings over the years, but here was an entire roomful of psychics for me study and learn from. Everybody there was pretty good at what they did, though there were those who stood out as the most advanced. The most advanced in our group was a middle-aged former military man named George. I got readings with five or more people a day. It was interesting to note the differences in style, in what they did and did not pick up on, and when it appeared that their personalities were getting in the way, causing them to draw the wrong conclusions or to interpret incorrectly.

Remember, whether seeing a psychic, a doctor, or a stockbroker, you can't assume what they come up with is correct and the best course of action just because they present themselves well. Second opinions are usually a good idea, particularly if you're not comfortable with what you've been told. In the end, people are people and nobody's infallible, no matter who they are, what position they hold, or how good they think they are. My apologies to those who believe they are infallible.

One day at the Faire, I had a half dozen readers read for me. The readings had been quite good and accurate and had offered me a very plausible look into my likely course for the future, according to where I seemed to be headed in life at the time of the readings. That night, I went home and thought very deeply on all of the comments the other readers had made to me and considered the visions they had offered. There were some major things that I'd been planning that these readings caused me to re-think. Before going to sleep, I had made some serious changes in my game plan and my outlook for my future. The next day, when things slowed down for a bit, I had new readings. In the new readings, the readers accurately saw the *new future* I had just determined for myself, hours before. If we truly "create our own reality," as the popular Seth books suggest, then this would seem to have been a living example of how consciously changing one's mind can change one's future. Interestingly, both sets of readings were helpful in clarifying my choices.

I did a few more Psychic Faires with the same group, before heading on my way to Arizona. The most memorable was in Saratoga Springs, New York. As we sat in the middle a shopping mall, waiting for the customers to start lining up, this very out-of-shape 60ish couple waddled by. The wife looked to her husband and said, in a very whiny New York City accent, "What are they doin', Harry?" "Oh, ah, they're, ah, physics!" (as opposed to *psychics*) Harry replied. "They're what?" asked the wife, sounding confused. Harry confidently explained, "They're a bunch of physics, honey. You know, they ah, they tell the future!"

George and his faire organizer girlfriend Carol were working this Saratoga Springs show together. This gave me a chance to get to know George a little bit. Carol and I had hit it off immediately, but it took George a while to warm up to me. George was a former soldier who'd used his psychic abilities in military intelligence. He'd been one of the first *remote viewers* (although, they may have been called something else in those days) who worked for the United States government. Remote viewing is the art of psychically seeing and otherwise experiencing people, places, and events at great distances, across space and time. [For more on remote viewing, read the book, <u>Psychic Warrior</u> by Dr. David Morehouse. Morehouse is a retired U.S. Army Ranger Commander who went to work for military intelligence as a psychic spy years ago. You can find him and his services at http://www.DavidMorehouse.com.] When George and Carol were working different shows for the faire, George would amuse Carol by reporting in on exactly what she'd been doing and where she'd been at any given time by using his remote viewing skills. We all flirt in different ways.

George was definitely the king of the psychic faire circuit. He was an exceptional psychic, as well as a charming and self-assured man. So it was no surprise that George's reading table was almost always busy, even when the rest of us were twiddling our thumbs. But what made me curious was that George even got tons of business at the faires where no one knew him and early on, when word-of-mouth hadn't had an opportunity to send people his way. I decided to study George and see if I could figure out why.

George and I happened to be stationed beside each at the Saratoga Springs show. As usual, total strangers walking through the mall would inexplicably stop when they got near George, stand mesmerized for a moment, and then slowly walk to the appointment desk and sign up for a reading with George. I studied the situation for clues to George's unique success. Was George flirting with them in some way? Was he intentionally looking mysterious? (An old ploy used by many cheap psychics to haul in the easily impressed members of humanity.) Did he simply have that certain *something*, that *star quality* that people are inexplicably drawn to like a magnet?

Then, I saw it. It was very subtle, and not at all obvious in any physical way. It was an *energy* that George put out. Was it conscious? Was it intentional? I watched closer, as the next group of shoppers passed by. And then I saw it very clearly. As this middle-aged shopper walked by, George reached out towards her with his energy field and took a hold of her. As she faltered in her steps, I watched the shrouded intensity on George's face as he continued to focus on her, holding her with his dynamic energy, though never looking at her directly until she finally looked at him first. Like many other clients before her, she was unconsciously following the energy force back to its source. George met her gaze for just a moment and then, once he knew she was intrigued, turned casually away as if something on his desk had caught his attention. George's fish was hooked, and she made her way over to the appointment desk and signed up for a reading with him. George was using *seduction*, the oldest lure in the world. I'd seen women and men play that game in bars and parties many times. The difference here was that George understood the psychic mechanics involved and had become a master of energy field manipulation in the way many great seducers instinctively are. Even if they don't totally understand exactly how they do it, they still know that they've got "it."

Those of us who pay attention to the metaphysical side of life realize that this more subtle energy field, invisible to the naked eye, is in its way just as physical as any arm or leg. This subtle energy field can touch objects and people in the three-dimensional world. Such is the actual physical basis for telekinesis, which allows for an individual to move or otherwise affect physical objects without touching them with their normal physical bodies, as in "spoon bending" and the like.

I decided to try the technique out for myself. I looked around the mall for a person to experiment on. I watched a few people go by and then saw someone that appealed to me. "Chemistry is probably a part of it," I reasoned to myself. "Surely it's easier to manipulate someone you already feel some connection to, than someone you don't." I had noted that George seemed to patiently wait and select his marks, before psychically reaching out to them. I imagine professional con artists, hustlers, and child molesters do the same thing.

A beautiful young woman, that I found myself quite attracted to, walked by and I went for it. She hadn't seen me yet, as she was looking ahead at something down the long shopping mall hallways. I reached out with my invisible psychic arms and grabbed hold of her. She stopped dead in her tracks. I held on firmly, watching her out of the corner of my eye. She turned and looked around the mall. Then she saw me, *unconsciously* recognizing me as the source of the sensation that had caused her to stop. I suddenly felt very guilty about what I was doing. I had tried many experiments of a mystical and psychic nature but had never before involved other people without their consent. I tried to end the connection and turn her away, but it was too late. She walked over to the appointment desk and signed up for a paid reading. When she walked over to my table and handed me her "paid" ticket, instead of to one of the other eight or ten readers on hand, I wasn't the slightest bit surprised. I had after all *selected* her, so she had unwittingly and unconsciously selected me.

I silently asked the Universe for forgiveness for this transgression, as I had used my mystical knowledge to willfully manipulate another person. This being done, I focused my mind and will in order to give her the best and most helpful reading I could possibly offer. I actually considered telling her what I'd done, getting her money back for her, and sending her away, but I recognized immediately that this explanation of what I'd done would either be way beyond her comprehension, or even worse, explaining this to her might make her even more compelled to intimately connect with me.

I definitely delivered one of the best mini-readings I'd ever done and the young woman genuinely seemed to have learned a lot about the problems and challenges in her life. She thanked me again and again and said how absolutely amazed she was that I could look up her birthday in a book and then tell her the things I'd been able to tell her. I felt a little better. But we weren't quite done. The original intense energy connection I'd intentionally made with her, combined with her having been pretty blown away by having her first ever astrology reading, made her want to know me better. In the Biblical sense, if you get my drift. It took more than a little willpower to resist her attempts to seduce me. She was a truly gorgeous young woman and I was definitely attracted to her. It also took willpower to choose to not call her, later that same night, as she'd left me her phone number and said she'd be home. But I wasn't about to turn a dicey situation into a dicey affair that had started with my intentional psychic manipulation of a total stranger.

From the moment I'd psychically reached out towards this passing woman, until the moment she'd reluctantly walked away from my table after her reading, George had been watching me from his neighboring table with amused interest. As soon as the young woman was out of earshot, George leaned over towards me with a new look of respect in his eyes. "Not bad, kid," he said to me. "Not bad at all." He'd taken in the entire drama and knew that I'd learned the psychic manipulation trick I'd used from observing him.

As interesting a lesson as this experiment was, I never did it again. The principle difference between what's classically been termed as "white" magick, a positive use of mystical understanding, and "black" magick, a selfish and manipulative use of that same awareness, is what you do with the knowledge you possess.

I choose to walk in the light.

CHAPTER FORTY-SIX

Taking A Ride On The Astral Planes

One of the friends I made doing the Psychic Faires was a terrific woman named Linda. Linda also lived in upstate New York and was every bit as exceptional as George when it came to her talent and ability in the psychic and otherworldly realms. Linda was one of those rare mystic who's mastered the amazing ability to maintain 24-hour consciousness. 24-hour consciousness is exactly what it sounds like. It means the individual is able to maintain his or her awareness of what's going on 24 hours a day, whether she or he is awake or asleep. When she's asleep she consciously knows she's asleep and remembers the details of her normal waking life and when she's awake she is able to recall the things she did in the astral realms when she was asleep. I've only known one other exceptional mystic with this ability.

Linda became something of a counselor for me. In particular, when I'd gotten involved in a martial arts dojo under a particular martial arts master. The master was an extremely high level black belt in one of the well-known Asian styles and also a practitioner of ceremonial magick, but in a way that I felt was more on the manipulative/black magick side. The master/sensei and I got along quite well and I really enjoyed the sensei's company. However, the sensei was also visiting me out-of-body and in my dreams without my *conscious* consent. The results of this close association included a dark and seamy lower energy that was progressively enveloping my life. This lower vibration manifested to me psychically as a kind of gray to black cloud that I could see from time to time around my energy field.

At first, I didn't want to admit to myself that the energy was connected to my martial arts teacher/sensei because I truly liked and honored my teacher and wanted to think only the best of the exceptional school and the people I'd become involved with. All that changed late one night, when I woke up, sensing my sensei's presence in the bedroom. At the same time, I felt this creepy, sickening, low vibrational energy drain leaving me via my solar plexus. I followed this thick swirling wall of energy leading away from me. At about ten to twelve feet above my bed towards my very high ceilings, I psychically saw four very ugly and distorted creatures (lower vibrational entities that live on the astral

160

planes) feeding off of my life force. This seriously creeped me out.

I immediately cut off the energy flow and started praying for spiritual protection to come to my aid. I demanded these lower astral beings leave. After a minute or so, they slowly withdrew. But there was something all too familiar about the sensation of their presence. This was not the first time they'd done this to me, I realized, it was simply the first time I'd remembered it in my waking life. I understood that somehow these lower astral *familiars,* the kind used by people who do manipulative magick such as voodoo, had been building a psychic relationship or bridge to me from the astral realms. I still wouldn't admit to myself the true and obvious source of this new connection.

The next morning, I still had that creepy feeling in my stomach. I looked up above me and saw these lower astral creatures were back. (Or perhaps they'd never left.) I again prayed and demanded that they leave, and again they withdrew slowly, almost casually, as if they had a right to be there. I decided I needed to call in the big guns. I picked up the phone and called for Eva at the Center of the Light. I managed to get her husband on the phone and he promised to do some praying on his end and then get my request for assistance to Eva as soon as he could. I thanked him and he wished me well.

About forty minutes went by, when all of a sudden I felt my attention drawn in the direction of the Center of the Light. I looked up and psychically saw this massive wall of energy rushing towards me from across the state border from Massachusetts to New York. This wall of energy took only a second or two to cover the fifty miles between us and then it hit my building like a tidal wave of light and power. Eva's wall of energy ripped through my apartment building, clearing out the lower entities and severing the astral ties that had apparently been quietly building for many weeks. Eva was a healer of a very high order and a very powerful soul on this and other planes of reality. I breathed a massive sigh of relief and allowed myself to be bathed in her light.

After I felt Eva was done with doing what she needed to do to help me out, I picked up the phone and called. This time I found Eva right away and thanked her for her help and motherly protection. "Anytime you need me, you just call," she said with the grace and compassion of the Queen of Light she truly was.

Later that day I had Linda over and she let me know what she thought, in no uncertain terms, "You know you brought it on yourself," she said. "What do you mean?" I asked. "You know why they came to you, and you know where it came from," she insisted. As she spoke, I saw the martial arts dojo in my mind, but still didn't want to believe that my sensei would be connected to such lower astral beings.

Linda made it unequivocally clear. "It's because you wanted power," she said. "And you were willing to compromise yourself in order to get it." Now, I understood. Having already known some of the most extraordinary and powerful mystics in the land by the age of twenty-seven, a part of me wanted to experience the power of those advanced individuals. Furthermore, having been a very awkward and un-athletic kid, I saw my chance to acquire both physical and mystical power by immersing myself in all that my sensei and the dojo had to offer me. I had watched as my own teacher's teacher, on his visit from the Orient, would control his assistant, calling her telepathically as he desired her presence, with her showing up with exactly what he had psychically communicated to her that he wanted.

I've always felt that if another human being can learn to do something then I can learn to do it too. I wanted to learn what these people had to teach me, but deep in my gut I knew that there was a darker, more sinister side to this particular martial arts family, lying just below the surface of all the friendliness and physical discipline. Even though I hadn't consciously acquiesced to all that would be required of me to eventually enter that inner circle, I'd been ignoring the warning signs and making excuses for attitudes and behaviors I didn't approve of. This otherworldly astral connection to this group of lower familiars (entities that can help one with control and manipulation in the world) had been part of my training from my sensei, though on a less-than-conscious level. This was a part of the training, however, that couldn't have happened unless some part of me agreed to it and allowed it to happen. With my friend Linda's no-nonsense assistance, I'd gotten the message. In that moment, I decided I would cut my physical ties with the dojo and my lower astral ties as well. As it was, I'd been considering leaving town and moving to the American Southwest for months, but something had been holding me back. Now that I fully understood what that something was, I quickly made plans to wrap up my affairs in upstate New York and move on to new life lessons in a new place.

My friend Linda and I continued to spend time together, but it would be several days before she stopped looking at me suspiciously. I knew she was making certain that I hadn't been deceiving her about my understanding of what I'd gotten myself into at the dojo. Before I left New York State, Linda and I had dinner together one evening at her apartment and found ourselves talking late into the night. There was always a bit of romantic tension between Linda and I, but we'd managed not to go there. It got so late that I ended up crashing on the couch, but we continued our visiting throughout the night on the astral planes. Linda, as I mentioned earlier, was able to maintain conscious awareness of her activities 24-hours a day, whether asleep or awake. Spending that night in her space allowed me to recall much more of my time out-of-body than was normal for me. The next morning, as Linda and I shared breakfast, I brought up our continued visiting on the astral planes the night before, still a little uncertain that I hadn't just dreamed it all. "Oh, you remember that, huh?" she answered ever so casually, her experience of such things seemingly being the most natural state in the world for her. A couple of months later I continued my mystical adventures, both in and out of body, after moving some 2,500 miles away to Arizona.

For those of you fascinated by the idea of the astral realms, I would suggest to you that there's a world of difference between having legitimate experiences on the astral, alone or with other souls, and just living in a fantasy world of dreams, a world where you don't have to take any emotional risks or deal with real life challenges. We've all got bodies here in this dimension, presumably for a reason. Pretending to have a life, while avoiding living a full and complete emotional life on this level of consciousness, is definitely not the advisable way to go.

CHAPTER FORTY-SEVEN
Reverend Fuller "The Dental Healer"

One of the other friends I made while in Albany was a woman in the midst of a separation from her husband. Her name was Charlene and she and her officially estranged husband Fred had a couple of very sweet kids. Both parents were good people who were interested in the mystical side of life, so we quickly and comfortably became friends. Living in the same building as Charlene was John. John was sort of the unofficial mayor of the neighborhood and was one of the first people to engage me when I first moved there. He'd graciously taken me around from house to house and to the stores and merchants in the neighborhood to introduce me. John had lived a fascinating and difficult life. A half-Gypsy (Roma) Roman Catholic, John was a passionate man of great intelligence, who'd been crippled by polio as a child and had turned to strong drink long before I'd made his acquaintance. In the fall of 1984, John turned sixty years of age, but looked decades older. I looked at his astrology chart and saw that he was about to experience the exact conjunction of transiting Pluto, the planet associated with death and transformation, to his natal Scorpio Sun. It was time for John to die and be reborn, one way or another.

When John was sober he was a kindly, wise father/grandfather figure to many and when he was drunk he was indistinguishable from the other old disheveled men lying in a stupor in the nearest alley. Part of John's personal agony and pain had been his physical deformities, but a deeper part of his personal demons was his conscience eating away at him for the dishonorable things he'd done in his life. In particular, John told me he'd been a high-level civilian involved with the United States military's Trident Nuclear Submarine project. John explained that the people in charge of the project were afraid of being shut down if the dangers the development program and its lethal byproducts posed to the environment and the general public ever became known. Many late nights, he explained, he had been responsible for overseeing rented tugboats, with their legal markings blocked out, hauling fifty-gallon steel drums filled with highly toxic radioactive nuclear waste and secretly dumping them into the Atlantic Ocean, just off the northeastern coast of the United States. This and other transgressions more private were the personal demons John drank to keep at bay.

Besides his Christian name, John also went by the religious name Kayum. Kayum had lived a deeply spiritual life for a time and now worn out by life at sixty he was seeking to renew himself. John/Kayum had a teacher who lived in New England. He explained he wanted to see his old spiritual teacher before his death, so we made plans to leave together on the morning of his exact Pluto conjunct natal Sun transit.

The night before we were to leave I discovered John drunk and bloodied and completely unprepared to go. He said he'd been rolled by a couple of guys outside the liquor store. He told me they'd beaten him up and taken his money. I cleaned John up, made him dinner, and put him to sleep on the couch before I left. I knew we weren't going to see his old spiritual teacher, after all. I didn't hear from him for the next two days after that, didn't see him around, and he didn't answer his door. It was late November and so I headed off to visit my family for the Thanksgiving Day holiday back in the Boston area. When I got back, I learned John's body had been discovered in his apartment. He'd apparently been dead for days. The neighbors had found him when they went to get him to include him in Thanksgiving dinner. As it turned out, the last meal John had eaten was the one I'd made for him. He'd apparently died that same night. From what we could tell, the last thing he'd read before his death was a poem written for him by our mutual friend Charlene.

Pluto, the planet of death and transformation, had made its visit that fateful night and John had made his transformation and gone towards his next spiritual rebirth. Occasionally, over the next few months, I would catch sight of John's ghost walking the streets of our little neighborhood, looking in on his former neighbors the same way he had when he was in his strongest and clearest place. John had loved the people of that neighborhood and they had loved him. He continued to look after us, even in his death, although I like to think he finally made the complete transition to the next stop on his journey.

Months after John's death, and just before I had my run in with the lower spirit entities in my apartment, Charlene and I took a short trip together to the Center of the Light for a special event. The famous Reverend Willard Fuller and his wife were going to be leading a night of prayer and faith healing on the performance stage at the Center. Reverend Fuller and his wife were Christian evangelicals who'd become famous for the amazing dental healings that some people experienced in the company of Reverend Fuller and his deep faith in God. As it happened, years earlier some people had experienced instantaneous healings of major dental problems in Fuller's presence. Over time, people with dental problems and other ailments started traveling far and wide to experience healing through Reverend Fuller.

When Charlene and I arrived, with Charlene's young daughter Meagan in tow, the Center of the Light's large performance hall was filled with an enthusiastic audience. The evening got under way and I was impressed to note that while Reverend Fuller went from person-to-person dispensing his healing energy many spontaneous healings appeared to be happening all throughout the crowded hall. Again and again I heard people calling out in amazement at the healings, dental and otherwise, they were somehow magically receiving. One such healing was for Linda Burnham, one of Eva's top students for years. I moved over to see what all the fuss was about. Something amazing was happening. Linda's friend Elaine and others watched with a flashlight shining into Linda's wide-open mouth, with Linda somehow managing to keep smiling from ear-to-ear during the process. As I stepped up to get a closer look, those around her happily moved aside to allow me a close up view of the action. There inside her mouth, brightly illumined by the flashlight shining directly into it, was a former cavity in one of her teeth apparently filling up with gold before our very eyes. Even with all I'd already experienced in my life, my mind fought with me to understand how what I was seeing was possible. As I had no other explanation, and as it was clearly happening right in front of me, I determined that the appropriate thing to do was to accept it. I lingered for a good minute to make certain that the gold, apparently growing to fill up the well in her tooth, continued to increase in volume. It did.

I walked away and sought out Charlene on the other side of the hall to tell her of the amazing thing I'd just witnessed. Charlene herself was busy grinning broadly, as she had also just witnessed a dental miracle. Her daughter Meagan, maybe eight to ten years old at the time, had been the recipient. Meagan had both upper and lower rows of teeth noticeably pulled out of alignment from years of sucking her thumb, a compulsion she'd continued into elementary school. Charlene and Fred had been expecting they would soon have to plop down the money for braces so that Meagan's teeth would straighten out and grow properly as she developed towards adulthood.

What had happened, while I was on the other side of the hall watching gold appear from the ethers inside Linda's tooth, was that Meagan's top and bottom rows of teeth had spontaneously straightened out, much to her mother's delight. Meagan, for her own part, was noticeably shaken by the miraculous event. She was a very smart little girl and according to everything she'd learned in her rather short life what had just happened to her should have been physically impossible.

After I moved to Arizona, Charlene and I stayed in touch for a while, but eventually lost track of each other, as I have lost touch with so many wonderful and honorable people during my private sojourn through the mystical side of human existence.

Reverend Willard Fuller, "The Dental Healer," as of this writing, in March of 2005, is alive and well in his late 80s and is still doing his amazing healing ministry. Dr. Fuller's ministry can be contacted through his website http://www.WillardFuller.com.

I did a quick web search on healing miracle-recipient Linda Burnham as well and discovered that Dr. Linda Burnham is still teaching and practicing healing, these days in Santa Fe, New Mexico. Naturopath Dr. Linda Burnham and her Burnham Systems Studies can be found on the web at http://www.BurnhamSystems.com.

~

P.S. – Always remember to brush *and* floss.

CHAPTER FORTY-EIGHT

Oh God, What Have I Gotten Myself Into?

It was a sunny afternoon in mid-August when my plane started its decent. From the air the hot, dry desert landscape of Phoenix, Arizona looked like a series of giant dirt piles with houses and roads placed around them. I was shocked at the starkness and lack of vegetation. "Oh my God! What have I gotten myself into?" I quietly asked myself. When the plane landed I picked up my gear, two suitcases and a large backpack, and headed for the exit doors of the air-conditioned airport. When the automatic doors opened, the 119°-Fahrenheit hot air (48°-Celsius) hit me in the face like a blast furnace. I had flown 2,500 miles across the country on faith and a one-way plane ticket. I had only $350 to my name, no job, no place to sleep, and I didn't know a soul for more than 1000 miles. Within hours I was feeling happy to be in a new place filled with new possibilities. And I felt certain I would be fine, for I had *visualized* what I wanted to happen next for me.

You see, before I left Albany, I'd created an image in my mind of what I wanted to appear for me when I got to Phoenix. I wanted a nice, inexpensive place to live near the college. I wanted to live in a house, not an apartment, with only one other person, not roommates. I wanted a job where I could work indoors, with nice people, for decent money. And I wanted a girlfriend. And I got exactly what I'd visualized for myself. Through a series of interesting coincidences I had a place to live the first night I arrived, within easy walking distance of the college, with one wonderful person, who remains a dear friend some twenty years later. I also had work within three days, the job I wanted ten days later, and I had a girlfriend inside of a week. Everything I'd visualized manifesting for my arrival in Arizona came to pass without a hitch. It was all happening perfectly as planned! Then, four weeks after I arrived, it all started to unravel, or so it appeared at the time.

I'd gotten a job working indoors in a boat-building factory (yup, smack dab in the middle of the desert!) with really nice people, and for a decent wage. The company built small yachts and was under very conservative management. I worked principally with one other guy, and it wasn't long before my kooky sense of humor came out, as it generally does when I'm with someone I'm comfortable with. I started this funny space alien routine, which my coworker found hilarious. He told his friends at the factory how funny I was and soon they were coming around and asking me to "say something funny about being from outer space," and so I would. They were a great audience.

But the religiously conservative Mormon management didn't think it was so funny. They'd heard about my sense of humor and my silly stories and decided that anybody who made up such crazy jokes "had to be on drugs." My boss and coworker went to bat for me, explaining that it was just all in fun and that I was a great worker, but the straight arrow management would have none of it. I was fired without cause or explanation, using a clause in the new hire contract that said they could do so. It suddenly felt like my new life was crumbling around me. I went to my new home, feeling devastated and defeated. "How could I have manifested everything, and then start losing it inside of a month? What did I do wrong?" I desperately needed to know.

Becky, a friend of my new girlfriend Mary Carol was visiting when I came home from that last day on the job. She suggested I call her friend Kevin, who was a great guy with his own roofing company and in need of help. "Why not work for him?" she suggested. But I was already lost. "If this fell apart, what else might go wrong?" I worried. Within twenty-four hours of losing my job at the boat factory I came down with Valley Fever, a disease caused by microorganisms in the desert air and water, which can manifest either like dysentery, or as pleurisy of the lungs, or both. I got the dysentery version.

All the fears I'd been suppressing for years came to the surface at this juncture, consuming my self-confidence along with my body. I became weaker by the day and for 3½ weeks I vomited constantly and was unable to keep any food or water down. By the final few days of my life threatening illness I'd become so thin that you could count my ribs just by looking at me. I'd become so weak that I had to lean against the walls and furniture if I wanted to walk across a room. By that age I had become adamant about only using natural healing methods, so I refused go see a medical doctor. I tried out various natural healing methods with the help of Mary Carol but nothing did any good. I understood that what I probably needed on the physical level was a major dose of penicillin but I wasn't going to let some bacteria force me to use pharmaceuticals. What I needed on the spiritual level, however, was not as easy to access.

I remember lying on the floor one day and thinking, "I'm dying." This was not surprising, given the wretched shape I was in, but what was surprising was that I recognized a part of me, way deep down inside, *wanted* to die. I analyzed my thought processes and discovered that I felt profoundly let down by God in my life. Not by the Great Spirit, or the Universal Mind, or the Divine Mystery, but by the old-fashioned, angry, dictatorial, Father God of the Old Testament. I explored deeper and realized that a very real part of me still identified with that violent, jealous, all-powerful father figure. This archetypal father figure ruled by whim and demanded unquestioning acquiescence to all of his laws or else a horrible punishment would follow. It struck me that, long ago in my early childhood, I had come to see my own father and the Old Testament concept of a Father God as one in the same. My father seemed every bit as dangerous, and potentially lethal, as the punishing God of the old Bible stories. When things appeared to be going wrong in Arizona, that old part of me felt I couldn't depend on God to keep what I thought of as "His end of the bargain" I'd made with Him, and if I couldn't depend on God then I didn't want to be here anymore.

My study of mysticism had given me some very sophisticated intellectual ideas about the nature of the Divine. But deep down inside, that little boy who'd learned of a very different and frightening model of a Supernatural Father figure still believed in that version of God. I recognized that this version of God had been drawn from the tribal dictator warrior kings of the ancient world who ruled by both law and by their personal whims of the moment. Those tribal fathers, like our own personal fathers, were a very human reality that became the dominant archetype for a dictatorial Heavenly Father for many peoples of the world. At a deep level of my psyche I'd misidentified with that ancient concept as if this were the reality and totality of God, a concept reinforced for many of us by our earthly fathers. In that moment, I consciously and willfully let go of that limiting and destructive concept of the Divine. I understood in that moment that I'd lost my new job because I was already wanting for something *better*. As would be revealed in the following weeks, the job Becky had told me about a mere two hours after I lost my job at the boat-building factory, would turn out to be the job I had really wanted all along, but had thought was too much to ask for. In that same instant of final realization concerning the truth behind my ailment, I was immediately made well, got up off the floor, and walked into the kitchen to make myself lunch.

CHAPTER FORTY-NINE

Believe It Or Not

What people believe about the nature of life and reality is as complex and as diverse as the people doing the believing. This also applies to what they believe about themselves. One of the things I've observed from spending time with a number of psychics, mystics, and spiritual leaders over the years is that most of them don't have much of a reliable feedback system for letting them know when they've been right and when they've been wrong. Even those who have regular clients or students who come to them for guidance often hear only about how "right" they were on a particular topic, but don't often get to hear about all the ways they may have partially or even totally missed the mark. This is partly why even many honest and honorable psychics will claim an extremely unlikely and unsubstantiated high level of accuracy in their predictions and readings. 95% accuracy is not that uncommon a claim by some of the best in the business, and by some of the frauds as well. Yet there is nothing that I've seen that would cause me to believe that such a high level of near infallibility is anywhere near as common as the claims of such ability are. This, of course, goes for any profession.

Often students or devotees following a particular teacher, preacher, or guru will make excuses for their spiritual teacher when he or she makes a mistake. They may even tell themselves the teacher must be trying to teach them something about themselves by giving the wrong advice. "Perhaps I've misunderstood what the teacher said?" they tell themselves, or "maybe the truth is so deep that I'm just not ready to see it?" These things are certainly possible, but all too often they are used as a way to excuse a teacher's shortcomings. Many are afraid to risk disfavor by challenging the one who's supposed to be so wise. Others have such a strong need for someone to lean on and take solace in that they won't speak up, even when they know in their hearts and guts that all is not right. One of the problems with not telling your teacher/guru/psychic/etc. that they're wrong is that they go on under the illusion that they're much more than they actually are.

To be fair, how are they supposed to know they're screwing up if everybody's afraid to tell them? So-called enlightenment is a matter of degree. It is not some plateau you reach that you never have to grow beyond. The student surpassing the teacher is a phenomenon that happens in all areas of learning, including the mystical realms. Of course there are those who artificially boost their profile by combining actual ability with sleight-of-hand and trickery. For instance, there are the people known as the *psychic surgeons* of South America who supposedly use their bare hands to reach inside a person's body and pull out harmful tumors without leaving a mark or causing pain, "tumors" that often look suspiciously like chicken gizzards. Every film, video, and photograph series I've seen of these so-called psychic surgeries have shown the healer with his or her hands pushed into the fat of the patient's body and always with the part of the hand that's showing appearing just at the bend of the joints of the fingers and always with what looks like a thick pool of blood around the fingers obscuring any sort of clear view of what's really going on. Never once have I seen an image of these supposed miracle workers' hands apparently clearly entering someone's body in a way that can't be easily faked with bent fingers and animal blood squeezed onto the body from a hidden sponge in their hands. As best I can tell, many of those practitioners actually do possess real healing energies and knowledge of natural medicines that can help their patients. But combining real ability with false magic and sleight-of-hand to increase the effect is not an honorable way to go about it, in my opinion.

In another part of the world there is a man who is famous across the globe for supposedly being able to produce physical objects out of thin air. His most spectacular feat is only performed once a year at a special festival that marks the occasion. People travel from around the world to witness the great man's "miracle." Years ago, I was given a book that describes this annual manifestation in a blow-by-blow description of the event, leaving nothing out of a performance that takes hours. The book was written by a man who came as a skeptic to the event and left as a true believer. Had the author studied magic tricks and sleight-of-hand as a child, as I did, he might have seen the obvious misdirection and not been taken in by the holy man's deception. *Misdirection* is a term used by professional magicians to refer to the act of making an audience focus on one thing, so as to allow the magician to do something else without that secret action being noticed. Even if onlookers are staring right at the action as it's being done, the illusionist makes it appear as if they're doing something else. This sort of thing can take a great deal of practice to master convincingly. Many magicians will use additional fanfare to further misdirect the attention of the audience such as scantily clad female assistants, sudden loud noises, and dramatic quick body movements in order to increase the likelihood they will get away with the illusion undetected.

When I began reading the book's blow-by-blow detailed account of the holy man's yearly miracle I was fully prepared to be amazed at the magical mystical feat of this extraordinary event. I had met several devotees of this famous holy man and knew that this modern-day sage was held in the highest esteem by some pretty influential people. When I recognized I was reading a description of an obvious fake, I was taken very much by surprise. I had expected to marvel at the great miracle and to be forced to try to wrap my brain around something that might seem to skirt the known laws of physics, like seeing the handiwork of dental healer Reverend Fuller. Instead, my reaction was much closer to, "Son of a gun, you sneaky little rascal!"

Here's the basic setup and how this apparent game of religious and mystical deception is played:

Once a year a great religious festival is held. For the followers of this world-famous spiritual master, the centerpiece of the festival is when the great man spends several hours supposedly *materializing* a slender six-inch stone lingam inside his body and then slowly pushing it up through his esophagus, to his throat, and finally out his mouth. People come from all across the globe to witness the yearly miracle. Once at the festival they spend many hours, or even days, fasting and sitting in meditation and prayer, chanting songs in the hot sun, and breathing air choked with the heavy burning of incense. By the time the great man arrives, a significant number of the many thousands of faithful and skeptical alike are lost in a mass sharing of expectation, religious fervor, dehydration, and blissful disassociation from their physical bodies. The spiritual master, with great pomp and ceremony, takes his place in the center of the crowd and proceeds to focus on the task of the moment, pretending to create a solid physical object inside his stomach and then pretending to push that non-existent object slowly up his esophagus and out of his mouth. This elaborate bit of theatre takes an additional few hours to play itself out.

Finally, after hours of playacting, the great man reaches a point where he pretends to be choking on the non-existent slender rock. At that, an attendant rushes to him with a vessel of water, made of stone or pottery, which, curiously enough, happens to be just long enough to conceal the object he's been pretending to have inside of his body all along. Once he's surreptitiously slipped the slender stone into his mouth from the water vessel, holding part of it at the back of his throat [professional sword swallowers do this six shows daily in Las Vegas], he then pretends to be finishing the job of pushing it into his mouth from his stomach, for an additional twenty minutes or so. This additional time delay ensures that any of the spaced-out, dehydrated, incense-drugged crowd that might still be suspicious don't draw the obvious conclusion that the small object he's about to produce from his mouth came from the water vessel he just drank from. Once the object is finally victoriously produced and triumphantly displayed for the crowd the great man seems to nearly faint from his great effort. The crowd gasps in fear for the holy man's life and his attendants rush to his aid to supposedly provide additional support. By this time, anyone who's guessed how the fake was pulled off is likely to keep their conclusions to themselves for the sake of not alienating themselves from the tens of thousands of devoted believers surrounding them on every side.

Now, if this yearly spectacle was all this man had to offer the world it would be pretty easy for most to dismiss him as a fake and pay him no further mind. But the fact is this famous fellow, by all accounts, has some very legitimate and highly honed psychic and healing abilities that he uses in his global interactions with his followers. These are the same exceptional mystical skills and *sidhis* (a Sanskrit word for psychic and occult *powers*) that allowed him to establish his massive international following in the first place. Much like the kinds of abilities our female prophet from Chapter 25 [The Chelas & Their Master] used to control her devotees, this occult master combines the psychic trainings and energy initiations of his mystical lineage with the ability to take much of the energy that is given to him every day, by the prayers and devotions sent to him via his picture and other objects connected to him, and use that excess energy to perform many of his amazing healing and psychic feats for his followers.

So why would somebody who such has exceptional psychic and healing abilities choose to perpetrate such a fraud every year? As best I can tell the answer is, at least in some cases, a matter of *tradition*. The healing, mystical, and psychic practices of many traditional cultures around the world have been in place for thousands of years. The knowledge and training gets passed down from teacher to student, generation after generation, but not every student is equal to their master. Some don't even come remotely close. One way around this problem of producing minimally gifted spiritual leaders is to add a bit of flash and glitter to the performance. These less-than-impressive individuals, after all, still have the job of looking after the health and spiritual welfare of their people. If the people believe that the spiritual healer, herbalist, shaman/magician has powers and abilities of great value, beyond the basic knowledge of nature and the body, they're more likely to continue to come to the trained healer in times of need. Of course, altruistic motives aside, there is always the old standbys of fame, money, and power to explain why somebody might perpetrate a massive spiritual fraud on their followers. Ask any rock star, movie star, corporate CEO, or powerful politician if they enjoy the trappings of fame and power and most of them will admit that the lifestyle has its definite upside. These days, we know from the news reports of disgraced priests, ministers, and cult leaders, that those supposedly in the service of the Divine are as susceptible as any to temptation.

The famous spiritual master who pretends to manufacture the stone lingam in his tummy every year is also famous for picking small objects out of the air and presenting them to his amazed followers. Go to any magic tricks catalog or magician's retail shop and you can buy dozens of similar illusions and the instructions on how to make it appear that you too can pull solid objects out of thin air. A teacher of mine told me of a friend of his who'd spent time in that famous guru's ashram. Late one night, his friend happened on a door in the ashram that had been momentarily left slightly ajar. When he stepped inside to see what was in the normally locked room he saw a number of shelves lined with brand new objects – the *exact same objects* the famous miracle man regularly claims to pluck out of thin air.

Might I be wrong about this famous spiritual master? Could he really be doing what he claims to in the grand ceremony every year? I'd love to think it was true, but I just don't believe it. Even though I've seen many extraordinary and amazing things in my life, and definitely have to admit that there are those among us that can do things that our rational minds have been taught to believe are impossible to do, I'm sadly aware that more than a few religious leaders choose the route of spiritual deception, sometimes even when they don't really need to.

175

CHAPTER FIFTY

Mind-Bending Spoons & Spoon-Bending Minds

One of the many interesting things I've had the chance to witness over the years is something called telekinesis. Telekinesis (also called psychokinesis) is the ability to affect material objects without making physical contact with them. The famous spoon-bending feats, made famous by Israeli-born Uri Geller, are an example of telekinesis. Now, to be fair to the psychic phenomena debunkers out there, it is very easy to fake the ability to affect objects with the mind, including fake spoon bending. Just like the spiritual master in the last chapter who apparently pretends to do things he cannot, spoon bending and other similar feats can be performed as illusions on stage, or close-up, by talented sleight-of-hand magicians. But saying that the ability to create an illusion is proof that an illusion must have been created is a bit like saying that an actor pretending to play a piano in a movie constitutes proof that the ability to play the piano doesn't exist. It's a nonsensical argument that somehow passes for reasonableness when applied to things we've all been taught to believe simply have to be impossible.

My direct encounter with spoon bending happened in the home of my friends Terry and June. They invited me over one day to meet another couple, friends of theirs who were traveling from another part of the country, who happened to be quite proficient in the art of spoon bending. Our group consisted of myself, June, Terry, June and Terry's three kids, their kids' three friends, and the spoon-bending couple. The youngest kid of our group was in early elementary school, with the oldest in high school. For the effort, June brought out some very heavy old silver spoons from the kitchen. We all got one to work with.

The spoon-bending couple demonstrated their technique for us, successfully twisting June's heavy silverware around in a corkscrew fashion so that the newly bent section of the spoons looked like that curly Italian pasta. I watched very closely, looking for the trick, but detected no deception or switch in the presentation. The couple then talked us through the process of quieting our minds and then focusing all our thoughts on our silver spoons. We were told to focus on the place where the shaft met the curved part of the spoon and to see it becoming soft and pliable in our minds-eye. Once we were able to accept the possibility of our spoon bending for us, we were instructed to turn our focus away from the spoon, let go, and simply twist the heavy metal around in our hands, allowing the metal to bend.

Terry and June's three children and the children's three friends were all able to open themselves up to the possibility and have their silverware bend for them. All six of the kids twirled the heavy metal spoons around again and again in curly cues, just like the traveling couple had demonstrated for us. We adults were apparently unable to let go with our minds and allow the magic to happen and got nowhere with our efforts. The children, ages six through fifteen, were thrilled at their results and successfully did it again on additional heavy spoons and forks. Terry, June, and I tried once more and failed again. Unlike the children, I suppose, we adults were too experienced in living in the "real world" for our brains to accept this mind-bending possibility, even after seeing it happen with our own eyes. The kids were still open, trusting, accepting, and therefore malleable for the task.

Over the years, I've come across two other people that can bend spoons by focusing their minds and wills. One, the sister of a friend, used to do it as child, but it only happened when she got really mad at a family member and that family member's silverware would bend on them. The other, a dear friend who chooses to remain anonymous in this book, has been able to do spoon-bending, but only with a great effort of will and energy. For her the process requires her to run as fast as she can, in order to increase her level of physical energy and intensity, while she screams at the top of her lungs, over and over yelling at the silverware to "Bend! Bend! Bend!" She keeps yelling, "Bend! Bend! Bend!" until the metal finally bends to her will and she succeeds.

Three hours after I finished the final edit on this book, I received an email about a new website http://www.LifeChangingTV.com. It's a new effort by Nicole Whitney and Dannion Brinkley, the folks behind the popular radio show News For The Soul, streaming on the Internet at http://www.NewsForTheSoul.com. On the new website, they've got various streaming video clips, including radio host Nicole Whitney demonstrating spoon-bending for the camera. Check out their TV clips and radio show on the web. They have some fascinating guests.

CHAPTER FIFTY-ONE

Psychic Tourism

I had a number of other interesting experiences while living in Arizona. I suppose you could say I did a little psychic tourism before leaving the state. I visited the beautiful and magical natural rock formations in the town of Sedona, which at the time was a sleepy little place sporting one ancient gas station with rusty pumps and a small number of shops catering to travelers. Ten years later, it had become a sprawling spiritual metropolis with hundreds of new residents, tens of thousands of yearly visitors, and even a New Age Chamber of Commerce to compliment the regular Chamber of Commerce.

I also spent a little time with a particular Spiritualist Church. One top church member's claim to fame was that she could see the famous ghost that had been seen there for more than seventy years. On my first visit, I happened to see the figure of the long since dead man, before anyone mentioned its existence to me. I unintentionally stepped on some fragile egos when I announced that their so-called ghost had long since disengaged from its astral corpse and that the only reason any image of it continued to persist there was that people who wanted very much to see ghosts kept re-animating it with their own energy fields. As far as I could see, there was no *manas* (mind) or consciousness left in this empty astral shell, so calling it a proper ghost was a bit overdoing it. Furthermore, I stated that if the dead person's spirit had still been connected to its astral corpse, they should have long ago acted to help that human spirit move on instead of calling it out again and again to show it off to guests. Actually the aging minister of the church and I hit it off quite well, which became another reason for her top students to be jealous of my presence there. I imagine it was something of a relief for the assistant and her friends when I moved on.

One of the problems people run into with all this psychic exploration and mystical seeking is that it's all too easy to lose your ability to tell the difference between fantasy, imagination, and real metaphysical phenomena. When you are one of the rare people who see, hear, sense, or otherwise experience these elements of reality and expanded states of awareness you can find yourself without any good way to check out the truth or falsehood of your apparent otherworldly perceptions.

When your sense of reality periodically finds itself needing to expand in order to make room for newer and more radical perceptions of life and truth it gets easier and easier to allow for pretty much anything to seem to be true. This is especially true if it appeals to your intellect, emotions, or values in some way. What might be theoretically possible and what is actually occurring in this world, or in some other world, can be radically different things. Think of those cult members a few years back that killed themselves in a mass suicide in order to board a supposedly invisible spaceship they believed was traveling behind the Hale Bop Comet and you get some idea of just how far out the human imagination can take us over the edge and into the abyss.

Along these lines, I was taken by shock while talking one day with one of the better psychics I've known. This woman was highly intelligent, successful, and a damn good psychic reader and spiritual teacher. In the midst of an otherwise very acceptable conversation, for the likes of us anyway, she told me the exciting story of how her German shepherd dog had "disappeared into the void," some one hundred miles north of her place and had reappeared 3½ days later, having, according to her, stepped back into this reality "through a rift in time and space."

Now, if her dog had disappeared in central China, surrounded by thousands of armed and hungry peasants, a place where they eat dogs for food, and reappeared 3½ days later inside a locked closet at CIA headquarters in Langley, Virginia, I would at least be willing to *consider* the theoretical possibility that this German shepherd might have slipped in and out of some sort of astronomers' white hole in time and space, as unlikely an explanation as that may be for what occurred. However, the facts of this dog's tale (tail?) are much more mundane.

This psychic lost track of her dog just off the main highway, about one hundred miles north of her home. After calling for her German shepherd for hours and getting no response she finally left without the dog and drove home. 3½ days later, the dog showed up outside her house, located just off the same highway, in good health and high spirits. The idea that her healthy, full-grown German shepherd could have covered that distance and then found his way back home in the time allotted was so unbelievable to her that she determined he must, instead, have popped entirely out of this physical universe for a few days and then popped right back in on her front lawn.

Now folks, I'm a middle-aged man who could comfortably jog a hundred miles down a highway in less than eighty-four hours (3½ days). That's just over one mile per hour. Serious Marathon runners regularly cover 26.2 miles in less than five hours all the time. Hell, most healthy adults even *stroll* faster than that. Nonetheless, this very smart woman unconsciously combined vanity (she's a talented psychic who couldn't find her own dog, therefore he *must* have disappeared into thin air!) with metaphysical fancy, to arrive at a very erroneous and silly conclusion. The truth is, when you've seen and experienced so many things that society and science tells you are impossible for you to see and experience you can find yourself more willing to entertain almost anything as being somehow also possible.

The problem of belief vs. empirical science is that belief requires no irrefutable proof. But to be fair to all of the various believers out there, many so-called empirical scientists regularly embrace their favorite theories as if they were already proven facts long before the proof ever arrives. Decades later, when the scientific theory is finally discarded as incorrect or incomplete and replaced by something newer by the next generation of cutting edge scientists some of these empiricists will continue to defend the older religiously embraced incorrect scientific theories until the day they die. Kind of like all other believers.

While still in Arizona, I decided that there must be some way of determining, with some reasonable level of certainty, when I was receiving real psychic intuitive information and when my mind was just wandering or inventing. Or, for that matter, when I was picking up on somebody else's wandering mind and mistaking that for truth.

I began taking very conscious note of each time I *thought* I might be getting something in a psychic manner. Whenever I felt something strongly, I would stop what I was doing and focus on that moment to see if there were any clues available to me. I repeatedly asked myself, "Did the ideas or information seem to come from a particular direction, above me, on my right side, etc.? Did they seem to show up in my head, in my gut, or did it feel like it was coming from outside of me?" I would take mental notes of each time I thought I might be receiving information intuitively and then watch for whether that supposed information actually turned out to be dependable or not. Within weeks, I discovered that I had a particular feeling in my body when the ideas that came to me were actually true and no such feeling when they turned out to be untrue. I experienced this as a subtle, but very distinctive, tactile sensation throughout my nervous system. This *energy buzz* felt like a low level electrical current running through my entire body. This, again, only when the information I thought I was getting turned out to be correct and real.

Since that time I have used this subtle gauge to let me know when I need to pay particular attention to a feeling or idea that comes to me. If I get that subtle buzz feeling, I take the thoughts or feelings more seriously and watch for any sign or sensation that makes me feel like I ought to act on the information in some way. If the buzz sensation is not present then I take it for just a regular human thought or emotion and respond to it or not depending on what I feel like doing about it. Readers: Do try this at home, it might prove very useful to you.

After this, I traveled briefly with a couple of psychic sisters from New Zealand; visited old friends and made some new ones; then headed back to Arizona; crashed at my friend Glenna's house; and finally returned to Massachusetts to pick up on the life I'd left behind 2½ years earlier. On the trip I had a rather interesting experience. I was driving across the U.S., in an old Toyota Celica when I had a break down at 4 AM, just outside of South Bend, Indiana. I had been running the car too long and hard for some 2000 miles on mountain roads, across deserts, etc. and it had just been too much for the old car. The engine caught fire and was destroyed beyond repair before a trucker came with a fire extinguisher and put out the raging engine fire, saving my clothes, my personal papers, and my precious books for me.

The tow truck that later picked up my vehicle hauled me into an old gas station. Out front there was this old beat-up chocolate brown American car with a "for sale" sign on it. I bought the car and continued on my way for the remaining 1000 miles of my trip. As I crossed the border from New York to Massachusetts I had this very strange and magickal feeling that I was shifting probabilities from one possible life direction back to my earlier one. It struck me, in a very meaningful way, that I was driving an old American car that was the same year and odd color as the car I'd left Massachusetts in 2½ years before. A vision opened up as I recalled how my old chocolate brown American car had lost its engine on that same highway just after crossing into New York State 2½ years earlier. That I was now driving a very similar car back across the border, having lost the Toyota a day earlier, seemed to be an energetic part of my recapturing, or reentering, the life I'd left behind. When I told this story to my Dad, it took on another curious dimension. While driving across the United States, I had repeatedly felt this very strong and distinct connection to my father and his tales of traveling across the U.S. as a salesman when he was my same age. I'm also his namesake, Thomas Francis Lyons Jr.

When I told him of my breaking down just outside of South Bend, Indiana he told me a very similar story of his car breaking down in the same spot, just outside of South Bend. I'd never heard that story from him before. In fact, I'd never heard of South Bend, Indiana until my car broke down there that day. I hadn't done much traveling yet. My Dad was a very intense man with a strong mystical side who was also quite fascinated by the larger questions and mysteries of life. Born the seventh son of a seventh son, an important place in Irish mystical lore, I feel my Dad never went anywhere near reaching his potential as a seeker and a seer. In many ways, our deepest connection was the fact that we both knew I was living a life of exploration into the mysteries of the Divine that he had largely turned his back on as a young man. Traveling the same roads, in the same ways as my father, and sharing some of the identical experiences seemed to add an important piece to who I am, genetically speaking, and to the totality of who I continue to become.

What does it all mean? Well, I guess I really don't know. Repeatedly, I'm reminded that no matter how much I learn on the mystical side of life, I'm merely scratching the surface of the infinite possibilities of consciousness and awareness of the ultimate truths of reality.

CHAPTER FIFTY-TWO

Walking Zombies &
Attack Of The Lizard People!!!

There are all kinds of wild and crazy stories that have come to us over time. Some of the more intriguing ones have been part of popular mythology for centuries. Stories of large ravenous wolves that seem to possess a frightening cunning and an almost human intelligence have mixed with tales of real-life wild-eyed human predators living on the edges of civilization to create the myth of werewolves and other murderous creatures. Ancient sailors catching terrifying glimpses of killer whales, great white sharks, and giant octopuses gave birth to tales of sea monsters of all shapes and sizes attacking ships.

The legends of bloodthirsty vampires even have their roots in reality. Dracula, the most famous so-called vampire of them all, was the grim nickname of an actual man, a vicious Eastern European warlord who controlled the Romanian principalities of Transylvania and Wallachia. His father before him was so evil and cruel that he was nicknamed Dracul, which in the local tongue meant the Devil or the Dragon. His son Vlad was considered even worse than his father and quickly became known as Dracula, or Son of the Devil. He was also known as Vlad the Impaler for ordering his enemies tortured to death by having their bodies impaled alive on large sharp posts around his city fortress.

Another old horror story, that of *zombies* or "the living dead," walking out of their graves, also turns out to be based on factual events. The truth behind the zombie phenomenon was brought to light in the 1980s by a fellow named Wade Davis who's a Harvard educated Ph.D. in Ethnobotany and who also holds degrees in biology and anthropology. Davis went to the island nation of Haiti and discovered that the zombie phenomenon was part of a punishment devised by a secret traditional justice system of voodoo priests. He learned that people in the village society who had grossly and repeatedly transgressed codes of decency, kindness, and fairness – but had not technically broken any actual laws of the federal government of Haiti – were sometimes passed judgment on by secret tribunals. If the offending person refused to change their ways and become an honorable member of local society, the tribal council might pass a kind of death sentence on them. The procedure is to cause the condemned man or woman to ingest, or otherwise come in contact with, a very powerful combination of nerve toxins that cause a dramatic slowdown of the heart rate and a temporary paralysis of the entire body. These nerve toxins are a combination of plant and animal toxins, a critical ingredient being taken from the toxin sack of the puffer fish, which uses the poison in nature to paralyze its prey.

Once they've ingested the toxins the tribally condemned criminal, temporarily unable to move, talk, or even blink their eyes and with an almost imperceptible heart beat, is declared dead and quickly buried to keep the body from rotting in the sweltering Haitian sun. Later that night, the voodoo priest and his accomplices dig the wooden casket out of its shallow grave. The subject, who's been buried alive, has survived due to the extreme slowdown of their heartbeat and respiration, which has allowed the small amount of air left in the casket to be adequate for the few hours they remained buried. The priests take their still drugged victim out of town, where he or she may be forced to live out their life in servitude as a slave on remote Haitian farms.

The cultural religious belief, before Wade Davis wrote two books on the subject and exposed the nerve toxin deception, had been that the voodoo priests were able to kill their victims and later dig them up and bring them back to life as "walking zombies." The victims, forced to work as slaves, were kept chained, with additional drugs secretly mixed into their daily food so that mental clarity remained lost to them. This narcotic effect created the dead-eyed zombie appearance. Having gone through the terrifying experience and not knowing that they were being continually drugged to keep them in a stupor the victims were convinced the voodoo priest had stolen their souls. According to their own beliefs they had become the walking dead and were forever more under the sorcerer's power and control. Anyone seeing these people would run away in fear from the undead souls. For the full story, read Wade Davis' books The Serpent and the Rainbow (1986) [frustratingly, this fascinating and important book was greatly distorted and highly fictionalized into a pseudo-horror movie of the same name, and released in 1987] and Passage of Darkness (1988) or go to his website http://www.Wade-Davis.com. At this writing, Davis is Explorer-In-Residence for The National Geographic Society.

Of course there are other stories of half human/half monsters that are significantly less dependable. A current favorite of many in today's conspiracy theory underground is a guy who claims that the entire world is run by a secret society of powerful leaders who are actually lizard people from another world, merely disguised as human beings. This particular fellow insists that pretty much everybody in power from former American President Bill Clinton to the leaders of all the nations and powerful corporations of the world are secretly reptilian lizard people who morph back into their natural lizard forms when they are amongst their own kind and no actual humans are in the room. This conspiracy worldview seems to be a mix of science fiction ideas combined with older conspiracy theories that state the entire world is secretly run by: a.) The Jews; b.) The Roman Catholics; c.) Old World European Family Dynasties; d.) The Trilateral Commission; e.) Microsoft Founder Bill Gates; or f.) All of the Above.

Hmmm. There just might be something to that Bill Gates, Microsoft theory… Anyway, the fact that some very rich and powerful people privately conspire together to gain more money and more power for themselves is not news to anybody in the financial world. However, there is no good reason to believe that every rich and/or powerful person in the world is collectively conspiring against the rest of us and even less reason to believe that they shape-shift into giant alien lizard people after their servants and office assistants go home for the day.

Okay, who am I to talk, right? Perhaps in the untold vastness of the mysteries of consciousness there really are power-hungry souls from other worlds that have incarnated in human form, that look kind of like giant lizards on some other level of reality. Who knows? However, I've seen nothing that would cause me to conclude that these things are happening in this dense, three-dimensional world we all hang out in.

Is there a rise of fascist tendencies in some of the world's governments and militaries, as this conspiracy theorist suggests? Many political observers would say, yes. Is there a concerted effort by many at the top of the economic food chain to keep the rest of us down and available to serve their selfish purposes? Again, there is abundant evidence of such actions and motives and that it's been that way for many centuries. Are these same power brokers wearing fake human suits to cover over their green, alien, scaly, reptilian lizard bodies? Ah, no, I don't believe they are. I think you can trust me on this one…

CHAPTER FIFTY-THREE

Putting The "Fun" Back In Fundamentalism

Back in the Boston area, I settled into my old favorite haunts. One of my first conversations on the streets was with a fundamentalist Hare Krishna devotee. I didn't even know there was such a thing as a fundamentalist Hare Krishna. Like many young progressive Americans raised in the 60s and 70s, I thought people who embraced exotic foreign religions that included gods, goddesses, enlightened masters, and reincarnation had cast off the mental chains of doctrinal belief and had opened their minds to ever increasing learning and spiritual growth. As it turns out, joining a religion is still joining a religion. Anyway, I got into what I'd expected to be a fascinating conversation with this young guy with a shaved head, funny-looking ponytail, and long religious robes who turned out to be every bit as intractable and dogmatic as the most extreme religious fundamentalist of any other established faith. When I tried to steer into less controversial waters, by discussing the symbolism of artistic renderings of Krishna that show his skin as being the color of a rich sky blue, the young man's face hardened and his arms crossed over his partially bared chest. "Lord Krishna was blue!" he told me, with no room for argument. Keeping an open mind, I suggested that perhaps the historical Krishna could have been one of those dark-skinned black men whose skin appears almost purple or blue. The young man's eyes narrowed. "Lord Krishna was blue," he said coldly, then turned away from me, looking for fresh passers-by on the busy street corner to convert to his religion.

Why was he so dead certain that the dictates of his religious group were absolutely true? Because that's what the group taught him was so. Absolutely agreeing with those absolute teachings was the price of admission to a group that offered many wonderful and magical things to enrich his life and they included an instant worldwide community of brothers and sisters to share it with. Perhaps, for some, blind faith is a small price to pay for being embraced by a community of millions?

I remember talking with another guy, one I'd grown up with years ago, just after he'd joined a very strict Southern Baptist church group. The guy had been kind of a punk back in public school, though I'd always had a soft spot for him in my heart. The worst defining characteristic

186

of his childhood persona was a self-centered, arrogant attitude that whatever he wanted he should have, whether he had any right to it or not. When he finally opened his heart and "accepted the Holy Spirit," in his conversion to this very nice Bible church, the change in him was profound and immediate. The energy center of compassion had opened in his heart chakra and he had been transformed into someone who now wanted to experience the joy of caring about others. "I know the Holy Spirit is real! Because I feel it!" he told me with great emotion, as he held his hands over his heart. Indeed the Holy Spirit of Love and Compassion had entered his heart and had changed his life forever.

However, hard-line fundamentalist beliefs can lead to terrible results. For instance, young Islamic men and women killing themselves and others in suicide bombings because their extremist version of their religion tells them that they'll be received as conquering heroes and great martyrs in heaven for killing the enemies of their faith. Some of the extremist Christian factions are no different, believing that all that do not belong to their dogmatic version of the faith are enemies of God and deserve no mercy. More than a few of those following dictatorial Eastern religious leaders fall into similar categories. Generally, the outsiders of their faiths are treated as simple-minded children who exist outside the circle of true grace and knowledge. Happily, many religious groups and their teachings do at least as much good as they do harm and some actually do quite a lot of good and very little harm.

On the other hand, some folks don't even know the specific tenets of the groups they support. I remember this spiritual retreat center where the affluent owner brought "enlightened spiritual teachers" in from around the globe to share with others, his literature telling readers of the greatness of the various spiritual masters being hosted. I attended one event where I found the spiritual master of the week particularly admirable. When I bumped into the host, I asked him about the master's teachings. "Well, he's enlightened," came the seemingly confident reply. "How did he become enlightened," I asked with sincere curiosity, "and what have you learned from him, so far?" Now, feeling on the spot, the wealthy sponsor started to falter, his face turning red with frustration. He apparently knew very little or nothing about his honored guest. "I don't know!" he finally stammered at me. "He's enlightened, all right? He's enlightened!"

One of the more interesting and entertaining groups I happened upon in my first few months back in Boston was a small but steady group out of eastern Canada. They believed that the center of the Earth is hollow and filled with kindly extraterrestrials that are busy building a new perfect world that they will one day share with all of humanity. Once the upper surface world is almost completely destroyed by war, they say, the space brothers will emerge from their secret places in the center of the Earth and instantly bring about a New Heaven and a New Earth. Why these kindly space brothers don't just do it now, instead of waiting for humanity to have World War III, was never explained well enough for my personal satisfaction. But on the upside of their teachings is their certainty that all the missing persons lost to loved ones over recent decades have not, in fact, met with grisly or untimely deaths but instead have joined the benevolent space brothers in their efforts of telekinetically building a New Heaven and a New Earth for use by the rest of us. This gives them a sense of something positive to look forward to in an otherwise grim and terrifying vision of a post-apocalyptic future, I guess.

Sadly, many who feel they've been let down by religion, or by the idea of God they've been taught to believe in, may decide that the only thing to believe in in life is nothing at all. Most passionate atheists, as far as I've observed, seem to be doing their best to fill an empty place inside themselves by declaring the non-existence of a Divine Presence they desperately wish were real, just as many devil-worshipping metal heads are often not so much embracing evil as they are rejecting the religious hypocrisies and abuses they've seen in their families and communities. But the Great Spirit continues on, with or without our embrace. One of my favorite T-shirts says it best by quoting both the Almighty and the late great German philosopher Friedrich Nietzsche:

"GOD IS DEAD" – *NIETZSCHE*

"NIETZSCHE IS DEAD" – *GOD*

The true believers I have the greatest difficulty relating to? They would be that handful of folks who still claim to adhere to the old Flat Earth Theory, insisting that the Earth is actually flat and not round. Are these Flat Earth people just having a little fun with us? I like to think so. But if they are truly serious, and if they really do know what they're talking about, then somebody had better inform all those Australians that they just might not be standing upside down, after all...

CHAPTER FIFTY-FOUR

My Mother & I Go On A "Stakeout" Together

After doing different things to bring in money, I got a job working for the world's first biotechnology firm, a place called Biogen. The company's founder won a Nobel Prize for developing the techniques that allow us all to read the genetic code of human DNA. One of my pals at Biogen was a West German medical research M.D. named Eric. Eric was the son of a classical physicist and saw the world in very practical, three-dimensional terms. We had great fun together, but he found it difficult to understand how I could believe in all this mystical and psychic stuff that was constantly happening to me. Eric had been raised to think of such things as nonsense. Yet there I was, this man with a very good mind and clearly quite sane who talked of visions that, according to his worldview, couldn't (or at least shouldn't) make any sense at all.

During a visit from Eric's German girlfriend Irene, Eric presented his "scientifically-based" explanation as to how I might "think" that I was having experiences that, according to his mechanistic worldview, had to be a series of completely random and unrelated coincidences. He presented his false psychic theory with the use of a Bell Curve model. At one end of the extreme, he explained, there were people like him who had virtually zero experiences of these "completely unrelated coincidences" that might be mistaken for psychic and intuitive events. On the other end of the extreme of the Bell Curve, he continued, were people like me who had an inordinately high number of "completely and totally unrelated coincidences." Irene and I both broke out laughing. At that, Eric gave up his attempts to prove to me that what I knew to be true from direct experience was somehow not true.

~

One day, during that same period of time, I'd fallen back to sleep late on a Saturday morning and had a most unusual dream. In the dream, I was involved in wild gun battles and dangerous car chases that included a very distinctive rollover on a highway embankment. The most curious thing about the dream was that I wasn't in the least afraid or concerned for my safety. In fact, I was having a great deal of fun. I awakened from this very vivid dream, quite uncertain as to what it might mean. Was it symbolic of my ever-increasing ability to face life as it comes, no matter the risks? It certainly didn't seem to be a warning of danger. The dream experience, after all, had been only fun and good times. As I awoke, I also had another very strong and distinctive feeling. The feeling was, "Call your mother, she's feeling very lonely."

So, I called my mother. We got together for lunch and then decided to go to a movie. We looked through the newspaper ads and saw there was a new film opening that weekend staring Richard Dreyfuss and Emilio Estevez. Neither of us had heard of it, but we decided it looked like fun so we made that film our choice. The movie was called *Stakeout*. It was a fun buddy movie about two cops on a stakeout trying to catch an escaped convict at the convict's girlfriend's house. Interestingly, about three-quarters through the movie the images on the screen became startlingly familiar to me. There was this gunfight shootout scene and a long car chase between the good guys and the bad guys. At one point, there was this very distinctive car rollover on a highway embankment. In a flash, it all came together in my head. I'd seen this movie before, in my dream late that morning! In my dream I'd apparently been *previewing* the day I would most likely spend with my mother. The gunplay and car chases in my dream had been scenes directly out of the film; a film that I didn't consciously know existed.

What was the big message I was supposed to get from my dream that morning? It was simply, "Go spend some quality time with your mom. Maybe see a fun movie, like this one."

CHAPTER FIFTY-FIVE

Visions Of The Tasmanian Genocide

When I first took the job at Biogen, I was sharing a house very close to work with some very cool, artsy people. When it became time to move on, I split the rent on a house with a nice guy from work named Gary. One of the books I took up reading in my new place was a best seller called The Fatal Shore by Robert Hughes about the British invading the continent of Australia and turning it into a giant penal colony for their prisoners. When I got to the part where it described the systematic genocide of the indigenous people of the island of Tasmania I became suddenly dizzy and profoundly depressed. In vision after vision I kept seeing myself there, as one of the native aboriginals, helpless as my entire race was being intentionally eliminated so that the invaders could have the land for themselves. I tried again and again to read beyond the passages about how the British had murdered the peoples of Tasmania with guns, poisoned food, and diseased clothing left as gifts until finally there were no full-blooded Tasmanian natives left alive. But I couldn't move on.

In my life in Massachusetts, my days became a blur and my nights tortured by nightmares and profound sadness. When I wasn't at my job, I slept. Constantly. My ability to function as a normal human being completely abandoned me during that period. After weeks lost in this apparent *bleed-through* from another lifetime I finally determined that one day, before I died, I would tell this story of human horror and tragedy to the world so that what happened to the Tasmanian aboriginals would not be forgotten. With that resolution, I was finally able to become me again, the personal me that identifies with this life in this particular place and time in human history.

I never could read beyond those early pages in the book, The Fatal Shore. To this day it still sits on one of my bookshelves, waiting for me to use it as a resource to tell the story of the Tasmanian holocaust to the rest of humanity.

CHAPTER FIFTY-SIX

The Death Of *"El Poco Diablo"*

My friend Mary Carol from Arizona had an older dog, named Poco. Poco was half Australian shepherd and half pit bull, a combination that caused her to look, to my eyes, a bit like a short, stout, collie. Mary Carol became Poco's human guardian years before we met when she and some hippie friends of hers were living in this place called Apacheland. Apacheland wasn't a real town, but instead was the remains of an old Western movie set, with many of the buildings existing only as false fronts held up by angled wooden supports. There was this guy there who thought of himself as a wild man and he had named the dog El Poco Diablo, which means The Little Devil in Spanish. But this sweet, loving dog never quite measured up to the devil part and after a while became known simply as Poco. Poco and I had been pals when I lived in Arizona with Mary Carol. We had enjoyed each other's company again when I paid Mary Carol a visit in her new home near San Diego, California.

I hadn't seen Mary Carol or her dog Poco for a least a year when I had a very vivid and specific dream that included both of them. In the dream, I was in a war scene and fighting for my life with my fellow comrades. Finally, as we were being overrun, we had to retreat on foot away from the advancing tanks and enemy foot soldiers. As I was running away from the flying bullets, the topography of my dreamscape changed to somebody's backyard in Southern California. A couple of houses and green lawns ahead of me stood Mary Carol and Poco, with Mary Carol waving a friendly hello. I acknowledged them as I was running past, at which point Poco reached out and grabbed my hand with her mouth. I stopped running and stayed with them. The advancing tanks having suddenly disappeared.

In the dream, Poco continued to hold my hand firmly in her mouth, so that I couldn't pull away. But her teeth didn't cut into my flesh, as only her gums seemed to be making contact. I realized that it wasn't that Poco wouldn't let go of me; it was that she couldn't let go. Her jaws were completely locked shut, so she was unable to open her mouth. Poco looked me directly in the eyes. As she did so, our minds made contact. She told me that she was going away and asked me to look after Mary Carol for her when she was gone. I promised her I would, and then Poco and I said goodbye to each other.

The next morning, I woke up and found the message light flashing on my telephone answering machine out in the hallway. I'd turned off the phone and the sound on the answering machine the night before because I'd really needed the sleep. Mary Carol had called after I'd gone to bed. She didn't say much in the message, only that she'd like to talk and that she'd call me the next day when she got home from work.

That evening we spoke on the phone and I learned that Poco was dead. It had been a couple of months since Mary Carol and I had spoken, so I hadn't even known Poco was sick. As it turned out, Poco had still been alive when her spirit had said goodbye to me in my dream the night before. Poco was pretty old for a dog and in her final year had suffered from the pain and weakness brought on from bone cancer. According to Mary Carol, the elderly Poco had taken seriously ill about four weeks earlier and had completely stopped eating two weeks later. Just before my dream, Poco's jaws had completely locked shut, making it impossible for her to take any food or water, for she could no longer open her mouth. Mary Carol had reluctantly taken this as a sign that it was time to let Poco go and put her out of her pain and misery. She had called me the night before, hoping for a little moral support and to see if I felt it was time for Poco to die, as well. Unable to reach me the night before, Mary Carol had taken Poco to a veterinarian the next day and had Poco "put to sleep" via lethal injection. I told her of my dream conversation with Poco and I know it made her feel a little better.

It's now been some twenty years since we became friends and, in keeping with Poco's wishes, I have continued to look after Mary Carol from time to time and she has looked after me. As for Poco, well I imagine she's playing poker and drinking fresh water with Lassie and some of those other famous canines up there in Doggie Heaven. I bet she's good at it, too.

CHAPTER FIFTY-SEVEN

Stepping Out Of Time And Space

For most of my life I've had the periodic experience of stepping out of time and space. That is, I find myself so expanded that my sense of self seems to encompass All That Is. As a child I called it hearing the Universe because when I was tuned in to this expanded state I would hear a specific series of overlapping musical tones, cluing me into a certain vibration. As I got older, the experience took on a new dimension. I'd awaken in a dark room in the middle of the night, feeling that extraordinary sense of expansion and of being One With All That Is. Many times I'd go so far away from the physical and into the Spirit that all I knew about myself was that "I AM."

The rediscovery of my physical-ness would cause me to have to re-acquaint myself with who and what I am supposed to be in this much smaller and limited experience of reality. Once I understood again that in this existence I was known as Thomas Lyons and that I was living in 20th and 21st Century Earth in a place called America, I'd have to sort out the specifics: "How old am I? Twenty? Thirty? Forty? Fifty?" "Is there a woman beside me in the dark, or am I sleeping alone?" "Where do I live?" "Is there a job I have to get up for and go to in a few hours, or am I free to spend the day studying and learning what I will?"

Once I felt grounded enough in my physical body to use it properly, I'd carefully feel around in the dark for a light source. Once there was light, I'd study the room to determine exactly where in space and time I had landed from my travels in the Forth Dimension and beyond and what, if anything, I needed to do in the next few hours. When I felt I was sufficiently re-integrated with the present, I'd go back to sleep. I think the reason all this was necessary was that I'd sometimes go so far away that I needed to re-align myself to the tangible in order to insure that the personality of Thomas Lyons would remain sane and able to function here.

A friend of mine named Ted, years before I first started having these stepping-out-of-time-and space experiences, had also found himself disassociated from his specific Earthly orientation in time and space. He spent a couple of weeks knowing he was One With All, during which time he was able to see multiple levels of realities and into the souls and other lives of both his small self (the Ted part) and of others. Ted's ability to see so much all at once, without the proper training and grounding necessary, left him unable to handle all the input he was receiving from this dimension and beyond. This led him to being briefly incarcerated in a mental hospital, as his family and the doctors slowly forced him back into being just Ted once again. Many people have asked the question, "If reincarnation is real, why can't I remember my other lives?" Ted's experience is one of the reasons why. We focus our psyches on one body, in one place, at one time, in order to be able to make some kind of practical use any given lifetime.

Another dear friend of mine periodically finds herself seeing and experiencing what appears to her as thirteen different dimensions of time and space, all of them available simultaneously. If she's driving her car and this vision opens up she may see an accident on the road in front of her and be unable to tell for certain whether or not the accident she's seeing happened in the past, will happen in the future, or is happening in the here and now. In those moments, she's been forced to slow down and cautiously determine which "now" she's supposed to be in, so that she can respond appropriately.

Those of you reading this book, who may be feeling eager to go out and have a whole bunch of mystical experiences like these for yourselves, know that we are, all of us, presumably focused in this particular here and now for good reason. As you move forward in your understanding of the Divine, just make certain you're living the life you came here to live, instead of trying to run away to another one you may not be prepared for.

CHAPTER FIFTY-EIGHT

My Early Experiments With Radio Activity

My job at Biogen had me split between two different departments, so I answered to two bosses: Nancy in Human Resources, and Peter in Stocks and Public Relations. They were great people, but working for a medical research facility clearly wasn't my long-term future. As it turned out, it wasn't their futures, either. I'd had an idea for years about doing a radio show on the nature of mystical experience. While at Biogen I started to look into making that happen. About six months into my time there, I had a very vivid dream that included both of my bosses, Nancy and Peter. In the dream I was in a large facility, like Biogen. However, in the dreamscape the facility was a minimum-security prison, with us workers as the inmates. Nancy and Peter were among the benign prison guards. The dream versions of Nancy and Peter both told me they were going to be leaving soon. I asked when I would be getting out and a voice from somewhere said, "In 137 days." Then I woke up and wrote down the dream, with the memory still fresh in my mind.

Three weeks after the dream, Nancy made a surprise announcement to everyone at work. A surprise to everybody except me, that is. She was giving her notice of resignation in order to realize her dream of opening a flower shop. Less than four weeks later, Peter announced he too would be leaving to join with an old friend in a new consulting business. I went home that day and double-checked the notes from my dream. If the final piece of my dream was also correct, I still had over three months left in my prison experience. By that time, I'd begun night classes at a broadcasting school. Exactly 137 days from the date of my dream I received a phone call offering me my first job in radio, with the option of buying time to put my program idea on the air.

I worked briefly at that AM talk station, while finishing school, and then got an offer to work full-time at WDLW, Boston's main country music station at the time. After only three months behind the scenes in production I was promoted to full-time on-air for six nights a week. I used my experience there to develop what I called *The Psychic & Spirit Radio Show* and spent a year trying to market it throughout New England. Every radio station I went to loved the idea of the show, but was afraid it sounded too controversial for their station. One station was just beginning a new format and was looking for new ideas. I pitched my program idea to the Program Director, which included a weekly segment called Earthwatch about saving the environment. He thought it was wonderful and invited me to come around the station in the near future. Six weeks later, that same Program Director came on the air with a new segment that became the signature of the new station's rock format. It was called Earthwatch and was exactly the environmental action segment I had presented to him weeks earlier.

That station used the success of the Earthwatch segment to help them become, for a time, one of the biggest stations in Boston. They became known as the station that cares about the environment and sponsored concerts on Earth Day, with hundreds of thousands of attendees. As for me, once the Program Director had stolen my idea and pretended to have come up with it on his own, he stopped taking my phone calls. I watched as caring for the Earth started becoming the popular issue amongst many in Boston. Finally I wrote him a letter saying, "What the heck, at least some good has come of my idea," and left it at that.

I left Boston radio after that experience with the intent of getting married to a great lady I'd met in another part of New England. But that marriage never happened. Her name was Elizabeth and I'd met her two hours after seeing her very clearly and distinctly in a vivid late afternoon dream. In the dream she appeared in a bright red dress, surrounded by great love and great emotional problems. I awoke, sitting bolt upright, deeply shaken and drenched in sweat from this prophetic dream of emotional trauma to come, but I dove into the relationship anyway after meeting her later that day. After that relationship ended, I did a little odd work in radio, including occasional time at one of the college stations where I interviewed the extraordinary healer and Roman Catholic Priest, Father Frank Rizzo, as well as Boston area psychic Victor Venckus. But soon other fascinating doorways of possibility were opening up for me, so I went off to pursue those new avenues.

Thirteen years later, I finally put *The Psychic & Spirit Radio Show* on the air in Southern California. A new version of the show, *Spirit Rock Radio*, is now being developed for syndication and will be coming to the airwaves later in 2006. Keep your ears open.

CHAPTER FIFTY-NINE

Omega – The Complete Shakti System

One day I came upon a stack of program brochures for an upcoming health and healing expo. A strong spiritual presence came over me and told me there was something very important for me there. I flipped through a brochure and found a brief description of something called Omega, The Complete Shakti System. As I stood in the entryway of this natural foods supermarket with brochure in hand, I suddenly saw the same vision I'd had on my parents' front lawn when I was eight years old, the vision that included the kind man with the beard in the brown suit, the map of his world travels, and the founding of the Theosophical Society in New York City in 1875. "These are the people you have come to work with," I was told by spirit. I understood our souls had been together in that earlier effort in the late 1800s. I made a mental note to attend the expo and did so 2½ months later.

The work known as the Omega Shakti System offered a series of powerful energy attunements. The Sanskrit word *shakti* means, in one sense, Universal Energy. At the healing expo, I went to the Omega Shakti booth and had a demonstration by one of its teachers, a tall fellow about my size named John. The energy flow that went through my body was distinctly different from Reiki and quite different as well from the other unique energies I'd felt years earlier from Eva, Reverend Fuller, Benjamin Crème, and various martial arts masters. Over the following months I would come to experience dozens of distinctly different energy signatures from this same system called Omega Shakti and recognize that there are many varied types of cosmic energies in existence, each as unique as any musical note or chord. I was told there was to be a First Degree Omega class in Boston in which I could become initiated into Omega, just as I had years earlier been initiated into Reiki by Phyllis Furumoto.

A few days after the demonstration at the expo I was using 2nd Degree Reiki on my buddy Shelby for pain. After connecting to the Reiki energy, I placed my hands on Shelby's head and started the energy flow. "Wow! What are you doing?" Shelby asked. "That's so intense. It's like five times stronger than your normal Reiki!" "You're getting a contact high off this guy I met a few days ago," I told Shelby. "He demonstrated this energy system called Omega Shakti on me for about three minutes and I've been carrying that energy with me ever since."

I contacted my friend Steve Dondoros, the guitar player, and found that he too had checked out the expo and had also been impressed by the work of Omega Shakti. A week or so later we both attended the First Degree Omega Shakti initiation and met Matt Schoener, the founder of this extraordinary system of spiritual transformation. The class elements were divided up into two days of instruction, initiation, and practice. When Steve and I left, after day one, we were so filled with this profound new energy initiation that we were laughing with delight like children. We drove through the nighttime streets of Boston and Cambridge with all of our senses in an extremely heightened state. The tactile sensual world was amazingly alive. My vision was so clear that I didn't need the headlights on or my glasses to see perfectly. I even found a stretch of road and shut the headlights off for fun. It was like I had the night vision of a cat. Steve, who has had major vision problems all his life, had the same kind of clarity of sight. When we stopped into a supermarket-sized health food store to get some late dinner, everything in the store was alive with color, sound, and vibratory information. The people in the store seemed super real and hyper-dimensional and every vegetable and colored package of organic food seemed uniquely alive with vibrant life force.

We completed the First Degree Omega initiation class the next day and would become intimately involved with this spiritual teaching organization for the next few years. At Matt Schoener's request, I became the New England area organizer for Omega for a time and held healing circles and support groups for the growing number of students out of my home. A lot would happen along the way, eventually leading to the premature and completely avoidable demise of this extraordinary organization and its important work. Happily today the work of Omega Shakti continues on through one of Omega Shakti's original teachers, Rosanne Amato, formally Rosanne Fischer. Rosanne had been Matt's right-hand woman and was intimately involved in the grounding and manifesting of much of the expanded energy components of the larger Omega system of energy lineages. The energy attunements and teachers of Omega Shakti, Temple Reiki, and Rosanne's unique Triple Helix energy system can be found online at http://www.Helix3.com.

CHAPTER SIXTY

The Extraordinary Life Of Matt Schoener

What I know of the life of Omega Shakti founder Matt Schoener is largely from what he told me in conversations over four or five years. Matt, by his own account, was born in an Austrian refugee camp near the end of World War II. When he was four years old, his family moved to the United States. Matt was very psychic as a child and could see and communicate with nature spirits, elementals, and other non-physical beings that the vast majority of us never get to see. Matt used to smile when he talked of unintentionally annoying his teachers at school. He said he'd have visions in history class and correct his teachers when his visions showed the inaccuracies in their statements.

Matt also liked to tell of an incident, when he was very little, when his parents were going through a period of constant fighting and arguing. Matt said he told his parents that they must stop arguing, for his sake, or he would have to take action. When his parents continued to bicker, little Matthew Schoener quietly packed up, left home, and made his way to another German immigrant neighborhood where he happily stayed for a few months with a very nice family. All the while refusing to tell them his real name or where he was from, so they couldn't send him back. When his parents finally located him through the immigrant grapevine Matt refused to return home until his parents gave him their assurance that the fighting would cease.

As a young man, Matt was an accomplished classical musician and music teacher. His mystical abilities also continued to develop and Matt's passion for Theosophy, the Divine Wisdom as taught by Madame Blavatsky, the Arcane School, the teachings of English-born mystic Alice Bailey, and Mahayana Buddhism led him to being both an exceptional teacher of meditation and of the occult mysteries. The word *occult*, by the way, comes from an old Latin word meaning, "that which is secret or hidden from view" and was used by some European mystery schools to refer to metaphysical knowledge that was taught in private. This secret knowledge was only supposed to be shared with those students believed ready to understand the deeper mysteries of life. Modern scientific astronomers still refer to a Solar Eclipse, when the Moon briefly hides the Sun's light from Earth, as an *occultation* of the Sun. The term means the physical body of the Moon has hidden the Sun from view, making it momentarily occult.

The study of the mysteries outside of the Roman Catholic Church came under attack by the Vatican in the European Middle Ages and the word occult became vilified by the Church, who condemned anyone studying the mysteries outside of the Church's doctrinal control as Enemies of the Faith. After the Protestant Reformation took root, protestants were those who *protested* against the policies of Rome, many of those newly *re-formed* Christian groups labeled any who studied the mysteries outside of *their* new church doctrines as enemies of their ideas of faith, ironically ignoring the famous dictate of Jesus to, "Judge not that you be not judged." Matthew 7:1]

While teaching an evening meditation class in Long Beach, California in the mid-1970s a distinguished gentleman, wearing unusual religious vestments, entered Matt's class and sat down. After class the unusual man told Matt he'd been trying to contact him *telepathically* for some time but that Matt had proved too dense for him to get through to. Matt referred to the man by various nicknames including Father Jack and Father Johannes, although he claimed the spiritual master's true name was unpronounceable to most English-speaking peoples. Father Jack was also said to have held positions in numerous religious orders, including the Coptic Church, the ancient Christian church of Egypt, but told Matt his truest affiliations were with the Great White Lodge and with the adepts and monks of the *Shigatze* Monastery, said to be located near a small village in the Himalayan Mountains of Tibet.

At Father Jack's invitation, Matt traveled to an *ashram* (monastery) in the American Southwest. There he spent nine days with the Master Spiritual Teacher. Towards the end of their time together, Matt says Father Jack performed a profound mystical energy initiation on him that literally knocked him to the ground. That initiation psychically transmitted an extraordinary amount of information into Matt's conscious and subconscious minds. The experience felt like he was having a stroke. Matt said he only had a few more contacts with this extraordinary man, before his teacher departed from North America.

Matt would go on to financial success and live the life of the mystic until a terrible accident broke his back and left him hospitalized and bedridden for a couple of years. During that painful convalescence in the 1980s Matt turned inward and came to a deeper understanding of the extraordinary gift of initiation transmitted to him years earlier by Father Jack. He recognized that he'd been simultaneously initiated into the "49 Sacred Fires," corresponding to the seven major chakras and the seven layers of the etheric body that surround us all. This included dozens of different levels of mystical attunement and enhancements to the various human energy centers. This elaborate series of energy attunements/initiations became the foundation of Omega Shakti.

In naming the work, Matt took the Greek word Omega (the end) as employed in the writings of the French Jesuit and mystic Teilhard de Chardin (1881-1955), who suggested a coming "Point Omega" of evolutionary transformation for the human race. This was a vision for the future in which Humanity would become more truly aligned with the Universal Divine Purpose as we reached the end of our old, outmoded ways of living and allowed for a new spiritual beginning for humanity. Astrologers might call this now current transformation "leaving the Piscean Age and entering the Age of Aquarius." The other component of the Omega Shakti name, *Shakti* is a Sanskrit word. Ancient Sanskrit is the mother language of Hindi. Shakti essentially means the Feminine Aspect of the Universal Divine Energy.

Matt would use these energies to transform his consciousness and heal his broken body. When I met him around 1990, Matt was dragging himself around with one of those metal walkers. Over the next couple of years I watched him transition to a cane and then finally to walking normally without assistance. He used the energies to help heal others and cautiously began taking on students. He would initiate those few students into one energy at a time and then closely study their progress to see how they reacted to and dealt with the powerful energy initiations. He also studied the types of changes the energy initiations sometimes compelled each person through in their personal lives.

Matt's work gained fame in the California energy healing communities. His strong personality, combined with his absolute certainty that what he had to offer was leagues beyond his contemporaries' powers in Reiki, Chi Kung/Qigong, Kriya Yoga, etc. brought him the admiration of many. Others envied him and despised his sense of superiority. Matt, who had been an exceptional teacher of Blavatsky's Theosophy, was thrown out of Theosophical Society meetings. Some decided Matt was just plain crazy. In reality, Matt was a true genius of energy manipulation and manifestation, though sadly his passion for ever-acquiring access to additional levels of expanded consciousness and magickal ability (through connecting to the powers of every mystical energy system and lineage on Earth that he could reach his mind and will into) brought about what can quite fairly be called a very real form of insanity. By the end of his days Matt was truly Mad as a Hatter, while easily remaining one of the most extraordinary occult and mystical geniuses of perhaps several centuries.

That which would ultimately bring Matt Schoener's life to ruin would be a combination of ego, a self-centered greed and lust for mystical power, a total disregard for the normal dictates of common sense, and his inability to accept the fact that he could be fooled by anyone, due to his overconfidence in his otherwise truly exceptional psychic and mystical abilities. Before the end of his life Matt would owe a lot of people a lot of money, a lot of favors, and a lot of apologies, none of which they would ever receive.

I personally never had a truly bad moment with Matt and will remain grateful for the rest of my days for the extraordinary experiences and gifts I received through my association with him and his abilities. Matt and I parted ways because I finally recognized the self-destructive path he was heading down and I tried to stop him for his own sake and for the work we all felt was so important and of such potential value for humanity. When he turned his back on me I knew I had lost an extraordinary friend, but I never turned my back on him. Until the day he died I, and many others, continued to hope his clouded mind would finally clear and that the important work called Omega Shakti would once again be fully available in its service to the world.

I'm happy to report that as of November 2004, Rosanne Amato, Matt's key partner for years in the energy manifestation, grounding, and initiations of Omega Shakti was in the final stages of preparing the new generation of Omega Teachers for service to humanity. Along with the Triple Helix trainings and initiations, Rosanne's own unique contributions to the world of human transformation and energy healing, Rosanne carries the newly purified and re-consecrated energy attunements of Omega Shakti forward for a new era of possibility.

CHAPTER SIXTY-ONE

Alternative Forms Of Energy

As I began moving through the levels of energy and consciousness initiations available in Matt Schoener's extraordinary Omega Shakti System I was keenly aware of the differences in the various energies. This included how they felt, how they moved, and what they seemed to be specifically good for. This ability to feel the different energy levels made me the first choice for public demonstrations whenever I was with Matt or Omega teacher John S. In support of Matt's boasting, the very First Degree of Omega itself seemed more potent and powerful than the Master Degree offered by many Reiki Masters. The energy in Matt and John's personal energy fields, bolstered by numerous levels of initiation, was extraordinarily dynamic and multidimensional.

Although there are many levels of possibility, a lot of people got what they needed from the first or second levels of initiation. Some had real trouble incorporating these extraordinary energies into their lives. Everybody seemed to find their level where the internal changes, initiated by the energy attunements, pushed them to learn and grow, sometimes faster than they were emotionally or mentally ready to. It took some a long time to process the energy of 1st Degree Omega, the primary focus of which is on the physical level of the body itself. Those who got seriously challenged at that first level seemed to be generally pretty closed down to begin with, the spiritual opening to their soul's higher energies bringing major disruption to their normal lives. Many more people were likely to find difficulties upon receiving 2nd Degree Omega, that which focuses more on the emotional life and relationships. Others didn't hit a wall until they moved into 3rd Degree Omega, with its focus on the mind and mental activities. Virtually everybody reaches stages of growth in this life that cause them to have to step back and take time to integrate what they're learning, Omega Shakti and some other systems of initiation like it just tend to push that processing along on a much faster track.

But for some the problems weren't with what level of initiation was which, rather their problems with Omega Shakti was the fact that it came from some guy who claimed its source was in a secret mystical organization that spanned the globe. I remember a conversation I had with a researcher at Harvard University. He'd spent years traveling back and forth between China and the U.S., studying and recording the work of traditional Chinese Qigong Masters and their energy healing work in hospitals. This fellow had years of first-hand knowledge and experience with these energy healers, who are an integral part of the Chinese public health system, and knew the truth and potency of their work with millions of Chinese patients every year. However, back in the early 1990s, the very fact that he was even taking this element of Chinese medicine seriously was tantamount to career suicide. When I offered to demonstrate the ability to relieve pain, acquired through my energy initiations in Omega, he virtually pleaded with me not to, at least until his research was complete and officially received.

Of course, not everybody is so cautious. Once I'd boosted my healing abilities with the first level of Omega, I regularly worked on friends, family, co-workers, and even total strangers I'd meet in coffee shops. At the time I shared a place with a guy named Eric, a professional saxophone player who practiced for hours every day. An unwanted side effect of Eric's dedication was a recurring tendonitis problem. His forearms and wrists would get so tight at times that it was both painful and physically difficult for him to continue playing. We tried the energy healing on Eric's forearms and it worked so well that every six weeks or so he'd come to me for an energy fix for the tendonitis.

During that time I held down three full-time jobs. I was determined to pay off my broadcasting school loans, so I was working five days a week (40 hours) doing office work, six nights a week (42 hours) as a Country Music disc jockey, and 32 hours a week (two double shifts on Saturdays and Sundays) as a security guard in an upscale law firm. Through sheer willpower I managed to survive on 3½ hours of sleep a day. After months of this I sometimes had to supplement my sleep by dozing between songs I played on the radio at my disc jockey job. Because of my ridiculously busy work schedule it was sometimes difficult for Eric and I to find that hour and a half every six weeks.

One day Eric was performing outdoors in Harvard Square and his tendonitis had gotten so severe that he had to repeatedly stop playing in order to massage the pain out of his forearms. A ragged-looking street person walked up to him and held out his hands, as if to offer Eric relief. Eric thought, "What the hell," and let the man give it a try. The disheveled man in tattered clothes confidently placed his hands on

Eric's forearms and in a flash of heat and energy Eric's pain was gone. (Remember, it took me an hour and a half to achieve the same effect.) As Eric looked from his forearms to the ragged stranger in amazement the man stated, "It's all God. It's all God," and went on his way. I never did learn if this street dweller was born with his ability, was trained or initiated into it, or had just opened up to it somewhere along the way. Anyway, "It's all God."

~

One of my favorite energy experiences was with a woman from India known by the spiritual moniker of *Ammachi* who seemed to express love as her principle quality. She's been called a saint since childhood and by all accounts has spent her life being of compassionate service to those in need. Ammachi was hosting a public *satsanga* in Cambridge during my second year with Omega. Like others seen as holy men and woman from her culture Ammachi offered personal blessings to all who wished them in her presence. At the end of her talk she blessed the crowd with a very loving vibration and then allowed a procession of hundreds to come up and receive a more personal energy blessing.

A lot of Eastern and Western mystics, those who have such abilities, bless individuals with a force of energy delivered to the center of the recipient's forehead. Ammachi, however, blesses her guests by holding them to her heart and giving them a warm and lasting hug, much as a mother would to a child. This technique has earned her the nickname "the hugging saint."

I'd come that day, in part, to observe anything that would clue me into how her specific energy sharings worked. It first appeared she was just delivering one hug after another, until I detected a subtle pattern in her movements. Ammachi would embrace most individuals with her arms wrapped around them and her hands on their backs, hold them for several seconds, and then let them go. With a little study, I realized that her hands often landed directly over specific chakras, the energy centers along the spine. She'd generally start with one hand over the heart chakra and then place her hands on different chakras, presumably depending on which energy centers, tied to certain physical and emotional issues in the individual, needed the healing energy the most.

During my entire time at the satsanga I'd been building my energy field so as to increase my sensitivity to whatever was happening. After seeing this woman tirelessly giving of her energy to so many, I decided I would give her some energy back. In short, I would bless the saint. I joined one of the long patient cues of attendees and ever so slowly made my way to the front of the reception line. When it came my turn to hug and be hugged by Ammachi, I placed my hands on her back and sent a wave of healing energy and light into her spinal column. She seemed surprised and pulled back to look me directly in the eyes. On her face was a delighted grin of appreciation. I gave her a warm smile and a wink and her eyes twinkled back. I honored her with the traditional bow of *namasté* and then took my leave. There were scores of spiritually hungry people waiting for a piece of her love and I didn't want them to be delayed any further.

Of all the people I've met over the years believed to be living saints, Ammachi truly seems to be an honest and legitimate incarnation of just that kind of goodness and decency. In the years I've been aware of her and her work I've yet to meet a single person who's got anything bad to say about her. Rather than living a lavish life of privilege, as some gurus have done, Ammachi takes in money from wealthy fans around the globe and funnels it into a remarkable group of charities. Her charitable work includes: homes for the poor, free legal services for those who can't pay, monthly pensions for those who have no one to take care of them, a medical college, a nursing college, job training, speech and hearing services, orphanages for abandoned children, rehabilitation programs for prostitutes, AIDS hospice, disaster relief, and the list of good works goes on. Ammachi's official websites with links to all of her varied charitable efforts can be found on the Internet at http://www.Ammachi.org or http://www.Amritapuri.org.

~

Post Script - A couple of months after I wrote this chapter, the woman known to millions as the "hugging saint" donated 1 billion rupees (that's more than $23 million dollars American) from her worldwide charities to help rebuild homes in southern India in the wake of the terrible December 26, 2004 tsunami that killed so many thousands of people and left so many more homeless in that part of the world.

CHAPTER SIXTY-TWO

Possession Is Not Just 9/10ths Of The Law

The idea of being possessed by some negative force or evil entity has been popularized by lots of scary movies and creepy novels. These fictionalizations generally go way over the top into the absurd and extreme, conjuring up events that just don't happen in physical reality. It is nonetheless my experience that possession, of one sort or another, is a legitimate phenomenon. A type of possession, for example, can be seen in some drug addicts and alcoholics, where getting their next chemical fix becomes all they can think about. There are those who completely lose themselves to their addictions while under the influence, becoming virtually separate people from who they are when they're sober. Many of us have encountered such people on the streets, seemingly deranged and lost in some other dimension, arguing with people or fighting with demons invisible to us. Later, after they've sobered up, they may seem docile and completely unaware of their earlier rage-filled outbursts. More than a few of us have had family members act out in violent and crazed ways, as if someone else had taken the place of the person we knew.

Where do their minds go during such episodes and what elements of consciousness might be taking their place? Modern psychology tells us these cases are a matter of unconscious or subconscious aspects that we only allow out when drugs or alcohol have lifted off enough of our inhibitions so that our "inner demons" can come to the surface. Although I acknowledge this psychological model, in some cases there is *another dimension* that I and others have observed up close that is indeed something quite other than just unconscious feelings acting up.

I know a very good woman, who was dedicated to her family, who watched her kind and beloved husband fall deeper and deeper into alcoholism over a period of years due to his emotional difficulty in handling some very ugly and painful things he'd seen and experienced in his life. Years of excessive drinking led to periods of blackouts, where he remembered nothing of his words or actions the next day. Finally came the emergence of a cruel and abusive personality, one with its own sense of self, quite separate from her husband. This *other* identity even had its own name. Increasingly, when her husband was drunk, this fully-formed other personality would take over. At first he/it was just disrespectful and verbally abusive. This escalated to threats and then moved to physical violence against her. In the morning the husband, who everybody knew was absolutely in love with his wife, wouldn't remember any of it. His loving wife tried again and again to get him to stop drinking and even packed up and left him on more than one occasion, returning each time because of the deep love they both shared when he was sober.

When the evil personality, an apparently disincarnate entity, became a regular player the loving wife even hid a tape recorder and secretly recorded the emergence of the alternate personality with his strange voice, disdainful attitudes, and violent ways. She dialoged with this entity that increasingly came through her husband late at night. The apparent entity told her he had claimed her husband's body. "He's mine!" she was told by the strange, hateful voice. "And if you don't leave us alone I'm going to kill you, you bitch!" When the recordings were played back for the husband the next day he was in shocked disbelief, insisting she must have hired somebody to do the awful voice, which he was convinced couldn't possibly be his. Of course, in a way, it wasn't his. This man's extreme drinking and disassociation from his body had, over time, opened a dark psychic doorway, a portal opened by self-destructive elements within himself, that allowed this other consciousness in.

One night, this loving wife barely escaped with her life after the other tried to strangle her to death. She fought off her attacker, though the black and blue bruises around her neck lasted for weeks. Wisely, she decided she not to wait around for a final encounter. But she still gave her husband of many years a choice. "It's me or the bottle," she told him. Her husband's sad reply was, "I can't stop drinking."

~

I had an older friend years ago that had another kind of demon in her head. She was close to seventy, yet still carried the trauma and guilt from a car accident she'd been in forty years earlier. Back then she'd been behind the wheel during an accident that resulted in her young daughter losing an eye. The daughter blamed her mother for the accident and the mother felt that they were never really close again. Decades went by and even though the daughter had forgiven her, the mother remained convinced that the distance between them was because of the accident. The older she got the more she feared and grieved that she would die without ever truly regaining her daughter's love. That psychic burden, her own inner demon, one day sought a final violent release and resolution.

As I saw it, a part of her thought that if she were punished, in the same way her daughter had been harmed, perhaps she would finally receive true forgiveness. I watched that torment grow inside her until one day I got the word that my elderly friend had been in a terrible car accident. She would recover, but there had been one tragic irreversible result. My friend had lost an eye. Was this a totally unrelated coincidence? No. This was a totally *related* coincident, what the psychologist Carl Jung would have termed a meaningful coincidence; a synchronistic event brought about by an aspect of my friend's unconscious self.

Curiously, just as there are many who seem unable to rid themselves of their personal demons, there are also those who intentionally let them in. In some magickal societies members go through training and ritual in order to prepare themselves to become vessels for entities from the spirit worlds. This is generally called "channeling" when used in a more positive way. Some traditional peoples perform ceremonies inviting totem animals into their bodies in preparation for battle or for other feats requiring great strength and power. Their hope is that the animal's spirit will lend its unique qualities and abilities to their own.

A perhaps more disturbing variation on this type of practice, certainly for many living in the "civilized" West, are the tribal practices of some African peoples who traditionally opened themselves up to either the spirits of their dead ancestors or to other spirits. These individuals, in special ceremonies, allow themselves to be swept away into a trance-like state, sometimes with the assistance of drugs and/or dehydration, and invite the "spirits" or "gods" of their cultures to enter their bodies and use them to interact more directly with this physical world. Some of these peoples ritualistically mutilate their bodies, performing feats with fire, sharp metal objects, and broken glass that would be far too damaging or painful for their bodies to endure in their normal state of waking consciousness.

One day I had an encounter with a guy in my gym that demonstrated a slightly different approach to spirit possession. I regularly worked out at the Gold's Gym near Fenway Park in Boston and there was this muscular, middle-aged German guy who always gave me this knowing look, like he had deep secrets to share and could see that I did too. I could tell this guy was used to psychically drawing people to him, using his formidable energy field to engage them and then pull them in. His energy field seduction thing was clearly a power play for dominance, a tactic I wasn't interested in responding to. After trying to get me to engage him a few times he finally walked up to me one day and took me on directly. "I can see your energy field, you know," he said, scanning me for how I might respond. "I know," I said back, "and I can see yours." He seemed momentarily surprised. "But you don't choose to walk in the light of service to others," I continued.

"There are many ways of using power," he returned, "let me show you." He looked me dead in the eyes, smiled a confident smile, and then his eyes changed so that *another intelligence* seemed to be looking back at me through this middle-aged businessman's eyes. "We have a special relationship, he and I," said the strange new voice of an apparent spirit entity, speaking through the man standing before me. "We work together, bridging the worlds so that I can help him achieve his goals and acquire anything he desires."

"And what do you get out of this deal?" I asked the presence speaking to me. I could now see him as a hazy form hovering over the German's left shoulder. He was clearly human, or that is he had been human the last time he had a body of his own. "I ask nothing, I am only here to assist," said the dark spirit entity.

"Bullshit," I fired back. "You lived a lousy life and got caught in the astral dimensions between this world and the next. You're just holding on because you're afraid of what might be waiting for you in the next level." I saw his arrogant expression drop away from the German's face. The German fellow himself seemed to lose confidence. The entity seemed momentarily wounded. I decided to see if I could make a further point. "You're using this silly man who thinks he's some kind of powerful magician because he's managed to bring a lowlife like you through! Why don't you try using your abilities for something good instead of wasting my time trying to seduce me into thinking you're scary and powerful?"

"You think your healing and helping others matters?" the evil former

211

human challenged me, "don't you understand how much real power could be yours? Look at the way others look at this man, with fear and respect! Look at his fine clothes and beautiful car! Don't you see how much you could gain by joining with us and forging your own destiny in the ways of power and magick? Think of how much we could do together!" Look, I know this sounds like bad movie dialogue, but this was this guy's actual pitch to me.

It was clear there would be no helping this disincarnate spirit on to the next level with prayers and angels. He was enjoying himself too much and the German fellow was getting off on the fear and awe most people responded to him with. I decided the best course of action was to let the German know how sad his little game really was, hoping that it might sow seeds of doubt in the value of his arrangement. "You're so pitiful it's embarrassing!" I struck again. "You go around acting all scary and sucking weak and vulnerable people into your little game in order to make yourself feel important! But, I know what you really are! You're sad and lonely and still using your consciousness to bully and to try to take power from others! If you were really powerful you wouldn't need to be stealing power from others!" The German and his apparent spirit possession seemed stunned. But I wasn't finished. "You're ridiculous if you think I'd ever have anything to do with you and your little game! Any moron can terrorize others! That's not real power! Try doing something worthwhile! It takes a superior person to change the world for the better!"

The muscular German and his spirit possession took a threatening move towards me and gave me their best menacing stare. "Oh, you've got to be kidding!" I laughed at them. "You think this guy is going to get away with attacking me right here in the gym? And you! You think I'm scared of you? You don't even have a body anymore, for god's sake! What the hell can you do to me?" The possessed fellow had lost and he knew it. Tears welled up on the face of the German muscleman. "You don't understand," he protested, "we're powerful! We really are! Together we can do great things!"

"Oh, yeah! You're sooo powerful!" I intentionally laughed at the duo. "Powerful to do what? Walk around scaring people weaker than you?" "You don't understand!" the trembling German screamed at me in a now shrill voice. All around the gym, people started looking at the guy like there was something seriously wrong with him. "You just don't understand! You don't know what you're talking about!" The German's face finally burst fully into tears. "You just don't understand!" the muscleman cried again as he ran out of the gym. Several guys just shook their heads and laughed and went back to their workouts. Outside the gym, he quickly jumped into his new Mercedes, the one he always parked out front for show, and sped away.

As I watched him drive away, I sincerely hoped I would get a chance to help that disincarnate spirit into the Divine Light. It was also my desire to encourage this capable mystic into working in the light and doing some good with the abilities he'd acquired. But, I never saw him again. The man who'd been such a fixture at that Gold's Gym location had been humiliated by his unsuccessful occult power play. Maybe he'd gone off to lick his wounds and then set his sights on weaker and more easily impressed individuals than myself. But in my heart, I hoped that one day the lesson that I sought to teach him would sink in and that he would finally reach out for the Light.

~

It's better when you don't have to hide in the shadows.

CHAPTER SIXTY-THREE

Transmitting Over The Psychic Airwaves

I remember driving with a co-worker when I was still at Biogen and the conversation turned to *telepathy*, thoughts traveling from one mind to another, *precognition*, knowledge of future events, *clairaudience*, hearing extrasensory data, music, voices, etc. that others can't hear, *clairvoyance*, extrasensory data perceived visually, as in *visions*, and other types of psychic experiences. These kinds of conversations just happen around me, what can I say? The guy I was working with was an engineer from the physical plant of the research institute. He was a solid guy, as grounded in normal reality as any, and couldn't make any sense of the idea of people being able to have such experiences. "I just don't see how it's physically possible?" he said, quite reasonably. "The 'laws of physics' don't just stop applying because your imagination wants them to."

"Well," I said, also quite reasonably, "just because we don't yet know the physical mechanism, the cause behind a given effect, is not proof that the event itself did not or could not occur. People raised in remote seclusion from the modern world, for example, might find television and radio impossible to grasp, within the known laws of physical reality that govern their daily lives, but just because they can't image how TV and radio could be possible doesn't stop it from being so." Really, think about it. The demonstration of satellite television might be perceived by such people as some kind of trick of the mind, mass hypnosis, a dream, sleight of hand, or even a phenomenon falling into the realms of divine miracles, evil magic, or madness. The fact that these people might have such extreme reactions to something that we take for granted everyday does not mean that they are too simple-minded, backward, or primitive to understand it. It just means that the mechanisms behind television and radio transmissions are currently not a part of their intellectual and scientific paradigm.

The mechanisms behind psychic phenomena such as mental telepathy, telekinesis, distance healing, etc., fall into the same category. These things do occur, but precisely how the magic is performed is simply not yet a part of our shared common knowledge. As far as I can tell, each of us is a mobile sending and receiving station. Our scientists merely need to find a way to detect these subtle mental and emotional transmissions. We will figure it out, of that I am certain. But we're definitely not going to uncover the physical mechanisms behind psychic phenomena like telepathy and precognition until we stop pretending that these things don't exist in the first place.

For centuries most people were convinced that human flight was a physical impossibility. A human body wearing a pair of wings, or a person sitting in a metal or wooden box with wings attached, couldn't possibly float on the air. Common observation of the laws of physics proved that anything heavier than air fell to earth, generally with a terrible thud. Visionaries like Leonardo DaVinci (whose wing designs were studied centuries after his death by NASA and which eventually helped create the hang glider) and later the Wright Brothers were considered either foolish dreamers or totally insane until the fact of flight was finally proven for all to see. The problem with the psychic transmission of information as it stands today is that the sending and receiving happens inside ourselves, where others cannot join us in seeing and hearing for themselves. Nonetheless, millions of people around the globe every day are experiencing the reality of such invisible information transference. When we finally stop dismissing psychic phenomena as impossible, and everyone associated with it as either frauds or crazies, and apply the same kind of scientific investigation into the causes behind such things we will discover them.

After my stint working three full-time jobs I decided to take it easy for a while and do something less strenuous, so I got a job as a truck driver and furniture mover. After years of sitting at desks, I needed the exercise. Working 40 to 60 hours a week carrying pianos, refrigerators, and sofa beds was still a lot easier than working 114 hours a week at three jobs, plus the migraines went away. Continuing to work with the various Omega energies, I found my psychic and intuitive senses were sharpening and the ability to demonstrate these various energies and their effects on others also created some interesting experiences.

My buddy Joby and I worked together at Stone Pony Movers. The guy who started the company was a big fan of singer Linda Rondstat and named it after her backup band. One day Joby asked me if I could demonstrate these energies on him. I'd recently been attuned to the first level of Agni Dhatu Samadhi Yoga, one of the Omega attunements, which allows me to create a sense of expansion, peace, and openness for those who are sensitive enough to feel such things. Millions of people are that sensitive and millions aren't, just like many people can hear when a musical instrument is slightly out of tune, while millions more aren't sensitive enough in their hearing to tell the difference. I chose to use the Agni Dhatu energy because I could demonstrate it without having to make physical contact with Joby in any way. We were, after all, driving down busy city streets in a large commercial moving truck, with Joby behind the wheel at the time. After about forty seconds of my sending him the Agni Dhatu energy, Joby was definitely feeling it. "Whoa!" he said with a growing smile on his face, "that's really intense! And you said you can do that to yourself, anytime you want?" "Yup," I responded. "Well," he shrugged his shoulders, "that explains why you don't bother to do drugs."

One of the more interesting side effects of my intentionally building up my psychic energy field, usually for hours every day, also manifested on my furniture moving jobs. I worked many hours every week and then spent my personal time reading, meditating, and doing energy work. After a while on the job, I discovered that almost every time I was about to say something, and then for one reason or another edited myself and decided to keep my mouth shut, somebody else around me would say exactly what I was going to say, word for word, within one to three seconds. Often what came out was completely unrelated to any topic of conversation under way. The mouthing of the exact words I had thought to say, but then didn't, was voiced by my co-workers, whether or not we had ever worked together before that day, or by the people whose stuff we were moving, or even by strangers walking past us on the sidewalk. I quickly realized that I was psychically broadcasting my unspoken thoughts into my immediate environment. Those silent thoughts were apparently being picked up by those around me and then re-broadcast verbally by those other people. This is just like a radio picks up invisible radio waves and then re-broadcasts what it has received through its speakers. I'd been on the receiving end of this experience many times, so I recognized how the process was working.

My unconsciously transmitted thoughts would appear in their minds, just like any other thoughts or ideas that might appear in their minds, though they were unaware that the thoughts and words in their heads did not originate there. This kind of thing was made popular in the fictional *Star Wars* movies as "Jedi mind tricks" in which the Jedi masters would intentionally impress thoughts into the minds of others, who then accepted them as their own because the thoughts had appeared inside their own heads. Apparently, truth can be as strange as fiction. I believe it was the fact that I was doing such intense daily psychic energy building exercises that caused my thoughts to have a much greater strength and psychic impact than they normally would have had. When I'd form the strong intent to say something in my mind and then at the last second not speak, those words would psychically travel out into my environment anyway and be unconsciously telepathically picked up by those closest to the signal strength.

Another type of psychic energy transmission I experienced in those same years was more the kind of thing you see depicted in scary movies. I'd been hosting a weekly support group for those who'd been undergoing the Omega Shakti initiations, giving people a safe place to practice their new healing and energy abilities and a chance to learn through interaction with like-minded others. Matt had recently been in town, working an expo in Boston, and he'd asked me for a particular favor. There was this very psychologically disturbed forty-year-old woman who had practically begged him to allow her to take 1st Degree Omega. Matt told me he could see that this woman had serious damage to her psychic energy field, which we both later learned was due to some thirty-to-forty electroshock treatments she'd undergone over a period of years as an outpatient in a state psychiatric hospital. Another contributing factor to the extreme amount of damage to her energy field was that she'd undergone something like six abortions in her lifetime. "If she's too much for you, I'll understand," Matt said. "I'm just concerned that she's such a lost soul that giving her 1st Degree Omega and then leaving her alone might do her more harm than good."

Of course I agreed to look after her. I met with her and helped her understand how she could begin to use the healing aspects of Omega to help mend the lifetime of trauma she'd undergone. After meeting with her several times, I decided I'd give her a chance to join our weekly energy-healing group. She definitely needed a lot more help than one person could give her. I figured I could get all the members of the group to work on her at once and maybe, just maybe, we could help reverse some of the overwhelming psychic damage to this lost soul. Well, as it turned out, this "lost soul" had spent decades working and manipulating the state welfare system of Massachusetts and its employees. Before long, she was using her highly developed emotional manipulation skills on me and the rest of my group to take anything and everything she could for herself, psychically attaching herself, like a leech, to everyone she could. Again and again I had to intervene and stop this self-centered psychic vampire from making every meeting just another night of manipulating people into catering to her. Finally, after many weeks and extraordinary patience, I had to put my foot down and inform her that she was no longer welcome. Almost everyone had stopped coming to the group because of her.

I continued to give this woman as much of my time and support as I could, but it was never enough. She also continued to show up at my place for the support group meetings, though I refused to let her in. She took to calling several times a day for me to council her with her problems, for free of course, and constantly begged for additional energy sessions. This went on for a few weeks until I finally told her I would not be available to her for at least two days. I had a tremendous number of things I had to get done and I just couldn't spend another day on the phone or in person giving to her.

Being the selfish taker that she was, she didn't honor my decision. As a result, I finally refused to answer the door or pick up the phone when she tried to make contact. On the second day of my moratorium on giving my energy to her, I came back from the corner store and found several messages on my answering machine. I'd only been gone twenty minutes. All the messages were her shrill voice screaming demands that I pick up the phone now, because she needed my help again! I did pick up the phone the next time she called and told her I'd had enough and that I would not respond to her calls ever again. After I hung up, she immediately called back and left a live message on my machine demanding that I talk to her. I refused to pick up. She called again and again, every sixty seconds or so, and I refused to answer. Each time she called back I could both hear and feel the rage building in her voice. Finally, I turned the volume off the answering machine so as not to listen to her screaming demands any further. I'd kept the machine in monitoring mode, up to that point, because I was expecting other calls.

As her insane anger continued to build, I could psychically see this extraordinary field of dark, violent emotion and rage assaulting my apartment from the direction of her home miles away. I used my own will to keep her energy out of the interior itself. I put some music on my cassette tape player to help tune out the hateful energy of this disturbed caller. The music tape I put on was my very favorite one. The phone didn't ring for several minutes, but all during that time I saw and felt her psychic energy field of anger and rage growing stronger and even more intense. Then the phone rang one final time with a *force* that couldn't be explained by any normal means. At the exact moment of that final ring, I felt this violent wall of rage break through into my apartment and saw the energy hit my stereo. The tape player jammed, spewing magnetic audiotape out into my living room, shredding and destroying my very favorite piece of music. After that final burst of rage, all went quiet and I didn't hear from her again.

Helping a fellow spiritual traveler in need is one thing, but allowing yourself to be used and abused in a dysfunctional relationship, of whatever kind, is not healthy or wise. Somebody who demands, uses, manipulates, or whines to get your energy is not your karmic responsibility or your religious duty just because they've landed in your lap. This includes relatives and people who call themselves your friends, but a friendship that only goes one way – from you to them. Anybody who tells you that you owe them your time and energy for nothing because you're supposed to be a "spiritual person" is just hustling you to get what they want for themselves. You need to consider praying for them and yourself so that the ties that bind you to them and them to you are severed and you are released from the grip of their selfish will. You need to allow yourself to retain the energy necessary to complete those things that *you need* to do for you and still have energy left over to help those who do truly touch your heart and spirit in a healthy and appropriate way.

Yes, when it comes down to it we are all responsible for looking after our own well being. After a few years of looking after things for Matt and Omega in New England, all on a volunteer basis, my personal finances were in a shambles. I looked over my bills one morning and saw that I was $400 shy of what I needed to pay my bills that month and the bills were due. "Okay God," I finally said aloud. "If you really want me to continue this spiritual work of service through Omega, I need $400 cash in my hand by the end of the day, no strings attached. Otherwise, I'll have to drop all this service work and refocus on my financial situation. I've reached the end of my rope and that is that." After that I went on with my day, which included my leaving the neighborhood for some errands in another part of town. On the way back to my apartment my thoughts were still fixed on my need to remedy my immediate financial problem without delay. As I was about to pass by the local convenience store I saw a man materialize on the sidewalk in front of me. It was my teacher, the spiritual Master who visited me throughout much of my childhood. I could see right through him, but it was clearly the same teacher I'd seen so often when I was a boy. I felt strongly that he wanted me to go inside the convenience store. I didn't feel like spending any extra money in my current financial condition so I decided to keep walking and get back home.

As I was about to walk through the ghostly figure of my teacher he became more clearly visible and blocked my way. "You asked for $400, now go in the store and get your money," came the message from his mind to mine. I realized that I was to buy a lottery ticket and win the $400 I needed. My rational mind told me this wasn't a very likely prospect, but the will of the Master was strong and insistent. "Okay," I thought back. "What the heck." I turned into the door of the convenience store. I felt a little odd about my task. I wasn't one of these people who spent money on lottery tickets. I decided to pick up a newspaper to look for extra work to make the money I needed and picked up a half gallon of milk at the same time.

I went to the counter and told the clerk I wanted to buy a lottery ticket. "What kind do you want?" he asked. "I don't know, what kind do you have?" He showed a bunch of rows of different colored tickets and I chose two $2 tickets from the available options. I paid the $4 for the two tickets, bought my paper and my milk and headed home. When I got back to my apartment I took out a coin and scratched off the silver patches on the tickets to see if I'd won anything. On the first ticket I won $4. "Well, at least I got my money back," I thought to myself. Then I scratched off the silver on the other ticket. The ticket told me I'd just won $400 exactly, which was exactly what I'd asked spirit for, right down to the penny. I walked back to the store and asked the clerk how to cash in the ticket. He told me that any prize under $500 could be cashed right there at the store. I cashed in my $4 ticket and my $400 ticket, got my cash and went back home, once again fully committed to doing the healing work of service that spirit was asking of me. And yes, if I could do it again any time I wanted to, I would. But unless I get that little psychic energy buzz that tells me it's the right thing to do I know I'd just be wasting my money like so many other folks every week.

CHAPTER SIXTY-FOUR

Otherworldly Adventures

There are apparently many variations on where our spirit bodies can travel to without our physical selves. The possibilities are probably infinite. Depending on what kind of spirit movement we're talking about we might call such adventures astral travel, soul travel, out-of-body experiences, dimensional shifts, or the transmigration of souls (i.e. reincarnation). Any way you cut it, we definitely get around.

I've been seen by others while out-of-body before and have had others show up in their astral bodies on my turf. One night, during the time I was living in South Boston, I woke up and felt somebody's hands inside my mouth! I monitored this strange occurrence for a moment and realized that some invisible dentist was working on my teeth and gums. I'd been having dental and gum problems that week, so I was pleased that somebody at some level of reality was choosing to help me out. But who could it be? I could see the astral hands belonged to a white man so I thought perhaps it might be Reverend Willard Fuller, the extraordinary dental healer, but it didn't *feel* like him. I decided to follow the astral hands back to their owner to find out who was doing me this favor. In a couple of seconds, I followed the connection across the United States and found myself in Southern California. There sitting in a room in the middle of the night was Matt Schoener, the founder of the Omega Shakti System. As it was, Matt had physically worked on my gums a few months earlier when I was having gum problems during an Omega conference in Pasadena, California. What he'd done had relieved the discomfort and I hadn't had any further difficulties until that week. I called Matt the next day to thank him for his out-of-body assistance. He graciously told me I was entirely welcome and recommended that I see a real dentist sometime soon.

I've got a friend who used to use her psychic abilities to help the police find missing children. They'd also call her when a crime seemed to have evidence of some kind of occult involvement. After she'd been successful on a few different cases she was asked if she would help on a different type of case, to track a serial killer. This particular serial killer left an upside-down pentagram with the bodies of his victims. The right-side-up pentagram, the five-five-pointed star inside a circle, is an old symbol that represents Man. The five points are for the head, hands, and feet. Although not originally a symbol of evil, the upside-down version of the pentagram with the head pointed "away from heaven" has become associated with evil and has become popular with sadists, devil worshipers, and other assorted creepy people.

My friend, married with children, was very apprehensive about taking on such a case. She finally relented, though her one condition was that her involvement remained a secret. One night on TV she heard her name mentioned as "the psychic involved" in trying to find the serial killer. That night she, her husband, and their daughters awakened from the same nightmare, with the girls screaming in terror. It seems the serial killer had seen the news and had decided to murder her. She could feel the evil presence of the killer around her home. Fearing for her family's safety, she very publicly withdrew from the case.

Of course not everybody that picks up information psychically, by whatever method, is going to be correct every time. People going out-of-body can misread a situation and draw the wrong conclusions, just like any other observer or analyst using any other method. One time, while with an Omega group on the island of Maui, I'd been hit on by a woman I'd met swimming. I'd been tempted to accept her offer to spend the night at her place on a different part of the island, but had decided not to. Instead, I went to bed extra early, unplugged the phone, and crashed out for the night to catch up on some much needed sleep.

The next morning at breakfast I was called over to join Matt and John S. of Omega Shakti at their table. Matt informed me that he'd been training John to psychically go out-of-body and that John had acquired information concerning my apparent absence the night before. When I could not be located by anyone the previous night, John had used his new psychic training to successfully pick up on my original intent to quietly borrow one of Omega's rented mini-vans, drive to a distant part of Maui, and spend the night with the woman I'd met while swimming.

John was, understandably, very proud of his new psychic prowess. However, John was somewhat crestfallen when I announced that, although he'd correctly picked up on my earlier intent, he'd made the classic mistake of a beginner by taking what he'd psychically acquired at face value and then had confidently drawn the wrong conclusion about what had happened next. John had combined his awareness of the woman I had met with the fact that no one could find me, added to it the fact that I hadn't answered my hotel room phone and wrongly concluded that he'd discovered the truth behind the mystery. We all had a good chuckle and Matt's psychic training of John continued.

During the years I was working with the Omega organization I'd often found myself awake at 4AM and had felt a distinctive force of energy moving through me, an energy that seemed to be many other places at the same time. One day I overheard Matt mention that he was up at 4AM that morning and had done his regular daily long-distance energy blessing, which he'd sent out to all those working with the Omega Shakti energies around the world. I realized that the regular 4AM energy rush I'd been feeling for months was from him. For some years, even after I'd parted ways with Matt, I would feel that same energy rush in the middle of the night and recognize that, at some level of reality, I was still being included in the blessings of Omega.

Just as John S. had psychically seen certain things about my personal life in Maui and drawn the wrong conclusion as to how things had played out, sometimes what we psychically see plays itself out even when we go out of our way to make sure it doesn't happen. Some might call this an encounter with Fate. Some things, it seems, are just going to play themselves out for their own reasons and we sometimes find ourselves playing a part in those karmic dramas, a part that some aspect of our greater self has presumably agreed to play.

One such incident happened to me while I was still working as a truck driver and furniture mover in the Boston area. My partner and I were on our way to a small job a few towns northwest of Boston. As I was driving up the main road towards our destination I had a sudden vision of a full-grown German Shepherd dog rolling under the giant wheels of our commercial truck. I immediately searched the area for any animals that might be too close to the roadway but saw none in danger.

I tried to clear my mind of the image but it persisted. I prayed for it to go away, but it did not. I decided that I would willfully change the energy of what I was seeing so that I could prevent it from coming to pass. I pulled the truck over by the side of the road and, after making an excuse to my moving partner that I was feeling a bit tired, I focused my mind on changing the energy of the vision. I did everything I knew how to do but was not convinced that I had affected any change in the situation. I hadn't felt the energy shift and I knew that without that feeling of a shift I couldn't be sure anything had happened.

To increase my chances of altering the energy of the undesirable vision, I decided to further change the timetable we were on. I told my partner I needed to eat something so I would feel better and be able to go on with the day. We pulled into a local coffee shop and hung out there for at least a half hour, having coffee and pastries. When I felt I couldn't stall our waiting customer any further we got back in the truck and continued on towards our destination. But first I checked a road map and found an alternative, albeit rather roundabout, route to our customer's home in order to further alter the course we'd been on.

About twenty minutes later we reached the center of town of our customer's residence. Because we'd taken such a circuitous route over back roads we didn't normally travel on I was a little lost. I had been watching the roadways with extreme focus every second since I'd had the vision of the German Shepherd dog going under our wheels. I was just as cautious when pulling to the side of the road to check the map. I compared a few road signs against the map and figured out how to get to our customer. I carefully looked around to make certain there were no animals in danger and then slowly pulled away from the curb. As I did so the rear tires on the right side of the truck went up and down as if I'd just driven over the curb. I immediately stopped the truck and checked my side mirror. The truck wasn't anywhere near the curb.

Suspecting the worst, I got out of the truck and found a dying German Shepherd dog lying just behind the rear right tires. I'd driven over him. As I bent down to the now dead animal a young, well-dressed couple rushed over to the vehicle. It was their dog. Much to my surprise, the woman told me right away that it wasn't my fault. She and her husband had argued repeatedly about the safety of their dog, with the husband insisting the dog would be fine in their fenced in yard and didn't need to be kept indoors. The dog, she told me, had gotten out of their yard and followed them on their morning walk and then had quickly hidden himself underneath my parked truck so that he wouldn't be seen by the couple and returned to his home. There was no way I could have known he was there, she assured me. What was their personal drama about and why had my spirit agreed to be a participant in it? I really don't know. Some things are just what they are and all the questioning and avoidance in the world simply won't change a thing.

CHAPTER SIXTY-FIVE

The Practice Of Distance Healing

On a visit to California, I underwent another energy initiation, this one performed by John S. I don't recall which Omega initiation it was, but I do recall a fascinating side effect. For about a minute or so, I was able to see in every direction simultaneously. I briefly experienced what has been called 360° sight. During that initiation my psychic faculties expanded, allowing me to see in front of me, behind me, on either side of me, below me, above me, and right through the walls, ceiling, roof, floor, and the very earth itself. This was totally cool.

Now, as much fun as this was one of the more practical experiences available via the Omega and Reiki attunements is the ability to send energy to others and do healing work at a distance. That distance can be across a room or across the globe. How is this possible? Well, one theoretical explanation says that the separation of one place from another, as well as the separation of one moment in time from another, is ultimately an illusion of the three-dimensional world of time and space. When one is freed from the constraints of the physical our minds, thoughts, intentions, and emotions can and do make contact to wherever and whenever we send them. More often than not, this is done unconsciously and without awareness of what we're doing, as most senders are unfamiliar with the mystical and mechanical workings that underlie our normal reality. Those who send and receive energy, thoughts, feelings, and intentions successfully and consciously may do so by praying, forcefully willing something to be, or by performing some kind of ritual of intention.

Most people would be surprised to learn just how many highly successful people know that they are affecting the world by their thoughts and by the activation of their will. This knowing often starts out earlier in life with an instinctive understanding of how the inner Universe works, followed in time by the more conscious recognition of the mechanics of intention through the consistent evidences offered by such cause and effect relationships. The true metaphysical magician is one who understands this truth and deliberately makes consistent and successful use of that mystical knowledge. Some very wise souls have suggested that although the inner workings of life are a secret they are an open secret, available right there before each of us to be observed and discovered by any who steadfastly seek to know the truth.

The technique of distance healing operates pretty much the same way as prayer operates. We intend for someone to be aided by our hopes, prayers, and best wishes and that intention sends the energy to the intended recipient. Whether or not that intended recipient makes use of the energy in the way we had hoped is up to them and subject to much more mysterious forces than most of us have any clue about. What can make organized energy systems such as Omega Shakti, Reiki, and the Triple Helix especially effective is the energy empowerments offered by the initiations and trainings. The initiations/attunements of such systems open a doorway to the specific energies of that initiation and make them more readily available for intentional use. Just as I trained as a healer at the Center of the Light and perform Angelic Life Force attunements, I've also learned various therapeutic healing techniques through Omega Shakti The most astonishing energy technique, for many, is known as Agni Dhatu Therapy. It combines the energy from one of the Agni Dhatu Samadhi Yoga initiations with an intensified mental focus attunement, which gives the receiver the extraordinary healing experience of cosmic awareness. (Agni means *comic fire*.)

I've got an old friend that I send distance healing energy to from time to time. Generally we talk when he's going through some personal crisis. He's a Baptist, so I don't trouble him with all this metaphysical stuff. Instead when I pray for him after our talks, as I promise him I'll do, I also send energy to him to help him gain a sense of perspective and clarity on his personal challenges. He's told me more than once that after he talks to me he somehow becomes very clear and calm and things just seem to make a whole lot more sense. I suppose he'll wind up reading this book and recognize himself in these paragraphs. I love him like a brother, so I imagine it'll be cool, though I've always tried to honor his religious beliefs so I always pray that only the highest and best for him comes of any distance healing energy I send his way.

One of the first people I tried my Omega Shakti distance healing work on was a woman friend of mine. I didn't want her to know when I sent the energy, so she wouldn't just imagine it was working. Instead, I chose a random time. When we talked next, two or three days later, she was all excited to tell me about the extraordinary changes that were suddenly happening in her life. She was electrified as she shared with me the amazing new insights she'd recently gained. "Jade," I said, "This is all pretty recent for you, isn't it?"

"Oh, yes! It's very recent!" she said, completely animated. "Sometime in the last week or so?" I queried. "Oh, yes! Even more recent than that!" she said, still excited to tell me more.

"Sometime in the past three days or so, maybe?" I continued. "Yes! You're right!" she said, with surprise. "Yeah. In the past three days."

"Could all of this new insight and understanding have started on Sunday?" I asked. "Yes!" she said. "It was on Sunday!"

"Sunday afternoon, perhaps?" I kept hinting.

"Yeah. It was Sunday afternoon," she said in amazement.

"Around 1:30 to 1:45 in the afternoon, would you say?" I finished.

"How did you know that?" came the fascinated reply. I explained about the distance healing experiment, and completely blew her away.

~

Another guy who'd signed up for Omega called me on the phone one day. He'd heard of my Agni Dhatu initiation and wanted to come by my place for a demonstration of the energy. "Let's try an experiment," I said to Brian. "Why don't you just sit quietly and meditate and I'll send you the energy from here." After I'd done the demonstration, Brian, who'd been doing Transcendental Meditation for years, told me that the distance healing energy session was the most amazing experience of his life. He signed up for more Omega attunements soon after that.

An even more astonishing demonstration of healing energy transferred at a distance is the ability of a handful of individuals to open up to certain vibrations by force of will and then bring those vibrations into their own energy fields, so that they can access the energies whenever they want. This is how Matt Schoener continued to grow Omega Shakti into ever increasing types of energy initiations and how Rosanne Amato continued her own energy healing work after she and

Matt went their separate ways. Rosanne is, in fact, one of a few individuals I know of that apparently managed to connect back to the original Reiki energy, discovered by the Japanese Mikao Usui over a century ago, and bring a pure and untarnished version of the Reiki vibration back with her. She's taken these energies and made them available as attunements through her Temple Reiki system.

Another who apparently managed to perform this feat of connecting back to the original pure Reiki energy is my friend Kris who works as a professional psychic in, of all places, Salem, Massachusetts. (A beautiful little historic seaport and tourist village, these days.) The way it happened, according to Kris, is that this very dynamic, though kindly older Japanese man came to her in spirit and initiated her in her home. She didn't know much about Reiki at the time and it wasn't until later on that she learned the man in her vision had apparently been the founder of Japanese Reiki. Kris demonstrated her new energy for me and I definitely recognized it as the Reiki vibration.

~

My final story for this chapter on distance energy transmissions came from when I was attending a one-woman show in a theatre in Boston. The performer was a friend of my actress/dancer friend Margaux, herself an Omega energy practitioner, and I'd gone on her suggestion. I was surreptitiously working with the Agni Dhatu energy on myself throughout the entire ninety-minute performance. As the evening progressed, I started to sense that the entire audience around me was beginning to be affected by the beautiful and expansive vibration of this energy. Towards the end of the show, the woman performer addressed the crowd, telling them that it had been the most amazing and special night. "There's an extraordinary spiritual energy that's here with us tonight," she told us. "I feel it coming from the audience and I just wanted to thank you all for this beautiful blessing." A number of her friends and supporters in the audience piped up in agreement that they had felt the unique energy that night, too. It was something they hadn't felt before during any of her other performances. Thinking she might want to know what had gone on, and by way of explanation, I sent the actress a note later that week, identifying myself as a friend of our mutual friend Margaux and clarified what had happened and where that extraordinary energy had come from. However, I wasn't surprised when I didn't receive a response from my note.

CHAPTER SIXTY-SIX

The Theosophical Society

The Theosophical Society was established in New York City in the fall of 1875. Its principle founders are generally recognized as Helena Pretrovna Blavatsky and Colonel Henry Steel Olcott. Blavatsky was a mystic and a world traveler from a Russian noble family and Olcott was a respected military man whose service included sitting on the three-man panel that investigated the assassination of U.S. President Abraham Lincoln. Theosophy means Divine Wisdom and the society was established to study and share the teachings of the world's religious and mystical beliefs. Its charter declares its belief in the equality of all, rich or poor, male or female, regardless of race, creed, skin color, or national origin. These principles of equality might seem self-evident today, but they were socially radical ideas for the times.

Madame Blavatsky, who also known to her close associates by her personal initials of HPB, was one of the most pivotal and colorful mystical figures of the 1800s. Blavatsky is credited with having been influential in introducing the West to the religious traditions, beliefs, and practices of the East. Reportedly, Madame Blavatsky's fans, during her lifetime and after, included a number of the world's notable thinkers and innovators, among them: Russian icon painter and occult philosopher Nicholas Roerich; mystic G.I. Gurdjieff; writers George Bernard Shaw, William Butler Yeats, Aldous Huxley, Oscar Wilde, and Frank L. Baum; revolutionary architect Frank Lloyd Wright; German educator and mystic Rudolph Steiner; Indian independence leader Mohandas (Mahatma) Gandhi; cartoonist and entertainment visionary Walt Disney; and the originator of relativity theory, physicist Albert Einstein. To this day, storefront psychics and gypsies still refer to themselves as "Madame so-and-so" in *homage* to the late mystic known to the world as Madame Blavatsky.

Up until my early thirties I'd known only a few Theosophists and had not paid the movement much attention. Its heyday having been in the late 19th Century through the mid 20th Century it has been largely overshadowed in recent decades by more modern, and more ancient, religious and mystical movements. Although many of its adherents would suggest that its traditions date back to the most ancient of times its official beginning as a modern organization was in 1875, New York. In my early 30s I was to get a crash course in the history and practice of Theosophy. After only brief study, and through a curious set of circumstances, I found myself suddenly on the Board of Directors of the Theosophical Society of Boston. The Boston chapter at the time was in the process of splitting from the International Theosophical Society, headquartered in India, it having moved there during Blavatsky's lifetime.

My principal interest in the T.S. was in learning more about the lives and metaphysical teachings that had so influenced Omega Shakti's founder Matt Schoener and which were said to be directly connected to his teacher, the spiritual master he knew as Father Jack. On a couple of different occasions my spiritual visions had informed me that Matt and his Omega crew were an important group of souls for me in this lifetime. According to my childhood visions, we'd been together back in the late 1800s, in the early days of the Theosophical Society. Then one day I met a guy named Richard, a student at the Harvard Divinity School, who was involved with a different Theosophy group called the United Lodge of Theosophists. This group was separate from the group headquartered in India and had a particular interest in another of the original founders of the Theosophical Society, an Irish-born lawyer and mystic named William Quan Judge (1851-1896).

Mr. Judge had a special relationship with Madame Blavatsky and was the head of the American section of the T.S. until his death in 1896. Richard told me he had biographical information on the life of Judge, if I was interested in learning more. As it turned out, some years earlier I'd owned a copy of the <u>Bhagavad-Gita</u> as translated by Mr. Judge. The Bhagavad-Gita is part of a Hindu religious classic, written in Sanskrit and given as a dialogue between Krishna, Lord of Devotion, and Arjuna, Prince of India. Richard also turned me on to other books containing compilations of articles written by Judge. One was entitled <u>Letters That Have Helped Me</u>. When I opened the book I got one of the biggest surprises of my life in the form of a posed photograph of the author. For the better part of an hour I just kept looking at the picture, somewhat in disbelief. William Quan Judge, the man in the photograph, was the same man with the beard and the brown suit I had been shown in the vision on my front lawn when I was eight or nine years old. My Master teacher had instructed me to remember his face and I'd kept his image in my mind for a quarter of a century.

At the first opportunity, I politely informed Richard that "I would love to get that biographical information," on the life of Mr. Judge that he'd offered to me. The biographical information amounted to a few dozen mimeographed pages chronicling the life and important moments of Mr. Judge's life of spiritual service. But I was mostly interested in learning exactly where on the globe he had traveled in his lifetime. I read through the pages as fast as I could and quickly confirmed what I knew had to be true. The map of the bearded man's world travels, the map I'd seen in my vision when I was a little boy, was a map of the life and travels of William Quan Judge. Suddenly, my appearance on the Board of Directors of the Boston T.S. made a kind of sense.

Was it possible that I the reincarnation of Mr. Judge, and/or of the Eastern mystic said to have been a part of his inner life, as my childhood vision seemed to imply? I earnestly began reading Judge's letters and articles for clues and was struck by just how similar our thought processes and writing styles seemed to be to each other. Now, I know from my dealings with a handful of Theosophy's Judge loyalists that the very idea somebody as common and as humanly flawed as myself might be remotely related to Mr. Judge would be considered somewhere between a joke and a sacrilege to some of his more devoted fans. But then, personally, I've never been much for putting people up on pedestals. We are all of us human and flawed. It comes with the DNA. Whatever is known about the life of Mr. Judge by those of us in this time period counts as only a small fraction of the true and complete life of the historical man.

Although I have not chosen to become a William Quan Judge scholar, I have studied his astrological birth chart, read many of his letters and articles, and do have my favorites from his surviving life's work. My favorite of all is a small book entitled The Ocean Of Theosophy in which he shares the essential essence of what Theosophy is in an amazingly concise and intimate way. Some of his adherents insist that he accomplished in a handful of pages what it took Madame Blavatsky a massive tome to achieve. Others have suggested that his very intention was to take the enormously complex work by HPB known as The Secret Doctrine and make its essence available in a simple form.

Here I quote from the opening passage of Mr. Judge's work The Ocean Of Theosophy, originally published in 1893 and available from the Theosophical University Press, online at http://www.TheoSociety.org:

"Theosophy is that ocean of knowledge which spreads from shore to shore of the evolution of sentient beings; unfathomable in its deepest parts, it gives the greatest minds their fullest scope, yet, shallow enough at its shores, it will not overwhelm the understanding of a child. It is wisdom about God for those who believe that he is all things and in all, and wisdom about nature for the man who accepts the statement found in the Christian Bible that God cannot be measured or discovered, and that darkness is around his pavilion. Although it contains by derivation the name God and thus may seem at first sight to embrace religion alone, it does not neglect science, for it is the science of sciences and therefore has been called the wisdom religion."

Mr. Judge further addresses Theosophy's teaching that there are wise, evolved souls, called Adepts, Ascended Masters, or members of the Great White Brotherhood, like the One who has visited me off and on since childhood, who play a critical role in the evolution of humanity:

"The most intelligent being in the universe, man, has never, then, been without a friend, but has a line of elder brothers who continually watch over the progress of the less progressed, preserve the knowledge gained through aeons of trial and experience, and continually seek for opportunities of drawing the developing intelligence of the race on this or other globes to consider the great truths concerning the destiny of the soul. These elder brothers also keep the knowledge they have gained of the laws of nature in all departments…if they were to come out openly and be heard of everywhere, they would be worshipped as gods by some and hunted as devils by others. In those periods when they do come out some of their number are rulers of men, some teachers, a few great philosophers, while others remain still unknown except to the most advanced of the body."

Do I claim to be Mr. Judge reborn? No. Whereas I can't prove the reality of it, if it is indeed true, as I believe it to be, I see no point in spending a lot of energy on the subject. If I've learned anything, living the life of a mystic, it's that belief in something, or lack thereof, is no criterion for establishing the truth. Besides, what's important is not what each of our souls may or may not have done in some other point in time and space, in some other life, or on some distant world. What's important is what each and every one of us does with the life we have today.

CHAPTER SIXTY-SEVEN

A Snake In The Garden

Matt Schoener of Omega had hit his stride and was rocketing towards the stratosphere with ever-increasing levels of attunements taken from various sources and traditions and added to Omega Shakti's list of possibilities. At the same time Matt's ever-increasing ego made him more than a few enemies. Years earlier, Matt had psychically snooped in on the keys to Reiki Mastership. Later, I heard Matt was being bad-mouthed by one of the main Reiki attunement providers in the West. In response, Matt had callously offered to make anyone who wanted to be a Reiki Master a Reiki Master for free. At the time, it cost roughly $10,000 and a serious commitment to a long apprenticeship program under Barbara, Phyllis, and others to become a Reiki Master, and it was considered a great honor to be chosen for the training.

Matt had also included Chi Gong (Qigong) attunements to Omega's amazing bag of tricks and loved telling the story of how he'd pissed off a powerful traditional Qigong Master in Hong Kong by initiating some of that master's own students into a level that had taken that master many years of daily practice and discipline to achieve. When I queried Matt about Omega's newly added Chi Gong attunements, he coyly spoke of a "wise Chinese Master" he had met with whom he had shared and traded knowledge of energy traditions.

With time, the levels of consciousness-expanding attunements that Matt assembled under the umbrella of the Omega Shakti organization became virtually overwhelming. Just keeping track of them all was becoming a feat unto itself. The list included sixteen or so degrees of the original Omega Shakti system, with upper attunement levels for teachers, as well as multiple levels of attunements for other energies.

The list of available energy attunements in the growing Omega Shakti system included: Parashakti, Ichashakti, Jnanashakti, Kriya Shakti, Kundalini Shakti, Mantrika Shakti, Daivi Prakriti, Agni Dhatu Samadhi Yoga, Quantum Molecular Rejuvenation, Exstasis, Grantha, Kalachakra, Electric Fire, Magnetic Healing, Marma-Shakti, 3rd Sight, Etheric Detox, Chi Gong/Qigong, Siva Shakti, Kali-Shakti, Ketamine, The Yoga of Enlightenment, Shamballa, the Divine Pause, Lights,

Enhancements, and Pattern Clearing attunements. Matt jokingly referred to one of the attunements by the name Gorgonzola, after the very stinky cheese, because the detox effect made most people smell pretty rank for a few days after receiving the attunement. After spending a few months introducing Omega to folks in Arizona, while being greatly helped out by my friends Kevin and Renée and friends June and Terry, I headed back to life in Massachusetts.

Meanwhile, things in the Omega organization were starting to go wrong. A con artist, claiming to be raising money to fund a project to save the Earth's ozone layer, had created some bad blood and mistrust by using some of the people in Omega to try and hustle others in Omega out of their financial resources. Matt was getting increasingly cocky with his growing mystical powers and had managed to convince himself that he'd completely transcended his personal ego. The belief that one can become one with the will of one's higher soul by leaving the personal ego behind is a major tenet and the ultimate metaphysical aim of some mystical schools of thought. However, from my observations, Matt had not so much transcended his personal ego as he'd pushed it into the background of his conscious awareness, by overwhelming his normal consciousness with constant influxes of energies and by flights into altered states of awareness. This can cause someone to think their ego has gone, when all that has happened is that it's gone below the surface, while continuing to function on the unconscious level. When unconscious motivations are what's driving agendas and coloring perspectives this can create a much more destructive part of the psyche in a mystic than if they'd just left their personal ego in charge.

The constant increase in energies, combined with the pressure of life on the road as a traveling energy merchant, was also bringing out some of the worst and rather domineering character flaws in Omega teacher John S's personality. John (God bless him) was becoming so difficult to be around that many students made it clear they wanted nothing to do with him. John attributed it all to their inability to handle his newfound power and remained blind to his own part in the problem. The endless plane fares, hotels, rental cars, and restaurants on the road were also putting an enormous strain on Omega's budget. Matt, John, Rosanne, Nancy, and Fred were working night and day to bring the energy initiations of Omega Shakti to every part of North America, and to a growing number of European and Asian nations. Another person high up in Omega had a sort of break with reality in which he determined that he was some sort of enlightened planetary sage. He set himself up as traveling guru, mostly to very attractive younger women, and began speaking of himself in the third person.

What was happening to many of Omega's leaders was curiously something that Matt had warned us all could happen to any of us who were involved with the initiations. That is, the pressures put on our delicate human psyches by the profound consciousness-expanding properties of each increasing energy attunement could cause a breakdown of the normal personality structures and lead to all kinds of psychological imbalances. Matt and John were increasingly pointing out the problems various advancing Omega students were having, as a result of moving so fast through these attunements, while remaining in complete denial as to their own symptoms of imbalance.

Then one day I had a very strange conversation with Matt. He told me that all of Omega's financial troubles were about to be over and that soon we'd have all the resources needed to bring the gifts of Omega Shakti to peoples all over the world. He said he couldn't tell me much, it was all very hush-hush, but he wanted me to have a chance to benefit personally from this extraordinary resource. All I had to do was pony up some money to help the process along. He explained that the Omega organization was strapped for cash, having already "invested" what it could in this very secret project. Once the financial floodgates opened, he assured me, I'd be rewarded with a very large sum of money for my comparatively small investment.

Okay. If it had been *anybody else* proposing such a vaguely outlined, unlikely sounding "financial opportunity" to me I would have laughed in their face and instructed them to take their scam elsewhere. But this was Matt Schoener, the founder of Omega Shakti, making this claim! So, like so many other trusting students of a great teacher or a wise leader before me I went for it. Like a fool. Because I believed in him. Matt was truly one of the most extraordinary people I've ever known. If he believed in it, then maybe there really was some Great Spiritual Presence secretly working behind the scenes to help us bring Omega to a greater portion of humanity through a large influx of cash? After all, what amounted to the collective attunements of Omega Shakti, and their real world effects, were in themselves so astounding that none of us could have imaged their existence before they came into our lives.

I asked Matt whether or not he'd *psychically* checked up on the people offering this unlikely opportunity. He assured me he had and that he could find "nothing wrong on the inner planes." Months went by and Matt kept alluding that all was going well on the secret financing front. "Just a little more patience," became the assurance. "Just a little more patience." Then one day I got an invite to attend a secret meeting in New York at the home of Omega teacher Nancy Wong. I still knew almost nothing about this financial scheme Matt had gotten us all into and this was my chance to find out what was really going on.

My buddy Steve Dondoros and I arrived together and found Matt, Nancy, and some other Omega regulars already there. There were also two strangers, a man and woman. They turned out to be the people that were supposedly going to financially rescue Omega Shakti and its noble humanitarian work. I listened to them give their speech and, without going into unnecessary detail, a lot of what this man and woman said and did that day just didn't add up. When I took Matt aside and expressed my concerns and doubts, he gave me a smile and a fatherly tap on the side of my face. "Don't you worry about a thing, Thomas," he told me. "I know what I'm doing." When I got the chance I asked some very pointed questions of the two strangers in our midst. Both Nancy and Matt quickly jumped to the strangers' defense and even mildly chastised me for being so rude to our guests. This, I felt, was definitely not a good sign. If these folks really were legitimate, what was the big deal with asking a few very reasonable questions?

Steve and I drove back to Massachusetts from that meeting in New York, both very concerned and yet still excited about the possibilities. We knew that something was either terribly wrong in the Omega Shakti organization or that something was about to be very right. We had been living in an extraordinary dream of mystical initiations and of healing service to our fellows and couldn't quite imagine that it could all come apart at the seams after we'd all worked so hard for the good.

CHAPTER SIXTY-EIGHT

The Emperor Has No Clothes

I'd hurt my back on one of my moving jobs. The healing process took a good eight months and without insurance or workman's compensation to cover me financially I slowly emptied my bank account during the recuperation process. Strangely, I wound up in a romantic relationship during that time. Her name was Karen and she was an extraordinary and talented young grad student studying art and psychology who I'd been friends with for about two years. One day Karen showed me piles of handwritten pages that she said just sort of came through her like a kind of automatic writing. She wanted to know if I thought the mystical concepts in them had any value. I found the work quite remarkable and strikingly reminiscent of the mystic Alice Bailey, someone Karen, a neophyte in mystical studies, had never heard of.

Alice A. Bailey (1880-1949) was a British-born mystic who'd settled in California after marrying an American minister. When she was a child she'd had a visit one day by a Spiritual Master who materialized before her in her parents' home. The bearded man with a turban on his head had told her that if she became a better person there was a very important spiritual work that was waiting for her. Bailey became a missionary in her younger years and after leaving her alcoholic first husband met and married a kinder man named Foster Bailey. Alice Bailey eventually did come to that promised spiritual work, ultimately completing some twenty-six volumes of highly metaphysical and groundbreaking spiritual treatises, much of it purportedly with the telepathic assistance of a Tibetan initiate named Djwhal Khul. Her writings include Initiation, Human and Solar (1922); A Treatise On Cosmic Fire (1925); and The Destiny Of Nations (1949).

The scope and volume of the work remains quite extraordinary and has spawned several New Age mystical and spiritual movements and groups. Most notably, those organizations that have demonstrated their devotion to the teachings and to the sharing of the mystical concepts put forth in the Bailey/Djwhal Khul books are the Lucis Trust and the Arcane School - http://www.LucisTrust.org; and the University of the Seven Rays - http://www.SevenRay.net. The books have even given the world a type of prayer that has become something of an anthem for many hoping for a better world in a coming New Age. The inspiring invocative prayer is called *The Great Invocation* and reads as follows:

THE GREAT INVOCATION

From the point of Light within the Mind of God
Let light stream forth into the minds of men.
Let Light descend on Earth.

From the point of Love within the Heart of God
Let love stream forth into the hearts of men.
May Christ return to Earth.

From the center where the Will of God is known
Let purpose guide the little wills of men –
The purpose which the Masters know and serve.

From the center which we call the race of men
Let the Plan of Love and Light work out.
And may it seal the door where evil dwells.

Let Light and Love and Power restore the Plan on Earth.

Recite that one three times a day and you may just find a whole new world of mystical understanding opening up for you over time.

Getting back to the troubles in the Omega Shakti organization – When Matt Schoener next came to town I arranged for he and Karen to meet. Afterwards, Karen let me know, in no uncertain terms, that she flat out didn't like him or trust him. Her intuition was quite good and she knew something was very wrong. Furthermore, she told me this so-called investment I was into on Matt's personal urging didn't feel at all right to her and that it frankly sounded like a bunch of crap. Months later Karen and I broke up, largely over money stresses and the fact that I'd been increasingly putting my trust in the future on Matt's promises. Karen's walking out on me was a cold, hard slap in the face. That slap woke me up. I decided it was time to have it out with Matt and the leaders of Omega. By this point I'd become informed enough in what this fake investment scheme was supposed to be to know that Karen had been right, it was all a bunch of crap. The trouble was that Matt had been completely hoodwinked by the con artists behind it. When I confronted him, Matt and his supporters had already poured hundreds of thousands of dollars into this absurd fantasy. And those hundreds of thousands of dollars were turning into millions of dollars.

I made my best effort, but there was no talking to Matt anymore so I sat down and drafted a letter to the top people involved in Omega imploring everyone to look at the reality of what was happening and asking them to help bring Matt around to sanity again. The response to my letter was a conference call between Matt, myself, and several of the top people in Omega. But instead of a sane and frank discussion of what had been going on, imploring Matt to use his common sense, Matt and the other Omegans had set up the conference call as a planned "intervention" for me. Because Matt couldn't believe that he, the master psychic and mystic, could possibly be fooled and used so completely by a couple of con artists he determined that it was I who was being misled. The conference call was intended to bring me back into the fold and once again show me the light. By the end of the call, Matt and most of the top people in Omega had turned their backs on me as hopeless as I was apparently unable to recognize the supposed truth of the great fortune we were all about to share in. But worse, I had essentially committed the greatest sin a spiritual chela (disciple) can against his wise teacher, I had told him he was wrong.

A short time later I received a call from Rosanne informing me that she'd done all she could to persuade Matt that he was being made a fool of. She had withdrawn from her place at the very top of the organization and would go on to continue the work of the Omega Shakti initiations on her own. Over the next ten years Matt traveled from place to place, keeping a low profile and depending on the charity of others as he waited for his great reward to arrive. His low profile was necessary to avoid the people from whom he had unwisely helped swindle so much money. To his dying day Matt continued to insist the fortune he'd promised us all would be arriving soon. Finally and quite unceremoniously Matt died of a stroke in the spring of 2004 in a friend's bathroom. Constantly messing around in other realities can have its price, especially when there's nobody around to help you find your way back when you get lost. In the final months of Matt's life, when he knew he was dying, he made clear his wish that Rosanne Amato would take over Omega Shakti and its great spiritual responsibilities. Rosanne has stepped up to the plate and is bringing the work back with a clear head and a dedicated heart. Stay tuned world…

CHAPTER SIXTY-NINE

Go West Young Man

I was devastated by the abrupt changes that happened in my life. For more than five years my entire focus had been helping to expand the work of Omega Shakti. Virtually everyone in my life was connected to that work. With Karen gone and having been abandoned by all the local Omega people who supported Matt's fantasy I had a major void to fill in my life. I'd gone back to studying film and spent the next two years working a television camera, sound equipment, and performing other technical jobs at Harvard University and other venues around Boston. I also did a little stage acting, experimented with filmmaking, and finally settled into writing screenplays in my spare time. As the writing bug grew I decided to head to California, like everybody else, and seek my fortune in Hollywood. On my way there I stopped into the San Francisco Bay Area to visit my old and dear friend Mary Carol and ended up spending the next three years in Northern California.

I found an apartment in San Rafael, about twelve miles north of San Francisco in Marin County. I'd felt a very strong psychic draw to this particular apartment and knew it was where I should be. That being the case, I was very confused when I was shocked awake about 1AM on my first night there by the incredibly loud sounds of several motorcycles, sans any sort of reasonable mufflers, all starting up their engines just below my bedroom window. The local bar directly across the street from my new place turned out to be a biker bar.

Even with all the windows closed, the sounds of the motorcycles reverberated off my apartment's thirteen-foot high walls and ceilings like World War III in stereo. After a second night of being shocked awake by the same motorized assault, I was at a loss for an explanation. Spirit had clearly shown me this was the right place for me to live. But how was I supposed to function with this constant shock to my nervous system every night? The next morning I walked across the street, with the strong inner feeling that somehow I would understand it all if I just got closer to the bar itself. As I approached the biker bar, I looked for some kind of mystical sign or vision that would explain it to me. When I reached the front door, a sign did appear right before my very eyes. Actually, the sign was already there, tacked onto the entrance door. The sign read:

"Come Tonight For Our Final Goodnight Bash!
We're Closing Our Doors Forever!"

~

I got a job managing a small audiovisual company in Marin County and went back to work on my screenwriting. I loved San Rafael and the Bay Area. There was even a very cool spiritual bookstore called The Open Secret a half a block from my front door. After less than a year at the a/v company I'd graduated to managing its San Francisco city office and found my daily commute from San Rafael less than convenient. I decided to create an image in my mind of the place I wanted to live in and then go out and find it. This is sometimes called a visualization technique. I'd been sort of enamored with the idea of living in one of those giant converted-warehouse apartments ever since seeing the French classic picture *Diva*, which featured characters living in two such amazing places. I went out and found just such a place in the Mission District of San Francisco and moved in weeks later. The place was enormous. My bedroom alone was literally three times the size of my entire apartment in San Rafael.

As part of my visualization, I'd also envisioned sharing a place with people who were in the film business, so both of my new warehouse apartment mates worked "in the biz." One, a very decent fellow, was a commercial photographer who did advertising campaigns for major automobile manufacturers, soft drink companies, and the like. The other guy told me he'd been in the film business for years. He even had his own theater with original movie theater seats, a full-sized screen, a massive film archive, and entire rooms filled with film canisters and walls of videos in that giant warehouse apartment to prove it. It wasn't until after I moved in, however, that I learned that the "film business" the other guy had been in for years was the porn business. Whoops! In my visualization I had forgotten to include everything I wanted and *didn't* want for my new home in the city. It didn't take long for the porn guy and I to recognize that we weren't meant to share the same space together, even the enormously large space of that converted-warehouse apartment. I soon started putting my psychic feelers out for another place to live in the city.

I kept my eyes and ears open for a different apartment to move into, while working my very busy job. As I sat in my office one morning in the popular Fisherman's Wharf tourist destination of San Francisco, I had a sudden flash about my future living situation. I had a vision that told me to go to the Whole Foods Market, located in a different part of San Francisco, after 5PM that same day. I saw that there I would find the right living situation posted on the community bulletin board. It was a rare slow morning at work, so I decided to jump in my car and head over to the store and get the information off the bulletin board right away. I figured, "Why wait until after five o'clock when I can do it now?" I got to the store and made a beeline for the bulletin board. I carefully searched through every notice there but found nothing that looked like what I had seen in my vision. I double-checked every notice again. There was definitely nothing there. A little voice inside my head said, "You were supposed to come here *after* 5PM."

I bought lunch-to-go and drove back to my office. When 5PM came around, I got back in my car and returned to Whole Foods. When I reached the bulletin board, there was a brand new house-sharing notice tacked up in front of the others. I knew this was the right one. I could feel it. I called the number on the notice and instantly hit it off with Pamela, one of the two folks I'd be sharing the new place with. When I arrived at the address it turned out to be a strikingly familiar spot. Months beforehand, when I was still living in San Rafael, I'd been driving through that part of San Francisco and felt overwhelmingly compelled to pull my car over, park, and walk around that very same neighborhood. I was drawn to it like a magnet. I looked at the houses and the neighborhood shops. I could see myself living and shopping there at some point in the future. But I didn't know when in the future.

Now, as I walked up to the front door of the three-story brownstone building to meet Pamela, I knew this was to be my new home. Less than two weeks later I left the Mission District and moved into this great little place in the Richmond District, just two blocks from Golden Gate Park. After moving in I would go for runs through the park down to the Pacific Ocean and back again, tour the libraries and museums located only a few minutes walk away, and find myself feeling greatly blessed for the new home the Universe had found for me.

CHAPTER SEVENTY

Oh, "Those" Kind Of Mushrooms

It was my drummer friend James' birthday and he was playing a gig at a club just down the street from where some friends of mine lived. I decided to show up at the gig to join him for his working birthday celebration. A couple of my friends were joining me, so we met early in the evening before heading over to the club. While at my friend's place, I was offered some mushroom tea. It was explained to me that the mushrooms were organic and that they made for a really mellow and soothing experience. I've been a fan of herbal teas for many years and was pleased for the opportunity to sample a new kind. I'd never heard of mushroom tea before, so I was intrigued to try it.

The mushrooms were powdered, creating a silky texture and a fine sediment in the hot tea. I was encouraged to consume all the sediment along with the liquid. I found the tea unusually delicious and before long I'd consumed three large cups, including all the tasty sediment. About twenty minutes into my third cup everything started to get really interesting. The colors and textures in the room became brighter and more alive and all of my senses were heightened to an unusual degree. It began to dawn on me why I'd never seen organic mushroom tea in any of the health food stores. Just like my old friend Tina, I was innocent enough in the ways of illegal drugs not to realize what I was getting myself into. I checked with my host and quickly confirmed my suspicions. The tea I'd been drinking was made from "those" kind of mushrooms, the psychedelic, psychotropic, and hallucinogenic kind.

"How very interesting," I thought to myself. "I've spent my entire life intentionally avoiding the use of hallucinogenic drugs and here I am with a quart of hallucinogenic mushroom tea making its way into my bloodstream." Finding myself in this unexpected situation with no real alternatives at my disposal, and being in the company of friends, I decided to allow this to be another altered state of consciousness research experiment. I informed my friends of my predicament and got apologies for the miscommunication and a promise to keep an eye on me for the rest of the night. Before long, I was feeling pretty antsy and needing to get out of the apartment. We ventured out into the evening and spent a while just walking and talking on the streets of the town. I was the only one in my small group who'd never had a psychedelic drug experience before, so I wanted to be cautious. The last thing I wanted was run into problems on the streets while on hallucinogenic drugs I knew almost nothing about. After a while my friends decided they were getting very hungry, so we headed off to the local Double Rainbow ice cream parlor for something to satisfy those cravings.

It was a beautiful spring night in California, so when we got to the ice cream shop we found it filled with children and their parents out for a treat together. My friends were laughing and having a good time with it all, but I was way too concerned to relax. Not yet recognizing that I was experiencing a classic drug-induced paranoia, and having no way of knowing how my appearance and behavior might look on the outside, I found myself extremely anxious and concerned that we might be creating a very uncomfortable and inappropriate experience for the parents and their children in the ice cream shop. We got our treats and I quietly insisted to my friends that we get out of the ice cream parlor and away from the young children and their families. We headed down the street to the club where James' band was playing and went inside. By this time, my companions were lost in their own psychedelic experiences and I was feeling pretty much alone and abandoned by those I had hoped to rely on for support.

I knew James had used the hallucinogenic plant *peyote* one time a few years earlier, so I figured he'd understand what I was going through. When I got the chance, I took him aside and advised him of my predicament. James assured me that I appeared perfectly normal on the outside, only noticeably quieter than usual. This, combined with the fact that I was now inside a rock 'n' roll club filled with other adults, many of whom were intoxicated in one way or another themselves, went a long way to allowing me to relax and just take the experience in for what it was. The hallucinogenic effects of the magic mushrooms were in full force when I got on the dance floor. It was fun to be dancing, though I had to be extra careful because the effects of the drug kept causing individual dancers to seemingly disappear and periodically reappear before my eyes. I'm a big guy, over 6ft. 5in. tall and 225 lbs., and I was concerned I might accidentally do some serious harm to one of the invisible dancers that my rational mind knew still had to be somewhere in the room.

By the end of the night I'd managed to sweat out and pee out the larger part of the psychoactive tea and felt comfortable that I had already peaked on the mushrooms. All in all, I suppose it was an interesting experience, although not one I have any interest in repeating. There wasn't anything that I saw, felt, or otherwise experienced on the drug that I hadn't experienced spontaneously on my own over the years. The principle differences between the drug experience and my own were:

1) My own spontaneously occurring altered states were generally filled with fascinating information, images of other realities, and often very important soul-level communications. The drug-induced ones were flat and not particularly interesting, by comparison.

2) The drug-induced altered states were rife with a creepy crawly sensation on my skin, a strong and persistent feeling of paranoia, and a desire for the experience to be over as soon as possible. My own natural experiences were profound, often reassuring and helpful, and didn't rob me of one precious moment in my regular world.

Now, I've got no personal moral judgment on the use of recreational drugs, anymore than I do for the recreational use of alcohol, but I've seen far too much human devastation from the use of both drugs and drink to take either of them lightly. Meditation and paying attention to the mystical coincidences in life may take a little longer to produce a fascinating and otherworldly experience, but the experiences are more likely to be something worth having when they come your way. The dangers of drug and alcohol use and abuse are well documented enough for anyone with any common sense to recognize that there's a world of difference between drug-induced states of altered reality and the real thing.

~

Sex and Drugs and Rock 'n' Roll?

(Um, no drugs for me, thanks.)

CHAPTER SEVENTY-ONE

Something Terrible Happens
On The Golden Gate Bridge

On my first visit to San Francisco, back when I was in my late 20s, I'd done some of the touristy stuff, including walking across the Golden Gate Bridge that separates the Pacific Ocean from San Francisco Bay. Now that I was living within the city limits, I decided I wanted to cross the bridge again. The Golden Gate Bridge, by the way, is named after the waterway that lies below it, which is called the Golden Gate Strait. Some historians write that referring to a grand opening that leads to an important place as a "golden gate" is an ancient tradition, though exactly where that tradition comes from is a matter of some historical debate. As for San Francisco's Golden Gate, the generally excepted story is that the strait was named *Chrysopylae*, which means Golden Gate in Greek, by a U.S. Army Captain named John Frémont around 1846. The strait, it is said, reminded him of a harbor in Istanbul (Constantinople) named *Chrysoceras*, which means Golden Horn. The bridge itself is painted a color called International Orange, not gold.

I got on the bridge's public sidewalk and started towards the north side and Marin County. The sidewalk is used by pedestrians and bicyclists and runs parallel with the automobile traffic. It was a beautiful mid-December day and the walkway was filled with people enjoying the crossing and taking pictures. But about ¾ of the way across I was overcome with a panic attack. As I paused to study the structure of the bridge, my attention was drawn to the 9½-inch gap that runs the length of the bridge between the steel I-beams that separate the sidewalk from the road. "Is that safe?" I asked myself with sudden alarm and concern. As I studied the relatively small gap in the bridge's walkway, a terrible vision opened up before my eyes. I was overcome as fear, horror, and disbelief ripped through my very soul. In the vision I saw a baby girl fall forward and fly right through the 9½-inch gap in the steel and plummet to her death on the land far below. I felt the little girl's parents' utter desperation, as the impossible scene became reality. After this my normal view of reality returned, but I was still panicked and confused. My head was spinning and I felt sick inside. "How could this possibly happen?" I begged of the air around me. "What can I do?

Who should I call? Is this really a vision of the future?" By this time, the people passing by were starting to look at me with concern.

I'd never heard of anything like this happening before, though I knew at least eleven men had died during the construction of the bridge in the 1930s and that some had used the bridge since as a suicide jump. I got down on my knees and looked through the small opening in the bridge structure to the land of the Marin headlands far below. "Could a small child actually fit through this opening?" I asked myself. It didn't seem at all likely, but it certainly looked at least possible. I returned home and then went to the San Francisco Public Library. No such accident had ever been reported since the bridge's public opening. Still, I considered contacting the local newspapers, television stations, and Bridge Authority and trying to make a case for installing some sort of safety measures to close the gap. But, what could I tell them? That I had a *vision*? And I wondered, "Did I really know anything, or was this just my imagination and natural caution going into overdrive?" I talked to a few people about my concerns, leaving out the part about how I saw it all in a vision, and they all agreed that something like this occurring would have to be the freak accident of the century.

Nine days later, it was all over the TV. "The Freak Accident Of The Century" had occurred. On Sunday afternoon, December 21, 1997, a two-year-old girl was crossing the bridge with her parents and 4-year-old brother when the girl stumbled and fell right through the 9½-inch gap in the steel, falling 170 feet to her death on the land below. I stood before my television set in horror and disbelief. The aerial view of the bridge, shown on the TV screen, indicated that the girl had fallen from the exact same spot I had been standing on when I had my vision about it. The video footage then showed a view of the place on the Marin headlands where the little girl's body had landed. It was the same vantage point I'd seen when I'd gotten down on my knees and looked through the gap in the steel to the land below.

Could I have done something to avert this terrible tragedy? Was that why I'd had the vision in the first place? Would anyone have listened to me if I'd made the attempt? I still ask myself these questions every time I think of that little girl and her family.

CHAPTER SEVENTY-TWO

Love Will Find A Way

As much as I loved San Francisco, it was already 1999 and I'd just spent an unexpected three years in the Bay Area. So I packed up my gear and drove the 400 miles south to Los Angeles. Once I got there I wrote all day long, working on film scripts and story ideas, attended lectures, art shows, movies, and other events to get to know the L.A. scene. I checked out the Self-Realization Fellowship, home of the devotees of the Kriya yoga linage brought to the United States by Paramahansa Yogananda, the author of the best selling book, Autobiography of a Yogi. I found the Hollywood branch of the S.R.F. assembly surprisingly more like a Protestant church service than an Eastern ashram, at least in its public devotional meetings, although I was delighted to discover the energy of Kriya Shakti was present during the church assemblies. The energy was sent out surreptitiously at specific intervals in the devotional services, but I was able to recognize the energy and pick up on the vibration. Good stuff.

I found myself drawn to a cool artsy coffee house near Venice Beach, which turned out to be the second home to a number of local writers. In less than a week of bringing my laptop to that café I made friends with Gert Basson, a South African writer who'd moved to L.A., and bumped into David Lampert, a comic writer and performer who I knew from film classes years earlier in Boston. Both of these guys would become my new pals. I decided L.A. and I would get along just fine. The one thing I didn't have was the love of a good woman.

There was a woman I'd crossed paths with in different parts of the country over the years, each time with us not quite connecting. This time she was with another man and once again I wondered why we kept missing each other. After pining away for her for a couple of months I decided it was high time that I got over it and moved on. I prayed and meditated for a solution to my heartache and loneliness. From that prayer I had a vision that I should go to the city of Pasadena in two weeks time and there I would connect with a woman who would be a potential spiritual mate for me. Pasadena was hosting a Psychic Faire that weekend, so I figured it would be a good place to meet somebody who would understand the mystical world I lived in. In the vision I'd seen that I needed be there on Sunday, not Saturday, if I wanted to meet up with my mystery woman.

On the appointed day, as I reached the right part of town, I passed by a Starbucks coffee shop and saw that I would connect with my mystery woman there, but later on in the day. I made it to the Psychic Faire and hung out there for a bit, catching sight of a couple of TV stars doing their best to hide their identities and also catching sight of a very beautiful blonde close to my age. I felt very drawn to her, but my intuition had shown me that I would meet the woman I'd come to connect with at the Starbucks, so I didn't say hello. Later, as I finished lunch in a local restaurant, I got a flash that it was time to head over to the Starbucks I'd seen earlier. I drove there and found a parking spot on the street out front. As I was parking my car another car pulled into the just-opened space behind me and out jumped the same blonde woman I'd noticed at the Faire. She made it inside before me and so I wound up behind her in line at the counter. We ended up sharing coffee together and talking for some time. I learned she was only in Pasadena for that afternoon. Had I come on Saturday, we never would have met. We exchanged personal phone numbers and email addresses and agreed to meet in two weeks when she would be in L.A. on business.

When the day came for her business in L.A., we agreed to meet at the Urth Caffé (yup, that's how they spell it) next to the Bodhi Tree Bookstore. We had a great time together, but she also had evening plans to attend a lecture. The lecture was actually the opening night of a workshop for couples. She invited me to join her. We drove to the romantic workshop in our separate cars and walked in together. As we entered, I looked across the room and saw the same woman I'd been pining over for months sitting with her current beau. Don't try to tell me God doesn't have a sense of humor. The presence of the woman I'd been trying so hard to forget confused the crap out of me. "Does this mean we really are supposed to be together after all?" I asked myself. I was still smitten. Needless to say, the potential relationship between me and the woman I'd met at the Pasadena Starbucks went nowhere.

Shortly after this trail of would-be romantic events, I started having a recurring vision of another blonde woman. I kept seeing her in a business suit at a house on the beach in Malibu, apparently employed by a tall elderly white man who lived there. It was clear the visions were indicating this woman as a possible mate for me, but I really thought an entertainment industry woman in a business suit probably wasn't the greatest match for an artsy, mystical guy like myself. Although the visions persisted, I made no attempt to go to Malibu to try to find the house, so the vision of the blonde woman just remained a curious sight that would pop into my psyche from time to time. Months later, I was driving to an audiovisual job in the desert, about 120 miles east of L.A., when I passed the city of Palm Desert on the highway and had yet another vision. In the vision I saw myself living in that desert area. "No, Universe!" I said immediately. "There's no way I'm leaving L.A. to live out here with a bunch of retirees and their country clubs! I don't care if I'm *supposed* to be here!" I said with determined finality. The sense of my living there persisted, but I doggedly ignored it. I was staying in L.A., or so I thought.

Instead of moving to the desert, east of L.A., I moved west to the Pacific coast. I took an apartment in Santa Monica, just down the beach from Malibu. It would be another nine months before I would finally meet the woman from the beach house vision. Then at a neighbor's party, I met an old friend of best-selling author Jess Stearn. Jess had become famous in the 1960s for a book entitled Edgar Cayce: The Sleeping Prophet. His writing about the American mystic and prophet Edgar Cayce (1877-1945) had made Cayce's prophecies and life's work internationally known, and making Cayce famous had made Jess Stearn both wealthy and a famous celebrity in his own right. A writer was being sought to bring the life story of Edgar Cayce to the big screen and I had just come back from adapting a novel for the screen in Sicily. It was arranged for me to meet the elderly Jess Stearn and his representative, a beautiful blonde-haired businesswoman, at Jess's beach house in Malibu. As you might have figured out by now, the beach house was the one from my visions and Jess's representative was Rhonda Clifton, the blond-haired woman in the business suit.

Rhonda and I hit it off right away and what was to be a brief meeting turned into a four-hour conversation about our respective lives. Rhonda, it turned out, had lived quite a varied and unusual life. We shared story after story of our interesting adventures, travels, and mystical experiences. Then Rhonda told me a story that was strikingly familiar. It started with Rhonda having been a single mom, giving birth to her daughter Tammie when she was only nineteen. For a time she'd lived in St. Louis, Missouri, where one of her duties involved picking celebrities up at the airport and bringing them for their guest appearances on the nationally-syndicated Mike Douglas Show. Rhonda told the story of bringing the famous comedian Georgie Jessell to the show one day. During the taping of the show, Jessell had called for Rhonda to be brought on stage, telling everyone that he was going to take Rhonda to Hollywood and make her a star. Rhonda was ushered on stage, all the while declaring, "No, no, no! I can't go to Hollywood and become a star! I'm a mother! I have to look after my daughter! No, no, no!" she'd said again, as she ran off the TV show's stage.

"I saw you do that," I told Rhonda with some amazement. "Twenty-five years ago I saw you and Georgie Jessell and that exact moment on the Mike Douglas Show." A quarter of a century earlier, I had been compelled by a strong spiritual force to turn on the television and witness those few seconds Rhonda had been on national television. That experience had never made any sense to me and I'd eventually put it in the back of my mind. Now here I was, meeting the same woman from that odd TV moment and my visions of the past year and a half. Clearly, Rhonda and I were meant to meet, but for what reason?

Rhonda and I agreed to set to work on adapting Jess Stearn's most famous subject, the life of psychic Edgar Cayce, for the big screen. As it happened, Jess had suffered a stroke two months earlier. Since that time Rhonda had gone from being effectively a combination of Jess' editor, publisher, manager, and agent to being a *de facto* personal nurse to her 87-year-old employer. They'd worked together for years and Rhonda just didn't have the heart to let him stay in a hospital. I went to work for the Stearn estate and started to fall in love with Rhonda, the woman in the business suit from my vision that I'd told myself couldn't possibly be right for me. Her endless love and compassion for the failing writer touched my heart. People who are as good and as kind as Rhonda are all too few in this world. I knew she was a rare jewel.

Shortly after we started working together, I had a very vivid dream that included Rhonda and another woman that I'd never met before. In the dream Rhonda was standing in front of me to my left and this darker-skinned stranger, with two small children, was in front of me to my right. As I looked back and forth between the two women, a booming voice came out of nowhere saying, "CHOOSE!" I considered Rhonda, and then the woman with the two children again. I realized that I was being offered two different choices for my future. But which one was right? "CHOOSE!" the booming voice said again. And then I woke up.

Two days after that dream, my writer friend Gert Basson and I decided to check out a local mystical study group. There was a very lovely woman, a writer herself, who really caught my attention as we walked in the room. The woman and I talked, exchanged phone numbers, and set a date to meet for dinner that week. We did get together for lunch, and somewhere towards the end of our meal the woman, married but heading for a divorce, showed me a picture of her two small children. When I saw the kids, brown-skinned like their mother, the dream from earlier in the week came back to me in a flash and I realized that she was the other choice being offered to me by the Universe.

I was dizzy with confusion as we said goodbye, but only a few hours later my mind had cleared and I had made my decision. Rhonda and I were right for each other. I knew it in my heart. I chose Rhonda in that moment and after a while, and with more than a little hesitation, she chose me, too. We began seeing each other and after only a few weeks, and through a dramatic and unexpected set of surprise circumstances, we ended up living together in the city of Palm Desert, California, 120 miles east of L.A., just as my vision of a year earlier had shown. A little more than a year after that, Rhonda Marie Clifton, now Rhonda Clifton Lyons, and I were married. As it turned out the Great Spirit of the Universe had been right once again. (Funny, that.) Rhonda was truly the right choice for me and I feel blessed for the privilege of sharing my life with such a beautiful and loving soul as she.

Rhonda, like myself, is a mystic who's had extraordinary dreams and visions much of her life, with her mystical world really having opened up after a near-death experience she had when she was a teenager. After we started working together for the Stearn estate, Rhonda brought me out to Palm Desert to show me her place in the desert. The original idea was for me to occupy that property and spend the next few months working on the Edgar Cayce movie script.

On the way there, riding in the back of a friend's limousine, Rhonda looked me over and suddenly said to me, "Your people are here." "My *people* are here? What does that mean?" I asked her. "Your people," she repeated. "You know, from where you come from." I asked her to describe them and she gave a description of three unusually tall beings, actually they looked almost impossibly elongated from a normal human perspective. She said they were from another world, a world my soul had come from before it began incarnating here on Earth.

Now, I was tempted for a brief moment to shrug this off as just a bit of fanciful imagination on Rhonda's part, I didn't know her very well yet and hadn't come to realize what an advanced mystical soul she was, but the description she gave of these three otherworldly beings was *exactly* the description of the three unusually tall beings that I'd been seeing in dreams and visions my entire life. The thing is, I'd never told anyone about seeing them. Not a single solitary human being. I'd never know what to do about these three beings. They were always just there, observing everything I did and experienced, but never saying anything to me, never interacting with me, and never seeming to respond in any way other than with a very focused intellectual curiosity.

Rhonda explained that they and I were from a distant world of very wise sages, beings who remained in the same physical bodies for many centuries. What they did with all their time was to constantly focus on acquiring new knowledge and new understanding about the Universe and about the practically infinite number of planets, peoples, and civilizations in existence. This, she explained, was why they never interfered or interacted with me in my experiences here on Earth. My soul had come here many thousands of years ago, she told me, as an observer for my people. Somewhere along the way, according to Rhonda's vision, I had fallen in love with the people of this world and had decided to stay here and help them gain a better understanding of the nature of life and of the eternal truth of the Divine Spirit. No one has ever given me a better description of how I've felt about my life here in this world, and about the mission I've felt I was on from the moment I first remember thinking. No one else has even come close.

Even with all of the mystical experiences I've written about, I've mostly shied away from any discussion of beings from other planets in my approach to spiritual life here on this Earth, largely because there's been so much misinformation, government conspiracy theory talk, and paranoia surrounding the subject. As best I can tell, there are indeed aliens living amongst us here on our world. But to paraphrase a famous quote from one of the characters of an old political comic strip from years ago, called *Pogo*, "We have met the aliens, and they are us!"

CHAPTER SEVENTY-THREE

Dead Men's Ghosts

Rhonda and I met in late 2001. I'd just arrived back in the U.S. from working on the film adaptation of an unpublished novel with American expatriate writer Norman Harris in the beautiful town of Taormina, Sicily. Norm and I worked from his home at Fontana Vecchia, a rustic Sicilian villa overlooking the Mediterranean that's famous for being the writing home of former residents British novelist D.H. Lawrence and American writer Truman Capote. The 350-year-old villa, made of stone blocks from the town's ancient Roman aqueducts, was filled with history and the ghosts of the creative minds that lived there before us. But the ghosts on the minds of most Americans were those of the dead from the 9/11 terrorist attacks on New York City and Washington, DC. I had flown to Europe just a few weeks after those hijacked airplanes had done their evil work, at a time when most people were terrified to get on a plane. My attitude was that, after all the planning the terrorists had put into 9/11, they'd probably done their worst, at least for a while.

Back in the States, I was to find other ghosts flitting in and out of my life. I'd met Rhonda at Jess Stearn's beach house in Malibu and we had agreed to work together on a screenplay on the life of American mystic Edgar Cayce. After those initial discussions, I'd gone to the Bay Area to spend Christmas with my friends James, Lissy, and Mary Carol. One afternoon James, myself, and another friend were in a pub having a casual drink. As we chatted, I noticed a man watching us with some interest. He wasn't a very tall or athletic-looking fellow, yet he seemed to have an air of complete confidence and peace about him. His gentle, friendly face was immediately familiar to me. As I looked at him more directly, I noticed that I could see through him to the wall behind him. He smiled a slight grin at me. "Uh, guys," I said, "the ghost of Edgar Cayce's here."

I'd been feeling Edgar's presence around me since the meeting about the screenplay on his life. I felt his spirit wanted to help me get it right. When I got back to L.A., I informed Rhonda I'd seen Mr. Cayce's spirit in San Francisco. Rhonda smiled and told me that I wasn't the first person to see Edgar Cayce in connection with Jess Stearn. Apparently on a few occasions since she'd gone to work for Jess, some seven years

254

earlier, the ghost of Edgar Cayce had been seen at Jess' house by *sensitives* each time discussions of a possible film about Cayce's life were under way. He'd also been seen during the writing of Jess' book Edgar Cayce On The Millennium, which was written to clarify some of the confusion surrounding Cayce's predictions. Jess' books had helped make Edgar a household name across the globe. It seemed logical to me that Mr. Cayce's strong spiritual presence would take a continuing interest in what happened to his legacy.

I went to work for the Stearn estate, but as it happened my mother suffered a heart attack weeks later and I was off to Massachusetts to be with her and my family. Rhonda, a very capable mystic in her own right, had told me, just after we met, that spirit was showing her that one or both of my parents was likely to die in the next two years, so when my Mom fell suddenly ill I was taking no chances. My mother recovered, but my Dad, who'd seemed strong as horse, died less than two years after Rhonda's prediction, suffering a stroke at age 73.

Author Jess Stearn died four weeks after I returned to California. With his estate in contestation, and with rumors that the Cayce foundation people were supposedly working on a movie of their own, our movie project on Cayce's life went on the shelf for a future time. Rhonda and I moved to her place in Palm Desert the month Jess died, but it wasn't long before I saw Jess again, this time in spirit form. I was awakened one night to see Jess standing with the lower half of his body passing directly through our bed and him impatiently glaring at me. It was actually kind of humorous because it looked to me like he thought he was going to scare me. People who no longer have bodies no longer scare me. "Oh. Hi Jess," I said to his tall imposing figure. Rubbing the sleep from my eyes, I gently shook Rhonda's shoulder. "Ah, Rhonda," I said softly, as she slowly became alert, "Jess is here."

I continued to see Jess every now and again, but we didn't really communicate. Jess had depended on Rhonda's hard work, intelligence, and loving support during the final seven years of his life, so I knew he wasn't coming by the house to visit with me. On November 4th of that same year (2002) I would have occasion to see the ghost of another man at our home, a man I'd never seen before. As best we could tell, this ghost was that of Rhonda's late firefighter husband, Gary. Gary had died a couple of years before as Rhonda held his hand, day and night in the hospital, in the last weeks of his life. Rhonda loved Gary, but had left him years earlier because of his drinking and late-night violence. Cirrhosis of the liver finally killed him. The day I saw him, Rhonda and I were on our way to go hiking. I was sitting by the picture window in our bedroom, when a man I'd never seen before passed by. I had a very strange feeling come over me about the man, so I impulsively jumped up and bolted down the hallway and threw open the front door to engage him. But there was no one there. Our place sits on a steep hill, with a clear view that goes more than a quarter mile away from the house, so there was no place for anyone to hide. "Where could he possibly have gone?" my mind tried to understand as I scanned the landscape for a man that had apparently disappeared.

Less than an hour later, as Rhonda and I sat at a red light on a local highway, a tourist in a rental car drove right into us from behind, sending Rhonda to the hospital and turning our lives horribly upside down from that day on. When I later described the disappearing man to Rhonda, the one that had given me such a strange feeling in my stomach just before our accident, Rhonda said I was describing her late husband Gary. She'd seen his ghost from time to time, as well. Despite the late-night drunken episodes that ended their relationship, Gary had truly loved Rhonda. Rhonda knew that Gary's spirit wanted her to join him on the other side and that a part of her had been drawn to doing so. His appearance, just prior to the accident, seemed to be his spirit coming for her. For months after the accident Rhonda was barely in her body. I knew I had come close to losing her. As I write this (on November 4, 2004) it's been exactly two years to the day since the car accident and Rhonda is still recovering from the damage done to her.

As I mentioned, my father died on October 1, 2003. My Dad had recently been diagnosed with diabetes, but seemed otherwise healthy and strong. The last time I'd seen him before he got sick he was in his late 60s and could still rip a thick telephone directory in half with his bare hands. My Dad was a very tough guy. Earlier, in the fall of 2002, with my mother recovering from a heart attack and Rhonda's prediction of at least one of my parents dying before early 2004, I looked at the astrological transits to my natal chart and noted major aspects indicating just such a possibility. When I checked my Dad's birth chart against my mother's, I saw a very strong likelihood of my Dad's death indicated in both of their charts. With all three charts bearing such strong indicators, I checked the charts for my sisters and found strong indicators in their charts as well. Armed with this information, I called my mother and let her know what I was seeing so she'd be prepared for my Dad's possible death in the following year. The transits in my Dad's chart could have indicated a major transformation of his life and attitudes, with him remaining alive, but knowing my Dad I wasn't counting on such a turn of events. About six weeks after the call to my mother, my father had a stroke. The damage from the stroke was minimized, due to his having had the stroke while at a doctor's office, but the stroke took away at least 90% of his eyesight, leaving him almost totally blind.

There's an old expression that goes, "God works in mysterious ways" and I couldn't help but note that my Dad had been given a chance to experience life from my mother's point of view. My mother, you see, has been legally blind since college and had been almost totally without sight for more than twenty-five years at the time of my Dad's stroke. My parent's were married almost thirty years before divorcing, but my Dad had never really appreciated how difficult life had been for my mother all those years, that is, until he experienced it for himself.

Even though the doctors said he'd recover just fine, my father informed my brother Jim and myself that it was time to get his affairs in order because he knew he was going to die before his 74th birthday, which was less than a year away. He said he could feel it in the depths of himself. One devastating medical complication after another would hit my father over the next nine months and my Dad's prediction of his own death before his next birthday came true. While my Dad was busy moving towards his death, I was hard at work producing and hosting a three-hour radio program I had on the air called *The Psychic & Spirit Radio Show*. I worked night and day seven days a week to knock out the weekly mix of interviews, news, music, and features, all with only a laptop, a CD player, a cell phone, a cheap audio mixer, and the technical know-how to make it work. One morning, about 5AM, I'd already been working on the show for hours when I looked across the room and saw a very muscular white man with short hair and an old-fashioned cap watching me. I was startled for an instant, and immediately readied myself to defend my wife and I against this intruder, when I realized that I knew him from somewhere.

The man didn't make a move towards me, but smiled at me with the confidence and self-assurance of someone who knew he was powerful and impressive. I studied his ruddy Irish face and dapper suit coat. He appeared to be someone out of 1940s or 1950s America. After a few seconds, I figured out he wasn't actually physically in the room with me, so I stopped scanning the room for a weapon to use against this big man. Recognition of who he was dawned on me slowly, however, as I remembered having seen pictures of him somewhere years ago. It turned out that the spirit man in front of me was my own father, but looking the way he'd looked in the physical prime of his life. This wasn't my father's ghost, strictly speaking, for he was still alive at the time, although in rapidly failing health back in New Hampshire. This was my father visiting me out-of-body in his astral form and outside of normal time as well.

I'd read, in the works of mystic Jane Roberts (the Seth books) and others that people who were very elderly or in extremely bad physical condition might choose to experience their astral journeys in versions of their bodies from a happier and healthier time. This would account for my father visiting me as the strapping young man he'd once been. That same summer, my wife had contacted Chicago-area psychic Irene Hughes, who she knew from years earlier, about the possibility of Irene being a guest on my radio show. When she told Irene my name was Thomas Lyons (I'm named after my Dad) Irene had quietly said, "Oh, dear! I see death around that name, possibly coming very soon!" Rhonda quickly assured Irene that it was my father, Thomas Lyons Sr., and not Thomas Lyons Jr. who was nearing his death.

A couple of months after seeing my Dad's *younger astral self* in our living room's entryway my Dad's condition took another major turn for the worse. By that point he was on kidney dialysis, caused by his being treated with too strong a medication for his stroke recovery, and had lost a hundred pounds. I knew it was nearing his time, so I hopped on a plane to the East Coast to see him once more, in the flesh, before his death. While I was back East with my family, Rhonda in California got the news that her mother had died in Illinois. Five weeks after Rhonda's mother's death we learned my Dad was dead as well. I returned again to Massachusetts for my Dad's funeral and stayed with my good friend and old radio buddy Shelby at his place in Cambridge. The morning of the funeral I was looking for something and Shelby told me I could find what I needed in a certain desk drawer. As I rumbled through a very messy drawer, I felt a strong hand come out of nowhere, grab my right wrist and elbow and jam my right hand into the desk drawer with great force.

I quickly pulled my now bloodied hand from the drawer, completely dumbfounded. One of my fingers had been cut by a stray razor blade in the messy drawer when my hand had been forced inside. My mind and heart raced as I searched for an explanation for what had just happened. As I focused on the throbbing in my finger, I heard a *distant voice* yelling at me from somewhere. I turned my attention to the voice and saw my dead father materialize by my right shoulder. His face looked furious with frustration as he shouted over and over into my right ear, "Listen to me! Listen to me! Listen to me! Listen to me!" Now I understood who had jammed my hand into the drawer. My father could be quite subtle and savvy, when the occasion called for it, but when all else failed he could always fall back on brute force and the extraordinary power of his will to make his point known. "Dad, I can hear you!" I said to the impassioned ghost standing beside me. "Dad, it's okay! I can hear you! I can hear you! What do you need?"

My father's ghost, looking more like he had in recent years, before his health had failed, relaxed and put his large hands on my shoulders. His spirit eyes became all misty as he showed me a vision he wanted me to see. In the vision, I saw my dear friend Catherine, a wonderful, red-haired Irish-American, a woman filled with life and love and goodness, during various moments in her life. I also saw images of my father's Irish-born mother. She had died in childbirth when my Dad was only four or five years old, but I knew her face from family photographs. In the vision my Dad was showing me, I saw the continuity of my grandmother's life, her death, and her subsequent rebirth as my Irish-American friend Catherine. My Dad pointed from his mother's image and then to Catherine's. "She was my mother!" he said to me with great emotion. "I wanted you to know. She was my mother!"

My father had come to me from the other side of death having apparently discovered the reality of reincarnation when he got there. According to my father's ghost, the woman I knew as Catherine, who'd always felt like family to me, had, in a former life, been my own paternal grandmother. His intended communication achieved, my father's presence slowly faded from my view. "I just wanted you to know," he said to me one last time. And then he was gone.

Both of my father's parents had been born in Ireland and then had emigrated to the U.S. My Dad's mother, born Mary Costello on one of the Aran Islands off the west coast of Ireland, had been raised speaking the ancient Irish language and had only later learned to speak English, the language of Ireland's British conquerors. My father's mother had been christened as an infant in an old Catholic church in the town of Spiddal on the Irish mainland in County Galway. Now, curiously, at Christmas time 2001, I'd called my friend Catherine to catch up and discovered that she and her wonderful man Erik had gotten married since we'd last spoken while they were on holiday in Ireland. Even more curiously, Catherine told me they'd been married in the west of Ireland at a Catholic church in the coastal town of Spiddal, near the Aran Islands. Catherine, who knew nothing of my family's past, had managed to get married in the same church my long since dead grandmother had been christened in more than a century earlier.

At the time she told me, I thought it a most remarkable coincidence and wondered at the deeper connections between Catherine and I that I'd always felt were there below the surface. I told Catherine about my grandmother and she too found it a most extraordinary coincidence. When I'd told my Dad the story, it had brought up deep emotion about the mother he had barely known and had always longed for. My father's memories of her loving spirit and earthy purity had always remained with him. Everyone who'd known her had always told him, "Your mother was truly an angel." Now, I suppose that's a very Irish Catholic thing to say about someone's dead mother, and my Dad had always insisted his father had been a saint, as well, but by all accounts she was indeed an unusually kind, loving, and compassionate woman. Furthermore, on the saintly front, his father had truly sacrificed most of his life to raising their six sons by himself after his wife's early death in times of great economic and emotional hardship. I remember my father's father as a man of deep emotion, but reserved on the surface, great intelligence, and a profound sense of dignity. His hands, like my Dad's, were thick and strong from a lifetime of hard work.

I've chosen not to give much information out about Catherine, as I've tried to protect the privacy of many I've written about in this book. Though just like the tales of my paternal grandmother she is truly a most remarkable, loving, and beautiful spirit. The day Catherine and I met, we already seemed like family. I was living in an apartment in South Boston, Massachusetts with my friend Margaux and our sometimes apartment-mate James, the same drummer friend of mine who later moved to California. Margaux was in Germany at the time, and we had a vacant bedroom to fill. I had just arrived home and as I took off my work boots in the outer hallway James called to me from the kitchen at the other end of the apartment, "Welcome home, Thomas!" he said. "Hey James!" I replied. "Thomas, my friend Catherine's here!" James called out. "Hi, Thomas!" said this joyful voice filled with life, still out of my sight in the kitchen down the hall. "I love your apartment!" she continued without hesitation, "Can I live here with you guys?"

From the moment I heard her first words my heart was filled with warmth and joy. I knew I had met a friend. This is generally how I find my friends, actually. Usually, from the moment we meet or from the first time I hear their voice, I just have a knowing feeling inside me that we are friends. It's a recognition of the essence of their soul. "Yes!" I called back down the hallway. "Really?" she said. "You mean it?" "Yes, Catherine," I said. "You can move in." And then I walked down the hallway to meet her in person. And that was that.

Is reincarnation truly a reality? Do our souls really travel from one time and place to another, taking in new experiences in this dance we call life? It sure looks that way from where I'm standing. But not only do we apparently learn and evolve during physical incarnation, we also can continue to grow and evolve outside of the physical world. Since my father's passing in late 2003 he's visited me on several occasions. I'd see him sometimes in the kitchen or living room of our home or sitting beside me in the front seat of the car while I'm on my errands. For the first few months after his death his ghost seemed bent on using me to tidy up the loose ends of the life he'd left behind. "Dad," I had to tell him more than once, "you already had your chance to do those things when you were alive and didn't do them. And right now I'm up to my eyeballs in things I have to get done for Rhonda and I."

However, in the more than two years since his death (as I revise this book in December, 2005) he's gone from being focused on his own agenda to working to be a legitimate help to me and our other family members. He's actually become more like a spirit guide for the Lyons family. The last time I saw him was in early November, 2005 at my mother's place north of Boston. My mother and I were talking about our lives, in particular about when my siblings and I were children, and I looked to my left and saw a large golden orb of light a few feet away. When I looked deeper into the light I saw that it was my father, who I'd witnessed growing closer to the light of his soul and away from the lower trappings of his human personality during the preceding year. I told my mother my Dad was there with us. She seemed glad. She told me she'd seen my father several times in dreams since his death. Just a few days earlier, she told me, he'd come to her in a dream and they'd gone for a long ride together. She knew he was sorry for the bad things he'd done to her in life and wanted to make up for it by providing comfort to her from the spirit realm. As bad a husband as my father had been at times, he'd continued to love my mother after the divorce that he'd initiated. He'd later admitted to his mistakes and asked my mother to take him back, but too much harm had already been done.

The week I came back from my Dad's funeral my radio show went off the air for a while, replaced by a satellite radio service put in place to save the multinational corporation that owned the radio station chain a few bucks. Rick Shaw, the station's program director, offered to keep the show on in a much shorter version, but I realized it was time to take a break. A new version of my show called *Spirit Rock Radio* will be on the airwaves later in 2006 and astrologer James Coleman from *The Psychic & Spirit Radio Show* will be back on board with me. But right now Rhonda and I have books to edit and publish for our new company We Publish Books, on the web at http://www.Books1234.net, and authors to market and promote, including myself and this book.

Back on the subject of ghosts, I have seen others since my Dad's funeral. One of them was the ghost of Matt Schoener, the founder of Omega Shakti. I saw him a couple of times in the spring of 2004, but there wasn't any deep communication between us. I wondered if he'd finally realized that he'd been waiting on a lie the past ten years and that perhaps it was time for us to reconnect, but that didn't seem right. A couple of months later, I told my guitar-playing friend Steve about Matt visiting me out-of-body. "Matt's dead," he told me. He'd died of a stroke about the same time I started seeing him looking in on me.

This out-of-body/dead ghost thing can be a little confusing sometimes. It's easy to assume the person is still alive and just visiting out-of-body if you don't follow the energy back to its source, which I didn't do with Matt's ghost. The astral body we travel around in each night when we go to sleep is apparently the same astral body some of us still hang around in for a while after our physical deaths. A couple of times recently I'd seen a woman's spirit in our house and wondered who she was. The first time, I only caught a glimpse of her and noticed she looked a lot like my wife Rhonda. The next time, I got a better look at her. It was Rhonda, busy going back and forth to her office in her astral body while her physical self was still asleep down the hall.

Am I one of those people who just sees ghosts and stuff all the time? Well, sort of. The fact is I just see things when I see them and hear things when I hear them. It's not something I've learned to turn off and on like a professional psychic does. I'm quite certain that if I really applied myself and worked to develop these obviously natural abilities, I could gain a level of on-demand psychic skill and maybe even join the ranks of the world's professional seers. But I've never really had much inclination to do so. The fact is there's so much to focus on in the here and now of this reality that I'm kind of busy doing normal life most of the time. I figure when spirit really needs to communicate with me, it will happen, and it generally does. I suspect these natural abilities may have come with me from other lives and other realities.

As matter-of-fact as I've gotten about such things over the years, sometimes the experiences still take me delightfully by surprise. One night Rhonda and I were awakened by a loud "thump." We both sat up in bed and started listening and looking around the room, trying to find the source of the loud noise. There was moonlight coming in from outside so I could see the room fairly well, even with the lights off. As Rhonda looked around the room, two feet away from me, I realized I could see my own reflection in the mirrored closets that cover the wall, but I couldn't see Rhonda's reflection very well. When I looked closer, I realized I couldn't see her reflection at all. I looked at what I thought was her body sitting up beside me and then down to an identical Rhonda still laying, mostly asleep, on the bed. At that point I put two and two together and figured out what was going on. Rhonda often sleeps so deeply that it takes her a while to come back to her body and become fully functional and awake. The shock of the loud noise and vibration that had awakened us both had brought her astral body back to her physical, but the instinctive need to check out the situation had left no time to get her actual physical body in gear. The woman next to me, scanning the room for the source of the noise, was indeed my wife, but she was the astral version of Rhonda and not the physical one. When I looked closer in the moonlit room it was all pretty obvious because I could see right through her. Such experiences are still fascinating after all these years. By the way, the loud "thump" sound was caused by a dead tree limb falling on our roof.

CHAPTER SEVENTY-FOUR

What's In A Name?

There's something called numerology, which exists in various forms in a number of the world's written languages. The idea is that the unique sounds used to make the words of a spoken language, and the written symbols that represent those sounds, have a deeper meaning, like everything else. These various systems of numerology, or number values, seek to uncover the meaning believed hidden in those words by translating those symbols into quantitative numerical values. I once shared an apartment with a Ph.D. candidate mathematician from Eastern Europe who declared to me, with stars in his eyes, "Numbers are the secret code of the Universe! Numbers are the hidden language and the building blocks used by God to create the Universe! Everything breaks down to numbers! Numbers are everything!"

Some religious groups have even tried using numbers from the Bible to calculate the exact age of the Earth by starting with Adam and Eve, then adding up the ages of every Biblical figure mentioned all the way up to Jesus and finally adding the Western calendar to that. According to this method the Earth is an extremely young planet, not much more than a kid really, still wet behind its cosmic ears. Other groups have tried using numbers from the Bible to calculate the End of the World, so far, with no success. Numbers and symbols have also been used to intentionally conceal meaning, such as with a military's use of coded messages or a secret society hiding its esoteric truths in words and pictures. Dan Brown's popular novels, including The DaVinci Code, explore at great length this sort of method of placing hidden meanings in visual symbols.

Surely the most well known use of hidden meaning in numbers, in the Western world anyway, comes from the last book of the Christian New Testament. This book is sometimes called the Book of Revelations, the Revelation of St. John the Divine, or the Book of the Apocalypse. The word *apocalypse* comes from a Greek word that means "to uncover" or "to reveal" though it has become synonymous with Armageddon, a final battle between good and evil, which itself originally referred, according to many scholars, to the ancient city of Megiddo in Northern Israel. Megiddo was repeatedly a battlefield for the Jewish people and the expectation of a final battle of Armageddon was the hope that one day the battles at Megiddo would end, with the Israelites as the victors.

The most famous (or infamous) number from that book is, of course, the number 666. The last book of the Christian New Testament, traditionally said to have been written by the Apostle John, has been interpreted in many different ways at various times in history. The bulk of this very esoteric, symbolic, and multi-layered book is said to be a chronicle of a series of elaborate dreams, experienced by the author, that point to potential events in the future of humanity. Some believe these events portend the end of the world, at least as we have known it, and the beginning of a new or better world. Other more mystical interpreters believe the images are symbolic and represent the trials and tribulations a human being goes through in eventually reaching the light of the soul, or what some would call the "Christ Consciousness."

All other debates and interpretations aside, many Biblical historians agree that the author was writing, at least in part, of events he expected to witness in his own lifetime. In that light, the "beast" that needed to be defeated was referred to by the numerological code number 666. "Let him that hath understanding count the number of the beast: for it is the number of a man; and his number is six hundred threescore and six [666]." {King James Version, Revelation, Chapter 14, Verse 18.} This great enemy of the Jewish people, in the first two centuries B.C.E. (Before Christian Era) and the first two centuries C.E. (Christian Era) was also called, in translation from the Greek to English, the "Anti-Christ." The New Testament, believed to have been written by Greek-speaking Jews, uses the Greek word for Messiah, "Christos" (Christ, in English), to refer to the one *anointed* by their God, in a ceremony conducted by the Jewish High Priests, to be their king on Earth. Messiah/Christ literally means "the anointed one."

The Jewish kings of that period were appointed by Rome and had to answer to the Roman Emperor. Because of that allegiance, the Jewish kings and their Roman rulers were called "false Messiahs," "false kings," or "Anti-Christs," by some Jews. The Roman Emperor, the Latin-speaking head of the empire, was also known, to the Greek-speaking Jews outside Jerusalem, by the nickname "that Latin man." Why use a nickname when talking about the Roman Emperor? Well, by using a nickname you could always claim that you were actually talking about someone else. In a world ruled by a military dictatorship, where merely saying something that could be construed as against the powers that be could get one imprisoned or put to death for sedition, using a nickname, a code name, could make the difference between life and death.

At the time the Book of Revelation was written, the Latin and Greek languages did not yet possess the written (Arabic) numerals of 0, 1, 2, 3, 4, 5, 6, 7, 8, and 9. Instead, numbers were commonly written down as "slash marks": / (1), // (2), /// (3), //// (4), etc. The written Latin (Roman) language also used letters of the alphabet to represent simple numbers and combinations of those letters to represent more complex numbers. We all learned those symbols in primary school as Roman numerals. Roman numerals are generally no longer used today, although they are still popular in some scholarly circles. Their most recent common use, as known to the general public, has been to indicate copyright dates on books and other published materials.

A book published in the year 1914, for example, would have been given the copyright date of MCMXIV in Roman numerals. The capital letter M being used to represent the number 1000, C was used for 100, X for 10, I for 1, and V for the number 5. The order that the Roman numerals were set out in was a bit of a code within itself: For the year MCMXIV (1914), the first M (for 1000 years) was followed by another M (another 1000 years), but with a C (100 years) coming before the second M, meaning "100 years before 1000 years", or 900 years. Added to the first M (1000 years) we arrive at 1900 years. Those Roman numerals are followed by an X (for 10 years) and a V (for 5 years), but with the an I (for 1 year) coming before the V, meaning 1 less than 5 (or 4), which, added to the 10, gives us 14 years, which is added to the preceding 1900 years to give us 1914 years of time passed on the Western calendar, or the year 1914. You can see why Europeans eventually adopted the Arabic numerals we use today.

The Greek language also had numeric values for the letters of the Greek alphabet. When the author of the last book of the New Testament referred to "the numbers of his name" being 666, it is believed by many scholars that he was using the same type of code, but using the Greek values. What was the name hidden in the code number 666 that identified the beast, the great enemy of the Jewish people, the false king, the false-Messiah, or Anti-Christ? Many historians believe it was a code name for the Roman Emperor, himself.

What's In A Name?

What code name, using the Greek number values, adds up to 666?

The Jewish nickname for the Roman Emperor – "Lateinoz"

Lateinoz was Greek slang for "that Latin man," the nickname for the Roman Emperor, used by the Greek-speaking Jews who wrote the New Testament books. Here is how the *numbers of the name* of the Jews' great enemy add up to <u>666</u> in Greek:

L (Lambda) = 30	30
A (Alpha) = 1	1
T (Tau) = 300	300
E (Epsilon) = 5	5
I (Iota) = 10	10
N (Nu) = 50	50
O (Omicron) = 70	70
<u>Z (Zeta) = 200</u>	+ 200
LATEINOZ =	666

[The number of the name of the Anti-Christ.]

~

Now, we all know the hopes and dreams of the Apostle John for the Jews to defeat the Romans never worked out. In fact, after two major wars of rebellion against Rome, the Romans put an end to the state of Israel altogether, creating Palestine in its place, and so the prophecies and dream of the Jews one day returning to the Holy Land were born. After this time, the writings known as Revelation/Apocalypse, the writings that are believed to include a symbolic or cryptic prediction of Roman defeat by the Jews, were put aside and largely ignored for many years. In fact, they came close to being completely eliminated from all finalized versions of the Christian Bible, like so many other mystical Christian texts. But, the writings did make it into the Roman Bible, and people have been trying to make the elaborate dreams and mystical symbolism laid down by the book's author make sense in their own lives and times ever since.

Centuries later, after the Protestant Reformation in Europe created another major schism in Christian belief, those who opposed what had become the Roman Catholic Church began to demonize the Roman church and its leaders, albeit, not without good reason. Those new Western Christian groups began to re-interpret the Biblical writings, from their new vantage point of moral superiority over the Roman Catholics, and some of them decided that maybe the coded name of 666 in the Book of Revelations was still relevant. In the new take on the book, the evil Babylon, a code name for Rome in the Greek New Testament, according to most scholars, became the Roman Catholic Church. The idea of the Anti-Christ was also reborn, symbolically, as the Roman Pope (Papa/Father) himself. How did they make the number 666 still apply? By making the Greek word for Latin(s) or "that Latin man," in the old Greek-speaking Jewish slang, now refer to the Pope, as head of the "Latin" (Roman) Church.

This same approach to making the Apocalypse of John contemporarily relevant to politics and current events has been used to identity the French Emperor Napoleon as the Anti-Christ, the German Chancellor Adolph Hitler as the Anti-Christ, and more recently both Osama bin Laden of Al-Qaeda, and Saddam Hussein of Iraq, as Anti-Christ(s). Ancient Babylon, by the way, was located within what are now the modern-day borders of Iraq. This historical fact made Saddam Hussein, in the minds of some current Doomsday Cult Christians who got tired of calling the Roman Catholic Church "Babylon," a great candidate for the Anti-Christ. Of course, now that Saddam Hussein's been defeated many of those still hunting for a bad guy they can claim "fulfills the prophecy" are checking out various other, mostly Middle-Eastern, heavyweights to prove that the "prophecies are coming true."

Now, one of the cool things (or terrible things) about supposed ancient prophecies is that many of them, particularly those couched in symbolic language, can be used by both sides of an argument to point to the evils and ills of the other side. Many of those supporting the idea that Iraqi dictator Saddam Hussein was the Middle-Eastern Anti-Christ they'd been looking for saw the U.S. President George W. Bush as a Christian hero fighting against the evil-doing Muslims. Conversely, the Middle-Eastern Muslims who attacked the U.S. saw themselves as Islamic heroes fighting against the evil Satan of the West. You see, since the defeat of the Ottoman (largely Muslim) Empire, there have been Islamic Arabic "prophets" predicting the defeat of the Western powers, who defeated them, and the rise of a great leader, anointed by God/Allah, that would make the world holy and right again by vanquishing *their* enemies. The Muslim extremists' fantasies of a "holy war" are not unlike the Armageddon scenarios of some Christian and Jewish extremists, only in the Muslim fantasy *they* win, with God/Allah on their side, instead of the Christians or the Jews winning, with the support of God/Jehovah/Yahweh on their side.

~

Perhaps one of the starker takes on the view that there is plenty of evil in the West, just as there is plenty of evil in the East, North, and South, is a website I recently stumbled across entitled: "Bush Is The Anti-Christ," located at http://www.BushIsAntiChrist.com.

This search for the identity of the Anti-Christ, and the de-coding of the number 666, uses numerical values for the Hebrew alphabet to make their case against current U.S. President George Bush:

G = 3 (gimel)
E = 5 (heh)
O = 70 (ayin)
R = 200 (resh)
G = 3 (gimel)
E = 5 (heh)

B = 2 (beth)
U = 70 (ayin)
S = 300 (shin)
H = 8 (cheth)
Total: 666 = The Anti-Christ

Maybe, they're just kidding?

CHAPTER SEVENTY-FIVE

Predicting The Future

People have probably been trying to predict the future ever since we've been able to conceptualize something beyond the Eternal Now of the present moment. In recent times, Quantum Mechanics has introduced the theory that there may be an *infinite number* of potential futures (probabilities) as well as an infinite number of pasts and an infinite number of presents. Our new understanding of the physical Universe tells us that even the slightest deviation from the track one is on can cause a dramatic change in any potential future one may have been anticipating, while at the same time we're told that the *original future* may also find its expression in another reality, in a parallel Universe. It would seem that the Mind of God and the manifest worlds may be infinitely vaster than even the most dedicated religious believer or traditional physicist could have imagined. This apparent scientific truth has been awe-inspiring to millions. But for millions of others it has been simply too much information to process and something that threatens the very foundations of the beliefs that their lives and psychological security have rested upon.

Where is all this apparent knowledge taking us and is it some place we really want to go? Does anybody know the future with absolute certainty? Not really, but we keep trying. In fact predicting the future is the bread and butter of many from stock market analysts, to meteorologists, to astrologers and psychics, to preachers warning of the imminent coming of the End of the World, which, ironically, they've been unsuccessfully predicting for many centuries. Understandably there's plenty of attention to be gotten and lots of money to be made if you are able to predict correctly, with any degree of success, in any of these areas. Curiously, there's just as much money to be made by simply claiming that you know what's coming next. Remarkably, you don't even have to be any good at it! You just have to have a strong presentation, or impressive sounding statistics, or a very compelling scenario to offer in order to dazzle, intrigue, instill fear and doubt, or encourage hope and positive anticipation in your audience of potential paying customers.

Some hustlers will intentionally mislead their fellow human beings into thinking they've got something to offer that they don't. For example, there's an advertisement for a psychic-readers phone-in service that's been running for years in magazines. This print advertisement features the real names and real photographs of some of the world's most famous legitimate psychics, with telephone numbers accompanying each of the psychics' pictures. When I was interviewing Chicago-area psychic/astrologer Irene Hughes for my radio show, she informed me that the phone number in that ad, listed by her name and photograph, doesn't actually connect to her. She gave me her real phone number, so my listeners could get in contact with her for a reading. She explained that, years earlier, she had signed a contract with that psychic service allowing them to use her name and photo. In exchange for the use of her name and image the ads tell the world what a great psychic she is. This raises her profile, spreading her fame, and theoretically gets her more clients. When someone who sees this ad does call the number accompanying Irene's name and photo, *somebody else* takes the call and somebody else does a paid reading for the caller.

This same regular ad also displays the names and pictures of other famous psychics, with accompanying phone numbers. Do any of those other famous psychics actually answer the phone when you call? Well, I don't know for sure about all of them, but this same psychic-reader call-in magazine ad was still running in March of 2006 publications, featuring the world-famous psychic and astrologer Sidney Omarr, even though Sidney Omarr's been dead since January of 2003. Now, it would be fun to think that Sidney was somehow managing to answer the phone calls from beyond the grave, more than three years after his death, but I think we all know that probably isn't what's happening. At least I *hope* we all know that isn't what's happening. For the record, I believe Sidney's syndicated column continues on with a ghostwriter (no, not that kind of ghost!), just as the late Dear Abby's advice column is now written by her daughter.

How do these people, whether professionals or amateurs, who believe they're seeing the future know for certain when they're right and when they're not? Well, for the most part, they don't. (Most of them, anyway.) Take me for instance. Although I'm not a proper psychic, so perhaps I'm a bad example, I do intuitively get information with some regularity. For instance, the very moment (in October, 2004) I heard the Boston Red Sox baseball team had beaten the New York Yankees in the pennant race, in four games straight, I knew that they were going to win baseball's World Series in the first four games. (And they did.) In fact I even had a vision of myself in a restaurant lounge north of Los Angeles watching the fourth and final game from a booth with my wife. At the time I had that vision, the business appointment that would bring us to that city (120 miles away from our home) to videotape a segment of a TV show in that very restaurant lounge had not even been set up yet. In fact, helping out on that shoot would be a last minute favor we did for the producers when another shoot we'd help to set up for them at a different location fell through the day before. The vision, however, appeared to me more than a week earlier.

On the other hand, during that same week I also knew, or *thought* I knew, that U.S. Senator John F. Kerry was going to beat sitting President George W. Bush in the November 2004 Presidential Election. I was definitely wrong on that one. My hope that Senator Kerry would win became my misleading *belief* in that particular scenario. The week before that same election, I was on the phone with a very talented professional psychic, a woman who has used her abilities to help the police solve crimes. In our conversation she confidently predicted that Senator Kerry would "win the election in a landslide." There was even this popular Eastern guru who, at the last minute, the day before the election, sent out an email claiming that some great spiritual beings and masters in the higher astral dimensions of reality had "changed their minds" from Bush to Kerry and had determined that Senator Kerry would be the winner after all. Apparently, even this well-known guru's "beings on the inner planes" can't correctly predict a popular election 24 hours before the vote.

Truly, predicting great world events that never actually occur has been a tradition for some time. For instance, the Jehovah's Witness religious faith has been unsuccessfully predicting specific dates for the End of the World for over a century now. Yet even with their repeated public failures, their religion continues to grow with new converts every year. What gives here? How can people be so illogical? Well, it may simply be because so many of us feel the need to be part of something greater than ourselves. Even if our belief is that there is no higher power and that life is ultimately meaningless we can at least join with others like ourselves, atheists, dogmatic skeptics, and grim fatalists and share that common bond of not believing in anything *together*. It can even be the kind of sharing that makes a true unbeliever all warm and gooey inside. Of course, this would be a scientifically testable gooeyness, really nothing more than a biological side-effect, a hormonal response to intellectual stimulus, experienced in the body as emotion, yet, in the end, utterly meaningless, but a warm gooeyness, nonetheless.

Of course, some people actually do sometimes get it right in the prediction department, at least part of the time. The popular Chicago psychic and astrologer Irene Hughes became famous decades ago for predicting the assassination of American President John F. Kennedy, a prediction given in confidence to a prominent politician who later supported her claim in print. She also grabbed significant headlines by predicting, in print, the exact date of the great Chicago blizzard of 1967, long before it was even considered a meteorological possibility. Another of Irene's predictions, recalled in Mark Thurston's book Edgar Cayce's Predictions For The 21st Century (published by We Publish Books in 2004) reminds us that, back in the 1990s, Ms. Hughes claimed that "the exposure of pedophiles and other non-Christian activities" would happen in a very public way to some in the religious orders during the period of Pluto moving through the Tropical Zodiac's sign of Sagittarius (1995-2008). We've all seen the reports of Catholic priests and others seducing children. She also predicts that a major spiritual awakening for humanity will come to the world, beginning at the end of the year 2012. Let's all pray she's right on that one.

World-renowned Edgar Cayce expert Mark Thurston's new book Edgar Cayce's Predictions For The 21st Century: *With Instructions For Living In The 21st Century That Cayce Envisioned* lays out the grand scheme of Cayce's vision of the future of our world, starting with a series of dramatic Earth changes and weather pattern changes that Cayce predicted would *begin to show themselves* by the year 1998. At the beginning of his book, Thurston gives us a list of what he calls the Ten Essential Themes of the Sleeping Prophet's futuristic visions:

1. A New Form Of Medicine Will Emerge - a kind of transformational healing - rooted in holism and deals with the body as an energy system. Each of us has a body, mind and spirit that interconnect. For healing to be complete and lasting, we will have a new kind of medicine that works toward the integration of all three elements. That means having not only physical treatments and procedures to promote healing for the body, but also having methods to transform attitudes and emotions, as well as disciplines to keep spiritual ideals and purposes clearly in focus.

2. Intuition And Psychic Abilities Will Become The Norm. As Cayce envisioned it in one statement about the essence of "Aquarian Age consciousness," people of the future will have "the full consciousness of the ability to communicate with or to be aware of the relationships to the Creative Forces and the uses of same in material environs." (Cayce Reading #1602-3) In generations to come, individuals will have a personal and direct connection with the spiritual world, in ways that allow that connection to be applied practically in daily life.

3. Science And Spirituality Will Cease To Be Antagonists. The convergence of these two great streams in human history will transform culture. "Research" and "enlightenment" will become partners, making possible a science of the spiritual world and a new sense of sacredness to the material realm.

4. Dramatic Geographical Changes Will Take Place, including very significant changes in weather patterns. In fact, it may well be that what Cayce saw in many of his Earth change prophecy readings, in regard to earthquakes and floods, may actually pertain to drastic changes in weather patterns to occur in the 21st century and beyond.

5. There Will Come To Pass On A Worldwide Scale A Kind Of Social "Leveling". This is very likely to be a difficult, painful, and even violent process, but conditions cannot continue whereby "there [is] one measuring stick for the laborer in the field and the man behind the counter, and another for the man behind the money changers." (Cayce Reading #3976-18)

6. Leadership On The International Scene Will Move To The Orient, And Even To Central China. China will one day become the cradle of Christianity; and "civilization must wend its way westward - and again must Mongolia, must a hated people, be raised." (Cayce Reading #3976-15)

7. Archeological Discoveries About Ancient Civilizations Will Radically Alter Our Sense Of Human History. What's more, these discoveries will show us how our ancient ancestors found ways to integrate science and spirituality.

8. The Continuity Of Life Will Be Fully Accepted As An Indisputable Fact. There is no death - merely a transition from one state of

consciousness to another. The fear of dying will be eradicated as a central human motivation.

9. <u>The Principle Of Oneness Will Become Paramount In Human Affairs</u>. The oneness of God will guide all religious traditions, the oneness of all energy will guide science, and the oneness of all humanity will direct politics.

10. <u>Christ Will Reappear Directly In Earthly Life</u>. The so-called "Second Coming" is perhaps a misnomer because the Christ Consciousness has never left us. Cayce envisions, however, the physical appearance of the Soul who came two millennia ago as Jesus. No date is given, but the prophecy is found many times in the Cayce readings.

Remember, Edgar Cayce gave all of these visionary prophecies out in his various readings before his death on January 3, 1945. According to author Mark Thurston, "Taken as a group these ten prophetic themes are an inspiring vision of the purposeful world in which we live. And perhaps in many ways it is a good thing that the years 1958-1998 have come and gone without some of the dire prophecies having been actualized. Now we have the chance to step back and get clearly in view a bigger picture of what Cayce prophesied for the new century and for centuries to come." Dr. Mark Thurston's enlightening new book on Edgar Cayce's Predictions For The 21st Century is available at http://www.Books1234.net and http://www.Amazon.com.

~

In mid-January 2005, another predictive astrologer gained attention for apparently having predicted the terrible *tsunami* (giant tidal wave) that killed so many on December 26, 2004. The fellow's name is Richard Nolle and he's got a pretty impressive track record of predicting major geological events, earthly disasters, and political happenings. In his November 2004 predictions for the upcoming month of December, Mr. Nolle wrote: "The last SuperMoon of 2004…augurs major turbulence in the Earth's crust, seas and atmosphere…that's bound to be one of the big stories for December. The end of the month, under the aegis of the high-declination full moon on the 26th, is likewise more or less certain to see an upsurge in strong storms and notable seismic activity…" After focusing on other more upbeat events, Richard Nolle finished his astrological predictions for December 2004 with these words: "The month ends on an explosive, uncertain note, if the Mars-Uranus square at 4 Sagittarius-Pisces is any indication…soldiers, sailors and aviators step up and put their lives on the line for a cause greater than self. Play it safe if you can…" Did he just take an extremely lucky guess in apparently describing the future terrible events so remarkably closely, or is Mr. Nolle, and other talented geopolitical astrologers like him, really on to something? Try reading his regular monthly and longer-term predictions at http://www.AstroPro.com and see for yourself.

Like in many other fields, it's often safer and easier to make strong declarations about a major event, such as the Asian *tsunami* of 2004, after it's already happened. The same Eastern guru who incorrectly predicted the U.S. election results only hours beforehand stated that the *tsunami* occurred because "God Is Mad!" that people have turned away from Him. A few of the conservative Middle-Eastern Muslim clerics suggested the terrible devastation that killed so many in Muslim countries, did so because those particular peoples were practicing a "too liberal version of Islam." On the other side of the religious extreme, certain Christian religious leaders gave their opinion that those same Muslims souls were killed as a punishment from God, simply for being Muslims in the first place!

~

What does the ultimate future of our world hold for each of us? It all depends on what each of us does with the *present*. Let's remember to keep our hearts and minds open to new possibilities and to pay attention to that "still small voice within" that guides us on our journeys. Practice love, kindness, and respect and except the same in return. Be honest and worthy of trust. Respect the Earth. Honor all life.

Do something *today* that makes a positive difference in the world, for every action truly does count, no matter how small it may seem. Keep holy each day, for we are meant to live as brothers and sisters in every moment, not just on a particular day of the week. Make peace, not war; for it is the only way we and our children will *have* a future.

- Namasté and Blessings to All

CHAPTER SEVENTY-SIX

Leaves Of Morya's Garden

Much has been spoken in whispers over the centuries of highly evolved Souls living amongst us. A few Great Souls have come out of the shadows and made their mark on history. Some, such as Moses, Jesus Christ, Mary, Gautama Buddha, Krishna, Apollonius of Tyana, Zarathustra (a.k.a. Zoroaster), Babaji, Mohamed, Black Elk, Lao Tzu, Confucius, Mahatma Gandhi, Mother Teresa, Bahá'u'lláh, and others have inspired entire religious and charitable movements. Still others, it is said, have made their way across time largely unnoticed. Since my earliest childhood, I have been visited on occasion by a Master Soul who is said to have made contact with many others over the years, most notably since the latter part of the 1800s. He has been called by many names, most commonly El Morya and Master Morya. There have even been a few spiritual groups devoted to him and his spiritual Brothers and Sisters. A couple of those groups, I feel, are truly doing the work of the Light. Sadly, others have mostly been the vehicles for power hungry so-called seers and prophets whose work is more akin to black magick than anything of value to the honest spiritual seeker.

Some historians claim this Master Soul is the creation of somebody's imagination and a fraud perpetuated on the world. Another purports to have researched and revealed his "true identity" with pictures to prove it, but I've seen the pictures this exposé claims are the true man behind the name and he doesn't look anything like the Master. Being someone who's had contact with this humble Servant of Humanity - contact that began more than twenty years before I learned anyone else even knew of his existence - assures me that these well-intentioned academics simply don't have the psychic and spiritual resources to learn the truth. Master Morya himself is believed to have communicated a number of books through a spiritual disciple named Helena Roerich (1879-1954), a Russian-born mystic and one of the founders of the Agni Yoga Society - http://www.AgniYoga.org. Roerich was married to another mystic, the Russian master painter Nicholas Roerich (1874-1947) whose inspired religious and visionary art and writings can be seen at the Nicholas Roerich Museum in New York - http://www.Roerich.org.

For many years I was not willing to declare with certainty that the Man who visited me as a child was, indeed, El Morya. I had seen a version of a famous artistic rendering of the Master produced in 1884 by artist Hermann Schmiechen, but had found the bug-eyed look on his face to not have captured his look at all. When told outright by Omega Shakti founder Matt Schoener that it was Master Morya who'd come to me over the years I insisted that if the famous image was accurate then it couldn't have been him. Only recently have I seen a truer copy of the original work of art (you can view it at http://www.Morya.net) and realized that the artist had indeed captured the Master quite well. Where the bug-eyed version came from I don't know, but it seems the person responsible thought they were making the Master's eyes seem deeper and more mystical by the alteration. Instead the change to his eyes make the wise sage look like a madman. Frustratingly, this bug-eyed version has become the most available image purported to be that of the Master and most fans of such portraits don't know of any other.

On a recent Internet search for images of the Master I came across a contemporary artist named Marie Klement who has also produced a very good image of Master Morya. Marie is a sensitive who has used her psychic clairvoyance to see and paint the images of a number of Great Souls. Her images include some of the more famous Spiritual Masters and Angelic Beings known to the world as well as privately commissioned paintings for clients who would like portraits of their own personal spiritual guides as seen by Ms. Klement. You can see some of Marie's beautiful mystical artwork and even order a spiritual portrait of your own at her website http://www.MarieKlement.com.

While I was preparing to do a few revisions, add a couple stories that had slipped my mind on the first draft, and fix some typos in this book (after it had already gone to print) our friend Richard came to me with a message. He said he'd been sitting in meditation when Master Morya had spoken to him. The Master, according to Richard, wanted him to tell me that it was indeed him who I'd been seeing since childhood. This message prompted me to do an Internet search for images of the Master, which resulted in my finding the work of Marie Klement and ultimately coming across the original image of Hermann Schmiechen's 1884 portrait. I also came across other images that claim to be those of Master Morya and some other famous Masters that look absolutely nothing like the great sages they're supposed to be portraying.

The following are a few words taken from Leaves Of Morya's Garden

(Book One), published by the Agni Yoga Society in 1924, and readily available today. I hope these brief, yet compelling lines will give you at least a glimpse of the true essence of this extraordinary Soul.

THE CALL

Into the New World my first Message. You who gave the Ashram, and you who gave two lives, proclaim. [Note: I believe the two referred to are the Roerichs.] Builders and warriors, strengthen the steps. Reader, if you have not grasped - read again, after a while. The predestined in not accidental, the leaves fall in their time. And winter is but the harbinger of spring. All is revealed; all is attainable. I will cover you with My shield, if you but tend to your labors. I have spoken.

I am - your Bliss. I am - your Smile. I am - your Joy. I am - your Rest. I am - your Strength. I am - your Valor. I am - your Wisdom.

By holiness in life, guard the precious Gem of Gems. *Aum Tat Sat Aum!* I am thou, thou art I - parts of the Divine Self. My Warriors! Life thunders - be watchful. Danger! The soul hearkens to its warning! The world is in turmoil - strive for salvation. I invoke blessings unto you. Salvation will be yours! Life nourishes the soul. Strive for the life glorified, and for the realization of purity. Put aside all prejudices - think freely. Be not downcast but full of hope. Flee not from life, but walk the path of salvation. You and We – here together in spirit. One Temple for all - for all, One God. Manifold worlds dwell in the Abode of the Almighty, and the Holy Spirit soars throughout. The Renovation of the World will come - the prophecies will be fulfilled. People will arise and build a New Temple.

In creation realize the happiness of life, and unto the desert turn your eye. Aflame with love for Christ, carry joy to Him. You bear wings of light. When departing life, you will see Me once more. Do not demean yourselves. Summon the courage to safeguard the mysteries. Comprehend the great gift of love to the One God. Try to unfold the power of insight, that you may perceive the future unity of mankind. The one salvation is to turn the spirit toward the light of Truth. The great gift of love lies in the one vision bestowed upon the fearless soul. You, my daughter [Helena Roerich], who have seen! Pure art is the true expression of the radiant spirit. Through art you gain the light.

About The Author

Born in the United States in 1958, Thomas Francis Lyons Jr. grew up in a small town 40 miles northwest of Boston. From the time he was an infant he had visions of a Master teacher that would appear before him and show him the mysteries of life. One of six children in an Irish-Catholic household, he also loved the mysticism of the Church and considered joining a Catholic monastic order. At the age of 16, after a three-hour interview with a local Catholic Church official concerning its beliefs and the origins of official church doctrine, he determined the Church's teachings and ideology were far too limiting for his needs.

Having had psychic visions, mystical encounters, and out-of-body experiences all his life he began learning everything he could about the other religious and mystical teachings of the world to determine who might be best able to teach him what he wanted to know. At the age of 19, he started meeting and picking the brains of some of the most prominent mystics and religious figures of his time, always with the aim of discovering any real mystical wisdom they might have to offer.

After half a century of mystical encounters and intellectual inquiry, author/mystic/healer Thomas Lyons feels he has something to say and some valuable lessons to share. *Modern Day Mystic* is the result of that impulse to offer his experience and perspective to others seeking to find their way on the path to greater spiritual understanding and peace.

Over the years author and mystic Thomas Lyons (host of the *Psychic & Spirit Radio Show* and the upcoming *Spirit Rock Radio* show) has worked as a truck driver, country music disc jockey, office secretary, natural foods store manager, furniture mover, cameraman, sound man, folk lift driver, and at dozens of other professions. He's also trained as an astrologer, an energy healer, worked for non-profit organizations, and received initiation into spiritual and mystical groups. Lyons works an *Agni Dhatu* energy therapist and as an Angelic Life Force teacher.

For more information on the current work of Thomas Lyons go to:

http://www.ModernDayMystic.com
http://www.SpiritRockRadio.com
http://www.PsychicAndSpirit.com

www.ingramcontent.com/pod-product-compliance
Lightning Source LLC
Chambersburg PA
CBHW060423100426
42812CB00030B/3284/J